We Must Say NO to the STATUS QUO

We Must Say NO to the STATUS QUO

Educators as Allies in the Battle for Social Justice

VERONICA MCDERMOTT

CORWIN

A SAGE Publishing Company

FOR INFORMATION:

Corwin
A SAGE Company
2455 Teller Road
Thousand Oaks, California 91320
(800) 233-9936
www.corwin.com

SAGE Publications Ltd.
1 Oliver's Yard
55 City Road
London EC1Y 1SP
United Kingdom

SAGE Publications India Pvt. Ltd.
B 1/I 1 Mohan Cooperative Industrial Area
Mathura Road, New Delhi 110 044
India

SAGE Publications Asia-Pacific Pte. Ltd.
3 Church Street
#10-04 Samsung Hub
Singapore 049483

Program Director: Dan Alpert
Senior Associate Editor: Kimberly
    Greenberg
Editorial Assistant: Katie Crilley
Production Editor: Amy Schroller
Copy Editor: Jocelyn Rau
Typesetter: Hurix Systems Pvt. Ltd.,
Proofreader: Sally Jaskold
Indexer: Judy Hunt
Cover Designer: Janet Kiesel
Marketing Manager: Charline Maher

Printed in the United States of America

ISBN 9781506345345

This book is printed on acid-free paper.

SUSTAINABLE FORESTRY INITIATIVE
Certified Chain of Custody
Promoting Sustainable Forestry
www.sfiprogram.org
SFI-01268

SFI label applies to text stock

17 18 19 20 21 10 9 8 7 6 5 4 3 2 1

Contents

List of Activities
and Figures

Preface

I can think of no more important curriculum topic or school culture and climate issue than social justice. Without a direct, purposeful, and critical consideration of how social justice plays out and is embodied in our school curriculum and classrooms and corridors, I fear that injustice, hate crimes, and ongoing marginalization will be our legacy. As educators, we can—and must—take the necessary steps to counteract the negative consequences bred from ignoring injustice, sidestepping hate speech, and tolerating marginalization.

I like to think of education as a gentle rain on a thirsty soul. I did not make up this definition. It came out of a discussion about education I was having with my husband, a non-educator. Among other things, my husband is a social worker, an Anglican priest, and a noncredentialed theologian. It was his theological side that kicked in. Did you know, he said to me, that the Hebrew word for education is *early rain?*

Of course I didn't know that, but the concept intrigued me. *Early rain* connotes a gentleness and new birth and nature providing exactly what is needed for flowers and plants and animals to thrive. *Early rain* transforms the landscape in fundamental and meaningful and essential ways. Should we expect less from education? What would happen, I wondered, if we thought about education as an early rain, something that is provided with gentleness, that is unbidden, that soaks down to the essential aspect of the human condition, the soul? What would happen, indeed, if our purpose as educators is to do what gardeners do: ensure that every plant in our care thrived; that every child in our care became more whole, flourished, and added to the general beauty and well-being of the world?

What would happen? The weeds of injustice, hate, and marginalization would disappear. They would have to. Weeds and plants rarely flourish together.

The more difficult question, of course, is how do we, as educators, address a world littered with a history of bigotry, misunderstanding, and hatred of *others?* How do we keep up with the ever-changing onslaught of new manifestations of bigotry, misunderstanding, and hatred that permeate the media, that worm their way into conversations, that play out in perverse policies, and that show up in malevolent individual and group actions?

In other words, how can we, as educators, make a difference? What do we need? What do our students need? How can we come together to honestly question and knowingly interrupt a system and ways of thinking that we have been conditioned to accept as normal?

GO TO THE PLACE WHERE NO ONE ELSE HAS BEEN

This book is an attempt to answer these questions. It is both a portrayal of my experiences as a White middle-class teacher, administrator, and professional developer on a lifelong quest to become an ally in the battle for social justice. This portrayal is dissected and sifted through a social justice lens as a way of elucidating the many concepts and theories that play into the work of a social justice ally.

In many ways, it is a storybook, and purposefully so. Stories leave room for interpretation and personalization.

Storytelling is a fundamental means of meaning making (Wells, 1987). It is part of our DNA. We love to hear and retell stories. Isn't that what we do when we get together with friends or when we need to illustrate a point? Stories anchor abstract ideas in an accessible medium. They take the sting out of emotionally charged experiences. They personalize and connect.

I know it is desirable, certainly fashionable, and undoubtedly comforting for authors to provide readers with a blueprint, an irrefutable-sounding, authority-imbued list of the ten next steps or five most powerful best practices or the three things you need to know in order to do whatever it is the book is about, along with a detailed description of what the desired outcome will look like, feel like, sound like and how it will operate. But I will not do that. I will not do this for one reason. I do not have a foolproof definitive recipe to become an ally in the battle for social justice. Nor should you. The reason is because it does not exist. A socially just world needs to be created. A socially just world is a work in progress. The end point, a new order, cannot be fathomed from our current vantage point.

My position is quite simple, but it springs from the coming together of many disparate ideas, the inevitable lessons learned from a lifetime of experiences, and the deep suspicion that complex issues defy simple solutions. There is no single, foolproof way to become an ally in the battle for social justice. There is no single, foolproof way to create the socially just world our marginalized students crave and allies desperately desire for them. If I provided you with a blueprint, a list of next steps or a litany of how-tos, I would rob you of your personhood, your uniqueness, your opportunity for soul searching, the joy of deep thinking, and perhaps most importantly, the chance for you to exercise your creativity, and that would be an injustice.

Ally work, the desire to change the world, is creative work. How can we, stuck as we are in a place where injustice thrives, know exactly how to build a better life, a society based upon the best in human civilization? In the post-apartheid world of South Africa, there is a strong recognition that the political transformation that took place in the 1990s requires a "second transition." This second transition, it is said, is needed to tackle the sticky residue of long-standing social and value systems that newly earned political rights left untouched.

I believe that ally work requires more than just a second transition. I believe it requires commitment to an open, adaptable, creative transition. Ally work is ongoing. It is messy. It is anything but linear and developmental. There will be setbacks, to be sure, but there will also be brilliant bursts of unexpected adjustment, glorious adaptation, and ingenious renegotiation. The results can be breathtaking, in much the same way emerging from fog that hides and distorts what is on the other side can be. Once the fog is traversed, once it is lifted, once the sun pierces its swirling cloudiness, what emerges is new and bright and glorious and often an unexpected and certainly unpredictable landscape. It is, in a very real sense, a new creation.

Ally work, like painting a picture, writing a poem, or composing music, requires fluidity, adaptation, constant adjustment, ongoing evaluation, constant revisiting. It is through these processes that works of art are created. The prolific artist, the productive writer, the inexhaustible composer possess a general idea, a nagging urge, a visionary desire to make something glorious out of the blank canvas, the wordless page, the note-less sheet music. The painter, the writer, the composer plunge in, they dig deep, and they trust the process. They fearlessly engage, charging ahead into unknown territory. They intuitively know that creativity is a place where no one else has been. Allies, too, need to fearlessly enter and charge ahead to that place where social justice thrives, that place where no one else has been.

Acknowledgments

In many ways, this book is a legacy project, the legacy others have left for me and the legacy I hope to leave for others. As a nod to the past, it highlights and honors my family, my mentors, my colleagues, my students, and the many systems that were in place to allow me to be in a position to write a book such as this. It also highlights and honors the work of countless allies who are deeply concerned about the kind of future our children and grandchildren will inherit. To all, a heartfelt thanks. You are all in this book somewhere.

PUBLISHER'S ACKNOWLEDGMENTS

Corwin gratefully acknowledges the contributions of the following reviewers:

Jennifer Abrams
Educational Consultant
Jennifer Abrams Consulting
Palo Alto, CA

Judy Brunner
Author, Consultant, Clinical Faculty
Instructional Solutions Group and Missouri State University
Springfield, MO

Becki Cohn-Vargas
Director, Not In Our School, Retired Superintendent
Author of Identity Safe Classrooms
El Sobrante, CA

Takesha Winn
Dallas ISD
Assistant Principal (Middle School)
Dallas, TX

About the Author

Veronica McDermott is a retired school superintendent who continues to focus her efforts on school transformation, social justice, and equity. She is a frequent keynote speaker and workshop leader at national and international conferences devoted to issues of leadership and learning for equity and social justice. She is the author of many articles, chapters, and opinion pieces, as well as coauthor of two books designed to change the way educators think about, talk about, and interact with our students who are not thriving.

Dr. McDermott received her PhD from New York University, a professional diploma from Long Island University, and her master's and bachelor's degrees from the State University of New York at Stony Brook. In addition to being superintendent of schools, she has served as assistant superintendent for curriculum and instruction; principal; district director of English Language Arts, Reading, Second Language, and ESL; and English teacher. She was also a regional director with a national professional development organization that provided high-quality, embedded learning experiences for urban educators.

Her legacy project is to eradicate the crime of squandered potential.

Introduction

THE COMPELLING WHY

I knew I needed to write this book at the end of the first day of a two-day preconference institute I conducted with a colleague in March 2015 at an international educational conference. Our session focused on transforming learning, leadership, and lives in schools labeled as underperforming. Our message was clear. There are multiple ways in which school, as an institution, reinforces marginalizing practices, ignoring along the way the vast potential of those marginalized.

At the close of the first day, one of the participants, a newly minted administrator who is in charge of Title 1 funding for a school district in the Midwest, asked if I had time to discuss something with her. Earlier in the day, she had explained that her district is undergoing a demographic change. Schools that historically did not qualify for Title 1 funding recently became eligible, but families from schools experiencing this influx of new Black and brown children (whose family incomes qualified them for free and reduced lunch) refused to accept the designation. The families who had been part of the school system the longest were willing to turn their backs on the extra funding and extra services, she said, because they did not want their schools to be labeled "poor." She indicated that she felt this refusal was at best shortsighted and at worst likely fueled by classism and racism.

This exchange led me to believe that this administrator was someone who "got" marginalization, someone who was far along in her understanding of what it means to be a strategic ally in the battle for social justice. After all, she named two of the multiple "isms" that serve to stratify society: classism and racism. I was certain I was dealing with someone who understood hierarchy, privilege, and oppression. All of that changed, however, when, at the end of the day, she relayed the following story.

She began by telling me that "everyone" was upset because a long-time, highly regarded principal was being forced to retire "under a cloud," when "all he was trying to do" was something positive by planning and executing a "slave day" at his school. "A slave day?" I asked dumbfounded.

Yes, she continued. The teachers and he wanted their students to "understand what it was like to be a slave," so they planned a series of events and several "re-creations" of the life of a slave. One "re-creation" included having students "sleep" in a space the size of those in which enslaved people slept. The problem, she continued, is that the Black community "got up in arms" when they heard about it. She could not understand why, nor could the other White educators who, she indicated, decided that they would never again address anything having to do with race for fear of getting it wrong.

I asked who was involved in planning the day. The teachers and administration, she told me. And how many of them are people of color? I asked. None, she responded. Did they consult with the Black families in their school? I asked. No, she said, there are none. What about anyone from the larger Black community? Again, her answer was no.

That is when I knew I HAD to write this book. Here was yet another example of a group of educators who view themselves as having big hearts, a group of educators of who want to be allies in the battle for social justice, but who make terrible, avoidable mistakes like the one here: that of appropriating another group's story.

They are not alone. In general, "getting" marginalization—and its traveling companion, oppression—is something for which many educators are ill prepared. We are, after all, educators, not sociologists; practitioners, not theorists; teachers, not researchers. Simply put, there are ongoing conversations, in-depth studies, and nuanced debates about the sociohistorical context upon which education rests that perpetuate inequality, but these conversations rarely involve classroom teachers or the school and district leaders who interact daily with students.

If you are a recent graduate—and lucky—you may have taken a course or two that addresses social justice issues in an educational context. There is no shortage of literature attesting to the need for preservice teacher education programs to include knowledge acquisition, attitudinal explorations, and pedagogical skill development for educators who are more and more likely to work with students who represent a range of ethnic, racial, cultural, social, and linguistic backgrounds. Unfortunately, though, these topics are often studiously avoided by professors who are ill equipped themselves to address them (Cruz, Ellerbrock, Vasquez, & Howes, 2014).

If you are predisposed to do so, perhaps you have sought out a conference session or two on issues of social justice. Over the years, there has been a proliferation of individual sessions, conference strands, and entire conferences devoted to aspects of social justice. As good as these sessions are, what is learned is often fleeting under the press of the daily grind, little ongoing support, and rare opportunities for in-depth discussions.

If you are fortunate, you may have a visionary leader who provides ongoing professional learning and discussion regarding social justice issues and ways to notice and dismantle unquestioned structural barriers to learning. Perhaps you are a member of a marginalized group trying to figure out how to bring others along, so that we end once and for all the slights, oversights, and deep spirit slashing that take place daily for many of our students.

If so, then this book is for you. It is an effort to put into words much of what I have learned about social justice and social justice activism in an educational setting. This work has become the focus of my efforts recently, and I have learned much as I share this work at conferences, workshops, and other professional development venues in the United States and Canada. In many ways, it is a story of my personal journey emerging from the fog of privilege to become an activist in the cause of social justice. It is a warts-and-all story. I came late into this work. It wasn't until I retired from full-time public-school employment that I had the opportunities and the resources to begin to reflect deeply on issues of social justice; to begin to see the many lost years that I spent as an English teacher, principal, and superintendent who possessed a big heart but who could have done so much more "if I knew then what I know now."

My goal is to lay bare my story, to take a sharp and critical social justice lens to the numerous experiences and exchanges that have brought my understanding to where it is now, to share the insights I have gleaned through reading and reflection, and to provide resources and ideas that I have found useful so that my fellow educators might see the possibilities and limitations of what it means to be a strategic ally in the battle for social justice.

I do this knowing full well that what I have to say is far from exhaustive. I am pretty confident that by writing this book I will be different at the end, one or two steps deeper into my understanding of social justice and how to best position myself to be an ally in this movement. Of course, my dream is that by engaging with this book, you, too, will be different. Your take on social justice will be more nuanced. Your desire to engage in the work will be more pronounced. Your confidence to wade in will be at an all-time high, so that you, too, will begin the work of bringing still more allies into the fight against oppression—no matter what form it takes. As long-time social-justice activist Anne Bishop reminds us, "We need unity to create a power base strong enough to change the system we live in" (Bishop, 2002, p. 47). And, make no mistake about it, "the system" does need changing, as I hope this book will show.

EDUCATORS ARE PRIMED TO BE STRATEGIC ALLIES IN THE BATTLE FOR SOCIAL JUSTICE

Educators are uniquely positioned to become strategic allies in the battle for social justice. This is particularly true of those of us who have chosen education as a career destination, not a waypoint. The very things that call us to the classroom, the very things that we do daily in creating learning experiences for students, the important spheres of influence and range of access granted to us as by-products of the roles we play represent key prerequisites that make us ideal candidates for becoming strategic allies in the battle for social justice. In other words, by disposition, by preparation, and by position, educators—whether teachers or administrators—possess strengths, which can be activated and intensified in the process of becoming more and more intentional social justice allies.

Identifying Educators' Strengths

Why start from strengths? Identifying and activating strengths costs nothing, but the payoff is tremendous. Affirming strengths creates a neurobiological sparkle of positive feelings, a cultural shift, and a renewed belief in one's capabilities to tackle a daunting task (Jackson & McDermott, 2015).

Figure 0.1 presents a summary of the strengths of educators that make them ideal candidates to become allies in the battle for social justice. The next section will go into more detail regarding each of these strengths.

In what ways do educators' dispositions, preparation, and position prime them for work as allies in the battle for social justice?

By Disposition, Educators Have Big Hearts

Our reasons for becoming educators are no secret. We care about others. We want to make a difference in the lives of students. We want to contribute to the future. We want to give back. These reasons are through lines that permeate why we chose to become teachers, whether

Figure 0.1   Social Justice Strengths of Educators

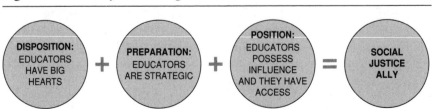

we fall into the *I-always-wanted-to-be-a teacher* camp, the *I-never-wanted-to-become-a-teacher-but-everyone-said-I-would-make-a-great-teacher* camp, or the *I-had-to-change-my-career-to-do-something-meaningful* camp.

Ask educational leaders why they chose to leave the classroom for the responsibilities of leading a school or district and the answer is surprisingly similar. Educational leaders respond that they care about others, they want to make a difference in the lives of students, they want to contribute to the future, they want to give back—but on a larger scale.

Educators purposely choose a career of service, not a career of entitlement. By disposition, then, we educators have the first prerequisite for becoming an ally for others. We have a big heart. We are inclined to consider the greater good, to be giving of ourselves. We are not shy about saying we love our students.

Danger lurks in this disposition, however, if it is not carefully thought through, supported, and developed over time. We know that having a big heart is not enough. How often have we seen youthful commitment to social justice sour, resulting in droves of disillusioned teachers leaving the profession within the first few years of their careers? How different would things be for their students and for them if they had opportunities to think through their motivation for wanting to work on behalf of others, their position in that work, and the far-reaching effects of the social and political structures that support inequality? In other words, a big heart, although valuable, is not enough to take down the seemingly intractable systems, the overwhelming number of enduring myths, and the biting venom of those whose interests are served by injustice.

We educators can—and should—build on our dispositional strength, our big hearts. This became clear to me several years ago during a multi-day conference addressing ways to transform learning and teaching for underserved students. A team of early-career middle-school teachers posed a critical heartfelt question, "Where do we start?" Noted psychologist Asa Hilliard, understanding their feelings of inadequacy and their sense of being overwhelmed, had a simple, profound response for them. "Begin," he said, "by loving your students."

A big heart, loving our students, is a starting point, an important one to be sure, but it is only a beginning. The kind of love Dr. Hilliard advocates implies more than warm, sentimental feelings for another. It requires will. Dr. Hilliard makes it clear that the kind of love he is talking about is the kind that drives teachers and school leaders to do "whatever it takes" to pry open opportunities that will propel traditionally underserved students to demonstrate their genius. Doing "whatever it takes" is synonymous with "the will to teach" (Hilliard, 2003). The will to teach requires conscious sacrifice, careful preparation, and purposeful action. Furthermore, purposeful actions that are driven by love mean that those taking action view the loved one's needs to be as important as their own, perhaps even more important than their own. Willful, love-driven action pushes back on the all-too-human egocentrism that would otherwise govern actions. Love calls us beyond ego. Many of us have experienced or purposely cultivated this type of love on a one-to-one basis. When applied to a classroom or school or larger community, this type of love functions on a larger, social scale. Love on a social scale is social justice.

By Preparation, Educators Are Strategic and Supportive

Besides possessing a big heart fueled by love, educators participate in the kind of preparation that helps them be strategic and to support others.

Educators are strategic by training. We know how to plan lessons with the end in mind. We know how to shape learning to meet a specific goal, criterion, or vision. More and more, teachers are willing to unbind themselves from the confines of imposed curriculum, unresponsive standards (common core or not), and questionable textbooks that do not leave room for discovery, for personal investment, for joy. These are educators in the real sense of the word *educate*, to *lead out* or *bring forth*, from the Latin *ex* "out" and *ducere* "lead." For educators who adhere to this definition of educate, our goal is to draw out or unleash the powers of the mind, to unlock student potential, to attend to those whose school and personal lives are lived on the margins. We search for and utilize practices, like those found in the Pedagogy of Confidence, that orchestrate multi-faceted learning experiences. The Pedagogy of Confidence strives to identify and activate student strengths, build relationships, elicit high intellectual performance, provide enrichment, integrate prerequisites for academic learning, situate learning in the lives of students, and amplify student voice (Jackson, 2011).

Educational leaders are strategic, too. Many are committed to reconceptualizing education and leadership. They fearlessly search for and use transformative approaches that foster distinctive and productive ways of being, living, and knowing aimed specifically and strategically at those students touched most profoundly by unjust, unyielding, and dehumanizing systems. The goal of these leaders is to cultivate strengths and foster the development of competence and confidence that lead to academic thriving and self-actualization for all students, but especially for those forced to exist on the margins (Jackson, V. McDermott, M. McDermott, & Simmons, 2015). They band together with like-minded educators, the students they serve, and the families who rely on them to become a powerful force that aims high in order to achieve more (Jackson & McDermott, 2012). These types of learning experiences and learning environments do not occur by happenstance. They are deliberately, fearlessly, and strategically implemented.

Educators are strategic in another way. We also know to keep our eyes and ears open so we can switch gears and employ another tack when the learning situation demands that we do so. In other words, we are focused, intentional, and adaptable, three components of being strategic.

By Position, Educators Possess Institutional Sway and Access

We also possess another set of strengths. We possess institutional power given to us by virtue of the roles we play in the world of education and in the lives of our students. Furthermore, these roles provide us with access to students, all kinds of students from the most privileged to the most marginalized.

Power is a useful starting point when you are engaged in a battle. Despite my reluctance to engage concepts drawn from the world of war and violence, in the end I purposely chose to use the word *battle* to describe what engaging in social justice work is like. We need to be honest here. There is a lot of history and there are powerful forces that will fight our efforts tooth and nail in order to preserve the current system. Therefore, we need to be prepared to fight back with the intensity required of a pitched battle.

What kind of power do we educators have? Our roles as educators provide us with unique opportunities to influence others by the countless decisions we make daily and the myriad interactions that occur during the course of a school year. In school, we choose our words. We choose activities. We choose who gets to speak—and who does not. We choose what to make a fuss over and what to ignore. Interestingly, we retain this degree of autonomy despite the current political climate that often makes us feel as if our voices have little or no authority, worth, or authenticity.

What we need to think through, however, is how, where, when, and under what conditions will we exercise this power. As members and products of society, are we unwittingly complicit in exercising power *over* others or are we striving to create shared spaces where power *with* others is the operative word? Grappling with the differences between power *over* and power *with* is a concern of this book.

Educators occupy positions that afford us the great opportunity to work with all sorts of students: students of color, students challenged by poverty, students facing bullying because of sexual identity, students looked down upon because of their parents' undocumented status or level of income, students labeled "handicapped or special," students living on reservations. In other words, our classrooms are microcosms of society with all of its glorious diversity. Our doors are open to all, we are prepared to embrace all, and we have the privilege of working on behalf of all who are marginalized, made to feel less than, ignored. Our efforts on behalf of social justice can—and I believe should be—directed at all oppressed groups.

EDUCATORS AS SOCIAL JUSTICE ADVOCATES

As a group, educators care about social justice. We see ourselves as contributors to the social order, the general welfare, and a better future. We consider ourselves just, if by just we mean that we strive to be fair, to have no favorites, to attend to all, to be even handed.

Educators are also oriented to support others. We work on behalf of others, the students we serve. Each and every one of our students is of interest to us, regardless of personal history, financial circumstances, ability level, or personal orientation. We seek out ways to address the various learning and emotional needs of our students, as well as ways to cultivate their strengths. And our interest in them rarely ends with academics. We care about all aspects of our students' lives: the social, the emotional, the physical. We have all attended out-of-school dance recitals and baseball games. We have all stayed long past our contractual hours to wipe away tears of a student facing a trying situation. We have all dipped into our pockets to provide school supplies or field trip money or a donation to a family whose house burned to the ground. We may have even stood firm and resolute to protect one of our students from a bad institutional decision. In these acts of support, we demonstrate that we are allies.

This is one form of being an ally, standing up *for* others. But it is not the only kind. Allies also stand up *with* others, often way in the background, so that others can stand up *for themselves.* This is the kind of ally this book seeks to develop.

More Than Pulling at the Norms

The question for potential allies in the battle for social justice, then, is in what ways and on what should we be focusing these obvious, shared strengths? Here is where social justice work gets tricky. Social justice work should do more than just pull at the norms. Our bold strategy should be to unravel the web of deception that holds together the intricately constructed system that fuels injustice and inequity in order to reveal it for what it is and ultimately rework the system to reflect a social justice vision. If you have ever tried to unravel a knot, you know how difficult it is to pull apart something tightly woven, to reveal where the various twisting and turning threads lead. If we act hastily, angrily, or carelessly—pulling at threads indiscriminately—we could create a bigger mess, a tighter knot. This may cause us to abandon the project altogether. To be successful in dismantling intricately woven systems takes patience, careful planning, and conscious effort. Social justice work requires a strategy that will help us identify the threads holding injustice together so that we can intentionally pull them apart.

So, yes, at first glance by disposition, professional development, and role, we big-hearted educators are uniquely positioned to be strategic allies in the battle for social justice. More and more, educators—and the general public—are acknowledging that two sets of schools exist in the United States, one for those deemed worthy of an education and one for those deemed expendable. More and more educators—experienced and new; whether they identify as Black, White, Hispanic, Asian, religious or nonreligious, gay or straight—are seeking out information on social justice. They take courses. They read books. They attend workshops. They are trying to "get it," but it is not easy. I know because I often work with teachers and educational leaders in settings specifically designed to pull at the norms that have created two sets of students in school, the marginalized and the accepted.

During these sessions, we have struggled to come to understand the sociohistorical context that has fueled our current educational system. We have looked at the myriad ways, intentional or not, that have made us complicit in perpetuating injustice. We have looked into, around, and under the sociological and psychological effects of marginalization. We have been buoyed by the realization that there is a plethora of ways in which we can rupture the status quo in order to create learning experiences that value all, include all, give voice to all intentionally and with great fanfare.

Moving to the Next Level of Practice

To get to this point, we have centered our work on a framework question: How can we intentionally harness our obvious strengths and advantages to move our work on behalf of social justice to the next level of practice? This framework question inevitably leads to other questions. If our *intention* is social justice, to what do we need to pay *attention*? How is this intentional focus likely to alter how we come to understand ourselves, the institution we serve, and the society in which live? In what ways might these insights alter the way we navigate our role as members of the educational community? How do we create a critical mass to advance the cause of social justice? What should we consider and expect? What are we likely to encounter?

Educators who are aware of their individual and group strengths are better prepared to grapple with these questions. By intentionally harvesting their strengths, educators move their work on behalf of social justice to the next level of practice. Identifying individual and composite strengths is an important first step for individuals and groups interested in addressing inequity. One way of identifying strengths is to conduct an assessment that isolates and identifies the current status of individual and composite strengths. The Social Justice Strengths Inventory (Figure 0.2) provides a template and process for determining the current state of individual and group strengths related to disposition, profession, and role.

Acknowledge the Current Reality

The strengths inventory is a useful tool to describe the current state of affairs regarding individual and group strengths. To begin to move our social justice work to the next level of practice, we also need to begin by acknowledging the current reality of the state of education as many of us experience it.

Most educators, like you, chose to be educators to make a positive difference in the lives of students. Many, perhaps like you, feel more and more bewildered, frustrated, and angry by policies and practices that make it difficult, if not impossible, to act on their vision. Many of us are fed up with media assaults that portray schools as failing, teachers as deficient, and students as hopeless, especially if these students are Black, brown, or challenged by poverty. Unprecedented numbers of educators are joining forces with parents to stand up to the "test and punish" mindset that has gripped education today. Still others are beginning to recognize the nefarious, narrow, for-profit mindset that is creating a two-tiered system of opportunity, education, and life in a country that has the capacity—and past history—to do much better than this.

If any good has come from the relentless assaults and questionable policies of recent years, it is that many educators, like you, see that something has gone awry, and, more importantly, they want to do something about it.

WHY THIS BOOK?

This book is for and about educators who, like you, want to make a positive contribution to right the wrongs that have been inflicted on others. They want to reach their marginalized students, whoever they may be. They want to create a better society, one that values difference, "gifts" all students (Jackson, 2011), and proves that demography need not be destiny

Figure 0.2 Activity: Social Justice Strengths Inventory

Directions:

- Using the template provided, isolate and identify your current social justice strengths.*
- Under each of the three branches, provide specific examples of your particular social justice strengths as they relate to or are demonstrated by your disposition, preparation, and position. Use a separate line for each item. Add lines as necessary. Each column does not need to have the same number of items in it.

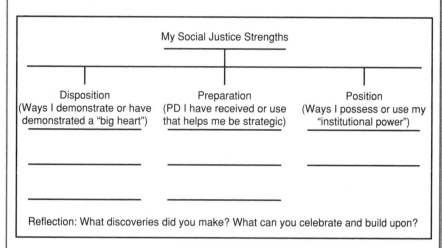

My Social Justice Strengths

Disposition (Ways I demonstrate or have demonstrated a "big heart")	Preparation (PD I have received or use that helps me be strategic)	Position (Ways I possess or use my "institutional power")

Reflection: What discoveries did you make? What can you celebrate and build upon?

Extension and Team Activities

- Ask a trusted colleague or workshop partner who knows you well to complete an inventory of your strengths. What similarities and differences did you note?
- Working in small groups (for example, by grade level, department, or randomly organized), create a composite of the strengths of your group. Share with other groups. What discoveries did you make? What can you celebrate and build upon?
- The individual and composite strengths uncovered by this activity can be used to jumpstart next steps. For instance, the survey might reveal that several colleagues possess a wealth of information regarding ways to identify, understand, and combat injustice and inequality by virtue of their participation in coursework, professional development sessions, or reading. These colleagues can act as resources in the development of book studies, professional learning experiences, and equity projects. A review of how individuals use their specific roles to advance the cause of justice and address marginalization provides inspiration and makes explicit ways in which others can use their roles in a similar fashion.

---

* The template is a Tree Map, which is used for categorizing information. It is one of eight Thinking Maps, each of which represents one of eight thinking patterns (Hyerle, 2004).

(Cooper, 2005). These are educators whose faculty-room and dinner-table conversations are peppered with words like *equity, social justice,* and *social contract.* They attend workshops with titles that invite them to address the needs of their underperforming students.

In short, they care. They also reflect the national profile of our profession. They are overwhelmingly White, middle class, able bodied, and heterosexual. They are trying to "get" it, but they often do not know where to begin.

This book is designed to help educators turn their sense of discomfort about the injustices they see around them into positive actions. It is a chronicle of how I came into this work, complete with mistakes, missteps, and minefields. It is about how you might position yourself to be an ally in the world of social justice work. This is a book about acknowledging the current reality, about coming to understand possibilities, about considering alternatives, and about thinking through how your unique gifts can contribute to social justice work.

Social justice work IS work. It involves openness to new ideas, trust in the process, and a strong stomach. It involves several stages that often overlap, frequently take unexpected twists, and always result in some sort of awakening. The three stages, which often overlap and are recursive, include becoming aware, sharing that awareness, and finding your place in the work. I call these

- Emerging from the Fog of Privilege,
- Exposing the Flaws in the Received Narrative, and
- Embracing "Allyhood."

I have experienced all three stages and I know from these experiences that my journey is far from over. I may "get" one aspect of social justice work, create awareness and support, and act on these insights alone and with others, only to find myself not "getting" another aspect of the work. This is the cycle of learning in general, and it certainly reflects how I grew into social justice work. I hope that through my experiences as a teacher, administrator, and professional developer, I can share the stories and reflections that have moved me into an ever-deepening, often baffling, wholly rewarding understanding of what it means to be an ally in the battle for social justice.

My intention is to share anecdotes and observations, run them through a social justice analysis, and introduce key terms and understandings from the worlds that inform this work so that others can pick up the mantle. As educators—teachers and educational leaders—we are well positioned to change the conversation, to act on behalf of others, to alter the life trajectory of the students for whom our hearts break, and then get out of the way so that our marginalized students and communities can—and will—use their voices to reshape society. Together we can be a powerful force in the battle for social justice.

My intention, then, is to be a catalyst for a movement. Through real-world examples, open discussion of possibilities and limitations of actions taken, generous sharing of resources, and embedded opportunities for reflection, I hope to open up a space for considering the many facets of social justice work as a means of mediating your next—and very personal—move to the next level of practice as a strategic ally in the battle for social justice.

ORGANIZATION AND OVERVIEW

This book is organized around what I now see as three major aspects of my ongoing development to become a strategic ally in the battle for social justice: emerging from the fog of privilege, exposing the flaws in the dominant narrative, and embracing "allyhood." Organizing the book in three sections might suggest that there is a simple, predictable trajectory to becoming aware and active in social justice work. My experiences, however, indicate that this would be a false assumption. There is no simple scope and sequence with a convenient check list that guides social justice work. I use three divisions to highlight what I experienced as I moved— and continue to move—to the next level of understanding. For me, this movement involves becoming aware, spreading the word, and stepping out of the way so that those most affected can take action.

Figure 0.3 Development of a Social Justice Ally

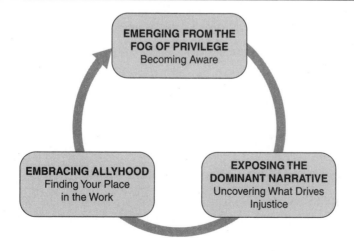

Part I: Emerging From the Fog of Privilege

Part I deals with becoming aware of privilege, locating it, and labeling it. I have chosen to call this initial foray into social justice work *Emerging From the Fog of Privilege,* a term that captures what I experienced and what I have seen others experience. Simply put, without reflection, privilege envelops us like a fog, blinding us to anything that is beyond the fog. From time to time, the fog may lift and we catch a glimpse of the world beyond our familiar foggy existence. The goal of this section is to help lift the fog, to shine a light on what we may be missing, in order to allow us to see injustice more clearly. This is a necessary and difficult step, one that often causes a variety of conflicting emotions and deep soul searching, as well as a new vocabulary to name—and in many instances rename—experiences that we see with a new light.

In Chapters 1 and 2, I will present a brief overview of my personal fog of privilege and move to an experience I had with a White teacher confronting the term *White privilege* for the first time. Social justice concepts are anchored in specialized social justice terminology. Chapters 3, 4, and 5 will present several key terms that will facilitate development of social justice concepts, including the ways in which privilege, power, and schooling are intertwined, often in very taken-for-granted ways, and some of the sociological and psychological effects of ongoing injustice. Chapter 6 acknowledges that engaging in this type of reflection is not easy. Among the myriad responses are avoidance, guilt, and feelings of inadequacy. The final chapter of this section is a challenge. It posits that you can't "un-see" what you have seen after the fog has lifted. In this way, Chapter 6 prepares us for the next major step, that of taking action.

Opening Anecdote: My Personal Fog of Privilege

1. What Is White Privilege?

2. Developing Social Justice Literacy

3. Privilege, Power, Politics, and Schooling

4. Dealing With Avoidance, Guilt, Feelings of Inadequacy, and Misunderstanding

5. Acknowledging the Social and Psychological Toll of Continued Injustice

6. You Can't "Un-See" What You Have Seen

Part II: Exposing the Flaws in the Dominant Narrative

Part II draws upon the rich and ever-growing body of literature that asks us to rethink injustice and schooling in order to expose the underlying assumptions and supporting narratives upon which the current system has been designed. Chapter 7 begins with an anecdote and discussion of the danger—and power—of a single, unquestioned story, as well as some of the dissonance created by exposing the "dominant narrative" to critical analysis. Chapter 8 looks more deeply into the tactics of deception and flawed theories used by those in power to maintain their power. Chapter 9 presents several ways in which educators can "trouble" the dominant narrative as it plays out in their own contexts. Chapter 10 proposes that in the face of injustice, silence is not an option. It also presents several ways in which educators can raise their voices to counter oppression. Chapter 11 is a how-to chapter, demonstrating ways to change the conversation as a catalyst to changing the culture of a classroom or school.

Opening Anecdote: The Danger of a Single Story

7. Embracing Dissonance

8. Tactics of Deception and Flawed Theories

9. Troubling the Dominant Narrative

10. Silence Is Not an Option

11. Change the Culture? Change the Conversation

Part III: Embracing "Allyhood"

The final section discusses what it means to be an ally, including how members of marginalized groups might respond to readers' efforts to engage in social justice work and claim the identity of an ally. Part III begins with an anecdote about the injustice inherent in expropriating other people's narratives. Chapter 12 asserts that allies are important in the fight for social justice, especially since there are so many forms of injustice to combat. Chapter 13 provides several examples of false starts, missteps, and minefields associated with social justice work as a way of illustrating the complexity of social justice work and a warning that there are risks—worthwhile ones, of course—associated with becoming an ally. Chapter 14 explicitly presents the basic characteristics of those who are successful in social justice work. Successful social justice workers are reflective, they cultivate resources, and they are resilient. Chapter 14 also explains how effective allies position themselves and what they can expect. Chapter 15 is designed to provide multiple examples of "allyhood," including discussion of key principles of social justice work that are reflected in these examples.

Opening Anecdote: Chicago Fifth Graders Tell *Their* Chicago Story

12. The Importance of Allies

13. False Starts, Missteps, and Minefields

14. Reflection, Resources, Resilience, and Position

15. The Many Faces of Activism in Action

Chapter Activities and Resources

In each chapter, activities and resources are provided that will help readers think through, under, and around the concepts presented.

All activities suggested in this book are intended to help readers engage, sustain, and expand their thinking about social justice. They can be done alone or with others. As with all meaningful and transformative learning, this process is supported and enhanced when learners have a chance to interact with others, sharing ideas and pushing each other to consider different perspectives. For this reason, most activities include opportunities for individual reflection, as well as extension activities that involve a partner or a group. In addition to being suitable for individual study, each chapter, then, can function as a class or professional development session.

Many activities involve accessing videos. The videos are generally short and integrally related to the content of the chapter. (Where this is not the case, it is noted, and instructions for which part of the video to watch are included.)

Several activities also involve accessing websites. These websites have been carefully selected to integrate with the content of the chapter. At the time of publication, they were checked to make certain the links work.

Rather than appearing at the end of each chapter, activities and prompts for reflection are integrated into chapters in much the same way professional development sessions intersperse activities and reflection prompts throughout a session. Activities are designed to move with the flow of the chapter, sometimes leading readers to new considerations or insights, sometimes to provide a space for reflection. It is recommended that the activities be done before reading the remainder of the chapter.

The strategies used in many of the activities, such as the Tree Map used in the Social Justice Strengths Inventory, can be applied to classroom settings, too. Where appropriate, I have provided a brief introduction to the rationale behind the strategy as it applies to learning and teaching in general, as well as a reference for further information.

Like the integrated activities, the resources mentioned in each chapter are included within the context of the chapter.

Anecdotes

Many personal anecdotes are included in this book. They represent a number of *aha* moments that I have experienced and that I believe provided me with some insight into various aspects of social justice. They are not meant to suggest or prove a universal truth. These anecdotes are intended to animate a point. They are intended as stories, not data.

These experiences extend over a long period of time, and, at the time many of them occurred, I did not seek permission to recount these events. As a result, all of the stories are true, but identifying features such as names of individuals or school districts have been changed.

Orthography and Terminology

Racial and ethnic groups are indicated with a capital letter, since these designations are proper nouns. Where exceptions exist, they are noted and explained. I have also sought to use terminology relating to different group identities that reflects what I understand to be the group's preferred terminology. Again, where exceptions exist, they are noted.

THE SOCIAL JUSTICE JOURNEY

The social justice journey is not neat and tidy, predictable and patented. Instead, it is highly dependent upon personal circumstances, differing contexts, variable supports. Certainly, my ongoing development as an ally is a story containing many twists and turns. By dividing the book into three sections, however forced they may be, provides a way to keep my story intact while I introduce key terms, concepts, and ways of thinking that I believe will prompt fellow educators to think through our cherished, but like all human creations flawed, institution of school in order to make it a place where all marginalized students can flourish. To flourish, our students need schools in which an emphasis on social justice is intentional and relentless, questioning the status quo is the norm, and finding effective ways to support marginalized students—and communities—is a joint effort.

This book is dedicated to eradicate the various "isms" that manifest themselves in schools: sexism, racism, ableism, classism, etc. It is not by accident, however, that I draw many of my examples from antiracism work, since I spent ten years as a regional director with a professional learning organization devoted to urban school renewal. It was through this work that I came to see and consider more deeply the manifold ways racism has played out historically, which then lead me to see more clearly the various manifestations of oppression against other marginalized groups that exist in today's society.

KEY CONSIDERATIONS FOR ALLIES

- Compelling reasons drive why educators need to be knowledgeable, thoughtful, well-prepared allies in the battle for social justice.
- Educators—by virtue of their disposition, preparation, and position—are uniquely placed to become influential allies in this battle.
- Using a formal procedure for isolating and identifying specific strengths provides individuals and groups with a solid understanding of their current reality and an easily identifiable source of resources that can be tapped for continued growth.
- Becoming an ally in the battle for social justice is an ongoing process, which includes three major and recursive stages: emerging from the fog of privilege, exposing the flaws in the dominant narrative, and embracing allyhood.
- **Looking Ahead**: In the next section, the metaphor of the Fog of Privilege is expanded upon and applied to my life trajectory, as a means of situating myself in the context of this work. At the end of this section, readers are invited to consider the ways in which their personal fogs of privilege converge and diverge with my story, as a means of examining the ways in which privilege has worked in their own lives.

Part I

Emerging From the Fog of Privilege

THE FOG PHENOMENON

A fog is a complex atmospheric phenomenon formed from difference, a slight difference, as it turns out. A minor four-degrees-Fahrenheit difference between air temperature and the dew point can obliterate the sun's rays, reduce visibility to zero, create unearthly shadows, and distort sound.

Fog is transformative. It twists reality. Despite its ephemeral quality, fog is tough. It outwits foghorns, fog lights, and radar. Fog is dangerous. It shuts down shipping lanes, airports, and highways.

Fog has a chilling effect. No amount of scientific know-how or wishful thinking can counteract its effects. Despite our best efforts, fog can envelop us, formed and maintained by conditions out of our control.

Injustice, like fog, is born from difference. Injustice is no less complex, distorting, tough, dangerous, chilling, or resistant than fog. This is why I chose to use the image of the fog of privilege to capture the essence of how injustice operates in the world. Injustice is a formidable enemy that will never go away until we understand how, like fog, it comes in on little cat feet—as Carl Sandburg says—and leaves in its wake filthy air that mixes up what is fair and what is foul—as Shakespeare says.

PART ONE OPENING ANECDOTE: MY PERSONAL FOG OF PRIVILEGE

I would love to say that I come from a long line of activists, that I have been at the center of many battles for social justice, that I have seen the inside of a jail or had my phone tapped for my actions on behalf of others, but all of that would be a lie. As a second-generation Italian American girl from a working-class family, I spent my childhood driven to figure out what the "American" norm was, to modify my behavior accordingly, and to seek the approval of the Irish nuns who ran our very traditional parochial schools. (Part of my high school uniform included white gloves, which I donned on formal occasions after having spent classroom time to learn how to greet a new acquaintance with a gloved hand and a curtsy.) To be a young woman in this environment invoked another set of strictures. I was expected to be docile, to "act like a lady" as my mother always cautioned, to anticipate moving from my father's house to my future husband's house—most likely situated on Staten Island—with no other stops along the way, such as university. In my Brooklyn, NY, neighborhood of the 1950s, *activism* was a word we never heard, used, or likely understood.

Even when the rebellious sixties arrived, the most activist thing I did was to spend a beautiful autumn Saturday afternoon outside a suburban supermarket holding a *boycott lettuce* sign. I was with my husband and the supermarket was not far from where we eventually bought our first home. After that, children, mortgage, and career became my life.

However, the social justice activist existed within me. Activism was usually close to the surface of the life choices I made, and from time to time it emerged in surprising and powerful ways. As a teacher in a four-year comprehensive suburban high school, status belonged to those who taught the upper-grade AP and honors tracks. The so-called "advanced students" were fine in my view, but I really preferred teaching the "lower track" students, whom I found to be more authentic, less grade-driven, and generally more fun to be with. When an in-school alternative school was created for the "10% of the population that caused 90% of the problems," I volunteered to be their English teacher. Now I can see that I was driven by a big heart but that the alternative school was nothing more than another manifestation of marginalizing students, forcing them to fit into the school mold, and doing so by exercising power over their movements and opportunities.

Movement was limited in that the teachers went to two classrooms dedicated to the alternative school rather than the students circulating to the teachers' rooms—in the interest of orderly hallways, no doubt. Opportunities were limited by an abbreviated day—get them home before they can cause trouble—and while they are in school give them an anemic curriculum, since their skill set is weak anyway.

As I look back on it now, I see another major flaw in the plan. No matter how many times you remove the "10% of the population causing 90% of the problems," there will always be another 10 percent. Although no one bothered to do so then, I am certain that had anyone looked into who was part of the alternative school, they would have discovered that the troublesome 10 percent came from the least wealthy part of town. I shudder today to think about the harm such programs did to students' self-esteem and sense of worth.

I am happy to say that by the time I became an administrator, I thought through a number of these issues and realized that my role enabled me to affect policy. I was insistent that students who were labeled special education receive the benefits of a robust curriculum. Special education, I came to believe, was intended to be placement, not a life sentence. When principals and teachers rallied to put students into more restrictive environments, I would often challenge them by asking, "And what will be different?" Of course, nothing would be different in either setting if teaching continued as usual. I firmly believe that professional learning that shows teachers how to push all students to the frontiers of their intelligence (Jackson, 2011) minimizes the need for labels, special settings, or other ways of institutional "otherizing."

Over time I even went so far as to engage in a bit of subterfuge on behalf of others. At a time when health care costs were skyrocketing and gay marriage was wholly unaccepted, I managed to work with sympathetic board members and supportive union officials to quietly slip wording into a negotiated contract that included extending health care benefits to unmarried, long-time partners.

It is only now that I see these efforts as social justice work. At the time they were occurring, I had yet to develop the social justice literacy and lens that I now have. What these examples highlight for me, however, is that none of us need to look far to find opportunities to work on behalf of social justice, and you, like me, may have been doing so without even knowing it. What interests me is what happens when you make the decision to become intentional about this work in a school setting.

Glimpsing the Light: "Never Discourage a Child" and Other Social Justice Lessons

A few years before I retired, I was asked to give a commencement speech at one of the departmental graduation events at the university from which I graduated. I was awestruck by this invitation. I remember telling the graduates so. After all, there was nothing in my early life experiences that would have suggested that I would go to college, let alone earn a PhD, and be the first—and only—woman superintendent of a large school district that began life in the mid-1800s.

How did this happen? Not by chance and not by personal effort, although both did play a part in the outcome. Family lessons certainly poured the foundation. My father, a big man with an even bigger personality, was an imposing, but kind hearted, presence. His favorite stories, whether they were set during WWII or in the workplace, often had to do with how he used his size to come to the aid of others. In other words, he was a softy. Even into his 90s, he could be moved to tears by cruelty, especially to children. I remember well his reaction to the school shootings in Connecticut.

When my daughter, like me, became a teacher, my father was visibly proud and he repeated the exact same words he had said to me some thirty years earlier when I got my first teaching job: "Never discourage a child." Not a bad mantra for any teacher. Coming from him, a man of obvious intelligence who had been discouraged by a teacher who said he was not college material, both my daughter and I knew we would never be dream killers.

When it came to raising his own children, he was encouraging, as was my ever-patient mother, who knew how to calm my back-to-school jitters each year by telling me that my teachers would never have promoted me if I really was not ready for the next grade level. Encouragement was also on the agenda of many of the teachers who I had throughout the years. But none of this encouragement would have led to a college degree if it had not been

Systems and Social Justice

We will never get social justice right until we acknowledge the powerful role systems play in who succeeds and who does not. Stories that suggest that all it takes to get ahead is individual effort are problematic. For example, one of the yearly stories carried by the media is the predictable June feature about a homeless child—most often a child of color—from some inner city who manages to be named valedictorian, to win numerous athletic awards, to be named employee of the year at the student's place of employment (of course, this model student maintains high grades working part time), and to be accepted at numerous Ivy League schools.

These feel-good stories are dangerous. They lead people to believe that overcoming enormous odds is a one-person test of endurance that is obviously doable by anyone willing to work hard enough. The thinking it leads to is this: If this homeless child can become valedictorian even though he sleeps in a car doing homework under a dome light, anyone can do the same. All it takes is individual initiative, or, what I perceive to be the dirtiest word in the English language, *grit*. Let's be clear. If you scratch beneath the surface of any of these end-of-school-year stories, you will find an array of people and institutions that intervened and supported these stellar students, just as I can point to family circumstances, social context, and political policy that gave me my chance to go to university.

for the rise of the state university system in New York, which made it afford-able for the children of working-class families like me to go to university.

Having the System on Your Side

For me, being White helped, too. Enormously. I wonder what would have happened to my university application or job application had I had an identifiable Black name. To be sure, SUNY Stony Brook, my alma mater, was as White as my neighborhood, as was the suburban Long Island school district where I got my first job. During the hiring blitz of those frenzied years of house and school building, there was only one teacher of color in the entire, large district, who, it turns out, became a friend of mine. Sadly, he left his position as an art teacher due to pressures he assiduously refused to discuss. There was also one Black family in the district. Everyone knew them. Dad was White and a professor at the uni-versity. Mom was Black from Cuba. All of their children went on to Ivy League schools and are leaders in their fields.

My unearned privileges did not end there. After university, having a supportive husband was essential. In fact, my husband, Jim, is another entire system of support. Jim provided the emotional support and encour-agement it took to give me the courage to break into administration and earn an advanced degree at a time when few women succeeded in doing so. He also became the mainstay at home. His more predictable hours and his willingness to do so made it possible for him to pick up those tasks I used to do: fetch the children, prepare dinner, and run the errands that go into maintaining a household and keeping a family together.

He also knew exactly what to say when I experienced blatant sexism in the form of a golf-playing board of education member who told me point-edly during my final interview for a superintendent's position that he was very proud of his wife because she was a "stay-at-home wife." Predictably, the position I sought went to a man who was less experienced and had less education than I. But, he had a wife who was a "stay-at-home wife"—and he played golf.

Fortunately, there were other men in the system (to be fair, some of whom also played golf) who judged candidates on their merits, not their sex, and who often went out of their way to promote women at a time when women made up the bulk of the teaching force but were almost totally absent from the ranks of administrators. Had I arrived on the scene five or ten years earlier, I am almost certain I would not have been afforded the same opportunities. Feminism was in the air, and even if I did not identify as a feminist at the time, like many educated, professionally trained, White women, I benefitted from the conversations taking place, the awareness generated, and the attitudes that were changing.

Story as Window and Mirror

One of the many ways I came to understand how my life trajectory was influenced by a constellation of institutional, political, and personal supports was by taking the time to think through my life experiences, comparing them to the experiences of others, and then applying the lens of social justice to analyze how privilege worked in my life.

As you were reading this section, you may have seen reflections of your own experiences, as well as experiences that are substantively different from the ones I experienced. Emily Style (1988) argues that curriculum should

Figure 1.1   Activity: Window/Mirror: Interrogating Your Story of Privilege

- Review the section titled "My Personal Fog of Privilege," which includes my story of coming to understand privilege.
- Select 3–5 incidents, experiences, or circumstances that resonated with you.
- Using the graphic below, briefly record the incident, experience, or circumstance.
- For each, consider whether the incident, experience, or circumstance is a window or mirror for you. A window provides a new frame of reference. A mirror reflects your reality.
- In the space provided, indicate in what way or ways that incident, experience, or circumstance functions as a window or a mirror for you.

Window/Mirror: Interrogating Your Story of Privilege		
Incident/Experience/ Circumstance	Window or Mirror?	Explain How It Is a Window or Mirror

Reflection

- What discoveries did you make? What patterns did you see? What questions do you have?

Extension and Team Activities

- Working with a partner or a small group, take turns presenting one section that represents a window for the presenter, then open the floor for discussion and comment. (Establish a reasonable amount of time to present and discuss the participant's window.)
- Repeat until all participants present their windows.
- Repeat the process focusing on participants' mirrors.
- As a result of this activity, what discoveries, patterns, or questions emerged?
- Share your discoveries, patterns, and questions with the whole group.

function as both window and mirror. In other words, curriculum should enable students to "look through window frames in order to see the realities of others and into mirrors in order to see his/her own reality reflected" (Style, 1988, p. 1). Furthermore, she asserts that education can help learners in the "great conversations" between various frames of reference.

The activity in Figure 1.1 asks you engage in a "great conversation," an internal dialogue, if you will, that helps you make explicit those experiences that are windows for you and those that are mirrors. By intentionally considering these two aspects, you will be able to think through some of the ideas presented in this section as they relate to privilege.

Through the Lens of Social Justice

As I think through the major life experiences that brought me to identify as a social justice activist, I see several themes that went unnoticed while I was going through these experiences.

Figure 1.2   What a Social Justice Lens Reveals

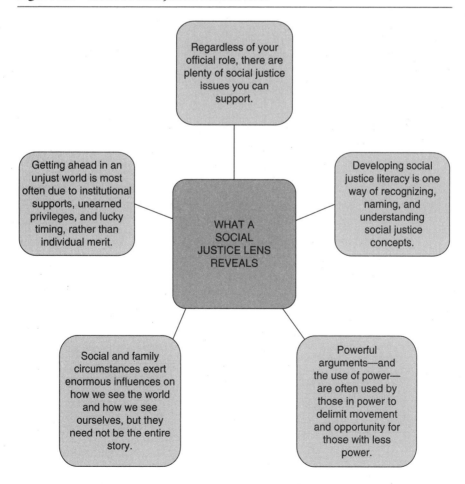

These five themes are insights that I gained as I began to seek out and pierce through the slight fissures, the less dense parts, of my personal fog of privilege. What emerged for me—and is still emerging—are the often achingly harsh realities of worlds and experiences and ways of being that others are forced into that I was spared and, even more importantly, that I never knew existed. In other words, unbeknownst to me, I was privileged by circumstances. Coming to understand privilege more deeply is the focus of the next chapter.

What Is White Privilege?

PIERCING THE FOG OF PRIVILEGE

The saying that a fish doesn't know it's wet implies that most of us take our lived circumstances to be the norm. That is one explanation for why so many of us live in a fog of privilege. It is not until something happens, someone says something, or something seems out of kilter that we begin to consider that there might be another reality, condition, or set of experiences that do not align with ours. The story that follows is a story in which a number of circumstances and people came together and served as a wake-up call, a piercing of the fog that enveloped an experienced, earnest educator. This anecdote has two major players, several risk takers both living and dead, an informative history, and a moral.

The Major Players

It was summertime. A group of one hundred or so educators from around the United States were gathered together for a four-day conference having to do with equity and the Common Core State Standards. What could be said about the two key players is that you could not find two people more different in terms of their understanding of issues around equity. We will call them Christine and Darnel. Christine, an elementary school teacher with ten years of experience teaching in one of two schools that qualify for Title I funding in an otherwise well-healed suburban district, represents the face of American educators: White, middle class, earnest.

Darnel, African American, comes from a district adjacent to a large city, a district with a changing demographic (code language for an influx of children of color), and a staff feeling off balance by these changes.

Acknowledging this reality, the district spent several years working with community members, staff, and students to develop a strategic plan designed to focus all resources on a unified vision for high intellectual performance for all students through equity. Darnel's voice and vision are clearly reflected in this document, not only because his role in the district is to direct initiatives around integration, equity, and American Indian education but also because he is a passionate, committed, and highly regarded spokesperson for those students who feel criminalized, vilified, silenced, and ignored—sometimes all at the same time. Darnel knows marginalization from bitter personal experience and from extended study, and his goal is to reverse the nefarious effects of a divided world, divided opportunities, and divided existences.

During the institute, Christine was apparently caught off guard during one of the sharing sessions when Darnel used the term *White privilege.* The bad news is that Christine has been working for over ten years in a school in which the majority of students are children of color, yet she had never heard the term before. The good news is that she felt comfortable enough to ask me privately, "What is White privilege?" Two promising notes: Christine listened intently (no push back) AND she asked me if I had any books or articles on the subject that she could read.

The Risk Takers

If risk taking involves being fearlessly true to your values and operating on the basis of these values, Darnel took a risk by frankly employing with a mixed group of educators a term that is either unfamiliar to many White people, like Christine, or that rattles White people. If risk taking means facing your fears and discomforts, Christine took a risk by seeking out the meaning of an unfamiliar, charged term. Thus, there are at least two risk takers in this story.

This story illustrates for me one of the principle understandings of privilege in general and White privilege in particular. Privilege is largely invisible to those who benefit from it. As a result, White privilege is not normally a part of the lexicon of White people, which explains Christine's lack of understanding. Another interesting point is that even though Christine did not understand the term, she did not feel comfortable asking Darnel directly what the term meant. Instead, she used me as an intermediary. In many ways, the manner in which this story played out parallels the way in which the concept of *White privilege* came to be framed and developed.

SO WHAT IS WHITE PRIVILEGE?

The History

Most scholars attribute African American sociologist and historian W. E. B. Du Bois with several observations that eventually led to the concept of *White privilege.* Among them, Du Bois pointed out that Black people in the United States live behind a metaphorical veil from which they both experience life and observe the life of White people on the other side of the veil. White people, on the other hand, pay no heed to Black experiences. Du Bois made this observation in 1903 (Du Bois, 1903). In 2013, Darnel, like Du Bois, demonstrated his insight into social stratification, his ability to navigate inside and outside the veil. Christine's question "What is White privilege?" reveals how far away she had been from considering the realities of other people's lives, how encased she was in life on her side of the veil.

Du Bois also pointed out another difference between Black and White experiences, which became foundational to the understanding of *White privilege.* In comparing the situation of poor Black workers with that of poor White workers, Du Bois asserted that despite their common economic situation, White workers received many "public and psychological wages" that resulted in differentiated treatment in many areas of life, including law and education (Du Bois, 1935). Clearly, Du Bois took many risks in making his observations public.

Over the years, many Black activists analyzed and discussed how Whiteness and Blackness play out in grossly uneven, patently lopsided ways, providing one group with advantages denied to the other, advantages that are frequently unacknowledged by those who benefit from them. It wasn't until 1988, however, that a White feminist scholar, Peggy McIntosh, wrote a groundbreaking article, which chronicles her responses to a simple question: What do I have that I did not earn (McIntosh, 1988)? Initially, she delineated forty-six items that made it clear to her that there are unearned advantages she could expect simply because she was born White. Among the items that made up the contents of what she called her *invisible knapsack* (McIntosh, 1989) are

- I can go shopping alone most of the time, fairly well assured that I will not be followed or harassed by store detectives and
- I can turn on the television or open to the front page of the paper and see people of my race widely and positively represented.

The *invisible knapsack* has many manifestations beyond those articulated by McIntosh. As a group, White people see themselves positively portrayed in the media and they generally enjoy positive relationships with law enforcement and the justice system. In a school setting, White children learn about their race in school, read more books about their race, are treated more leniently because of their race, and have more chances to attend better resourced, better performing schools because of their race.

White Privilege: The Backlash

The concept of *White privilege* was articulated more than one hundred years ago, yet it is a concept that is still not universally understood nor accepted. Increasingly, the term has moved beyond the world of sociology and into the vernacular. It is, however, a highly charged term in the minds of many.

One need not search long to find articles, videos, and postings vehemently protesting the notion that Whites experience privileges denied to their non-White counterparts or that all Whites are recipients of the same privileges or that the privileges White people enjoy are, in fact, unearned. The term *White privilege* can stir up much controversy and backlash. Allies for social justice need not look much further than this concept to find a highly contested, emotional battleground of ideas and convictions.

White Privilege: The Moral

The concept of privilege in general and *White privilege* in particular is critical to social justice work.

THINKING THROUGH PRIVILEGE

Privilege is a concept that applies beyond White, non-White relationships. It is a term used frequently in the world of sociology and in social justice work. Therefore, it is worth our time to unpack this concept in more detail. Many definitions of privilege exist, as do many examples.

The artifice of social divisions makes privilege possible. We see privilege in operation in the various ways certain groups are treated, talked about, and managed. We have also experienced privilege and its opposite, oppression, even though we may not have had the term to describe these situations we have observed and experienced. A few examples will help to bring the term *privilege* into focus.

- What are some of the privileges enjoyed by those with excess capital that those challenged by poverty do not possess? What forms of oppression might those who are challenged by poverty experience?

- What are some of the privileges afforded to those who are able bodied that those who are challenged by physical restrictions are denied? What forms of oppression might those who are challenged by physical restrictions experience?
- What are some of the privileges afforded to those who identify as or practice the majority religion that are withheld from those who identify as or practice a minority religion? What forms of oppression might those who practice a minority religion experience?

Certainly there are numbers of privileges associated with economic status, physical ability, and membership in a majority religion. Things like food insecurity do not exist for the wealthy. Able-bodied people rarely need to plan ahead of time how they will navigate to insure that they have access to their preferred grocery store, the closest pharmacy, or the nearest full-service bank. Fear of physical attack does not accompany members of religious majorities to their places of worship or set up residency in their homes or occupy their minds when their loved ones go about their daily routines.

Understanding how social divisions work to produce inequitable situations is critical to social justice work. Two resources for digging deeper into social divisions as a way of understanding privilege and oppression include

- the Power Flower, a tool developed by social change educators that visually charts where people stand in relation to those in power, and
- the Privilege Aptitude Test, a twelve-question exercise with follow-up activities developed by the National Civil Rights Museum in Memphis. This exercise is designed for students to contemplate how their lives are influenced by privilege. (Although the activities and intentions of this aptitude test are noteworthy, I find that the document would benefit from editing.)

Privilege: The Invisible Ink of Advantage

Coming to grips with privilege is not always easy for those who enjoy it. Determining what it is can often be difficult because of the intricate ways in which people relate to one another. So how can we come to conceptualize this notion without depending upon dictionary definitions or Google searches? Metaphors often capture the subtleties missing in a definition.

Privilege can be seen as the invisible ink of advantage that writes the life story of those who occupy the top of any social strata. It is the stuff that defines those privileged, that shapes the contours of their experiences,

Figure 1.3   Activity: Coming to Understanding Privilege

Part 1. The Power Flower

The Power Flower was developed in Toronto and has been widely adapted by many organizations and individuals because of the graphic way it demonstrates where individuals are in relation to those who wield power (Arnold, Burke, James, Martin, & Thomas, 1991).

The activity can be done with adults and secondary school students. The Power Flower is a sixteen-petal daisy containing a central core and both inner and outer petals.

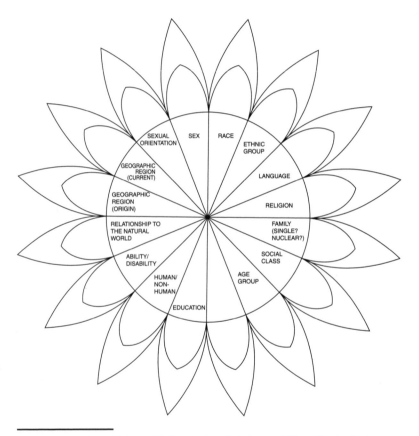

"Power Flower" from Rick Arnold, Bev Burke, Carl James, D'Arcy Martin, Barb Thomas, *Educating for a Change* ©1991 (Toronto: Between the Lines, 1991), p. 13. Used with permission of the publisher.

The central core represents sixteen social identities such as language, sex, and race. After the group identifies and labels the outer petals with what they believe is the dominant language, sex, religion, etc., participants then shade in the inner petals with their individual identifying characteristic if it matches the dominant category. For example, if in the language category the dominant language is identified as English and English is your language, you would be credited with possessing the dominant language characteristic. The object is to see how close or how distant each individual is to the dominant characteristics. The more matches an individual has, the closer that person is to being a member of the socially dominant group.

One of the organizations that has used the Power Flower in its efforts to help people understand the role of power in racism is the United Church of Canada. One of their publications includes a history of the project, an explanation of its purpose, and complete directions for completing the Power Flower activity (Ng, 2004). The document can be found online at the following website:

http://lgbtq2stoolkit.learningcommunity.ca/wp/wp-content/uploads/2014/12/ flower-power-exercise.pdf

Directions:

- Access the document and complete the activities as directed on the website.

Reflection:

- What surprised you?
- What insights do you now have about position in society and privilege?
- How does your position in society and access to privilege compare to those of your students?

Part 2. The Privilege Aptitude Test

Like the Power Flower activity, the Privilege Aptitude Test can be found online. The document includes a definition of privilege, a questionnaire, a scoring guide, and a discussion guide. This activity is designed to be done with students.

Directions:

- Review the document, which can be found at the following website: https://www.civilrightsmuseum.org/assets/2417/Youth-PrivilegeAptitudeTest.pdf

Reflection:

- After reviewing the document, determine what students you might want to use the survey with and why.
- What ways could you integrate this survey into the curriculum?
- What follow-up or extension activities might you consider?

that guarantees a lineage of privilege, but, like messages encoded by invisible ink, those privileged have no idea that a subtext exists. Privilege, like invisible ink, can only be made visible if special measures are taken to render the ink visible. Of course, no one would take this step unless one suspected something was hidden and needed decoding in the first place. Hence, most privileged people "read" a one-dimensional story of society, usually one that indicates that they possess special personal characteristics or, in some cases, favoritism based upon their higher moral state, which has contributed to their success.

There is a second aspect of invisible ink that bears upon notions of privilege. Another term for invisible ink, which was developed as an espionage tool during WWI, is *security ink*. Clearly, the intention of this alternate term was that encoded messages were written in invisible ink in order to ensure that the message remained secure. When applied to privilege, *security ink* takes on a slightly different meaning. In many ways, privilege is security for those who possess it. The invisible ink of privilege secures and insures a dominant or favored position for a select few. It also spells insecurity for those whose life stories are written without the invisible ink of privilege.

Privilege is more than just a possession some have and others do not. Privilege establishes, maintains, and operates what Paul Gilroy refers to as the "complex machinery of inequality" (Gilroy & Yancy, 2015).

KEY CONSIDERATIONS FOR ALLIES

- Privilege is largely invisible to those who benefit from it.
- Privilege is a constellation of unearned benefits that sustains inequality.
- Coming to grips with privilege is not always easy for those who enjoy it.
- Privilege could be defined as the invisible ink of advantage that defines, circumscribes, and shapes the life story of those who occupy the top social strata.
- *Privilege* is a fundamental term associated with social justice work.
- **Looking Ahead**: Besides *privilege*, there are other terms associated with social justice work that benefit from consideration, explication, and definition and that help ground the work. The next chapter will address some of these terms in an effort to come to understand what it means to be literate in social justice work.

Developing Social Justice Literacy

In the preceding chapter, we looked at the ways in which privilege, in general, and White privilege, specifically, take on particular meanings and suggest particular social constructs that divide groups of people. It is difficult, if not impossible, to talk about, think about, or interrogate injustice without understanding privilege. In other words, *privilege* is a fundamental concept, a basic vocabulary word that is part of the social justice lexicon. Coming to understand a basic term like *privilege* helps to ground our work, and it introduces us to some of the precise ways in which the language of social justice literacy operates.

The purpose of this chapter is to further ground our thinking about social justice issues by situating our work in the lives of real students, by becoming more fluent in the language of social justice, and by employing a social justice lens to "read" historical and current educational issues.

DEDICATING YOUR WORK TO A MARGINALIZED STUDENT

Before looking more deeply into what is meant by social justice and a socially just school, it might be helpful as you read this book to dedicate the work you are doing to a marginalized student who you have encountered during your career. (Alternatively, you can dedicate this work to a marginalized group of students.)

We will return to your dedication later in the chapter, after we have thought through, under, inside, and around how we might define a socially just school.

Figure 2.1   Activity: Dedicating Your Work to a Marginalized Student

Jot down and save your thoughts relating to the marginalized student or students you selected. Be as specific as possible.

- To whom have you dedicated this work?
- What is this student's name? (Alternatively, what are the names of some of the students who make up the marginalized group you selected?)
- Why did you select this student (or group of students)?
- In what ways does marginalization of this student (or group of students) manifest itself, especially in school?
- What do people say and do that leads you to believe this student (or group of students) is marginalized? (Consider teachers, community members, the media, and other students.)
- What do you know, or think you know, about the circumstances of the life of this marginalized student (or group of marginalized students)? Think through family composition, place of residence, religion, economic status, race, ethnicity, school classification, etc.

BECOMING MORE FLUENT IN THE LANGUAGE OF SOCIAL JUSTICE

Because definitions bring clarity, our goal in this section is to work toward a definition of social justice and what constitutes a socially just school. Definitions highlight essential characteristics or attributes. They aid in making distinctions. How we define something is an indication of how we are making sense of what we are defining.

Defining School: Being Duped and Duping Others

In the mid-1980s, when I first became an administrator, I stumbled upon a definition of school that I used many times in meetings with teachers, parents, and students. "School," I would say almost reverently, "is four walls with the future inside." I would pause, certain that all within hearing would take my Hallmark-card meaning. The school I was referencing was light and airy, well maintained, and orderly. My greeting-card school was a version of school in which students and teachers worked well together; smiled continually; and came to school well fed, well dressed, and well prepared for learning and teaching. Think sunshine and flowers in soft pastel hues. My definition was meant to appeal to tender feelings, to conjure up a romantic image—and it usually worked. It was also a sentimental hoax.

If I knew then what I know now, I would have realized that this definition, dripping in sentimentality and nostalgic longing for a condition that probably never existed, was far from the whole story. In fact, I have since come to be especially suspicious of anything soaked with sentimentality. Psychiatrist Carl Jung famously pointed out that "sentimentality is a superstructure covering brutality." These are strong words. They caused me to wonder—did Jung's observation apply to the schools with which I was associated? The only way to find out was to look into what was really happening in schools at the time.

What kinds of brutality did my definition gloss over? At the time, I think I understood but chose not to delve into and articulate that for many students and teachers, the experience of school did not fit the implied meaning of wholesomeness behind my dew-dripping definition. Not being particularly critical at the time, I could accept and promote this sentimental definition of school and totally overlook the more brutal reality: underserved, over-policed students; underresourced, overburdened teachers; over-zealous and wrong-headed policies; anemic expectations and ailing, irrelevant curricula. The list goes on.

As I was writing this chapter, I initially hesitated to use the term *brutal* to describe the reality of school for many students, but then two incidents occurred that prompted me to fearlessly label school as a site where brutality can, and often does, occur. One had to do with an incident that made the news. The other had to do with something I happened to be reading at the time. Both involved discipline in a school setting that morphed into brutality.

During the fall of 2015, people were shocked by the video of the security officer dragging a student out of her desk and across the room because she did not follow her teacher's directions to put her cell phone away. This, the nation asked, is the way we carry out discipline in South Carolina in 2015? The other incident that shocked me the very same week was recounted in a book I was reading about the plight of Canadian aboriginal and native peoples. Unlike the immediately and widely available video, the incident I read about was long denied and only came to light when the Canadian government was forced to publish a report that confirmed what victims had been saying for years. In Ontario, well into the twentieth century, discipline at one of the then still existing Residential Schools for Indians, as they were called, involved the use of an electric chair in which shocks were administered to wayward students, mostly boys it appears. These children's legs were not strapped down during these disciplinary sessions. The electric current would cause children's legs to fly out in front of them, a sight, unbelievably, that the adults watching found funny. Often, to get more laughs, they would increase the current, which often resulted in children passing out (Saul, 2014).

How, one wonders, did these school systems think it was okay to replace discipline with brutality? What other ruthless methods have been sanctioned in places like these? One thing is certain, however, events such as these have long-term and extraordinarily damaging effects on the well-being of victims and witnesses alike.

The Case for Complete Definitions

In some ways, then, my definition that school is four walls with the future inside was not wrong. It just was not complete. Depending upon the school, the future is markedly different for attendees. For some students, everything inside and outside the four walls is aligned for them to reach and exceed their potential, for them to thrive, for them to live fulfilled lives. For others, what happens in school prepares them for a life relegated to the margins, a life hounded by trying to cope with and make sense of unspeakable horrors experienced or witnessed.

My wish to paint a sunny portrait of school was little more than an exercise in manipulation and myth making. It was not—and is not—the complete and honest picture about what schools are and what they have been designed to do. There are—and always have been—hidden agendas, uneven opportunities, and well-thought-out distractions that get in the way of distinguishing between myth and reality. Another, more honest, conceptualization of school and schooling is the brutal reality that the unevenness of school experiences provides "a place for every child and every child in his or her place" (Tyack & Cuban, 1995, p. 20). Those who are on the inside, who most resemble those in power, are put in places where they are accepted and flourish. Those who are on the outside, who are Black or gay or wheelchair bound or Muslim or poor or non-English speaking, are put in places where they are treated as expendable, blamed for their condition, and viewed as being members of a group possessing intractable, unsolvable problems.

Definitions, then, cannot be taken on face value. They need to be thought through, reflected upon, and critiqued. A sociologist might ask a series of questions to ferret out the finer distinctions inherent in the definition of school as four walls with the future inside. For example, a sociologist might ask the following questions:

- For whom and under what conditions does this definition apply?
- For what kind of future or futures do school experiences prepare students?
- Are they the same for all students?

Obviously, I eventually came to a more nuanced understanding of the definition I once promoted. In short, I emerged slowly from the fog of privilege, denial, and lack of criticality that clouded my ability to see reality.

To do this work I needed two things: guidance in alternate ways of viewing situations and a vocabulary with which to explain the emerging picture I was seeing.

A critical aspect of engaging in social justice work, then, is to develop a lexicon of social justice terms that capture the way societies organize themselves and operate. This is a daunting task if you, like me, are an educator, not a sociologist. Over time, through discussion and reading, I became more and more capable of thinking through situations using concepts and vocabulary that capture social justice implications. Eventually, I have become more and more comfortable using my newly acquired vocabulary to support others to come to understand inequity in its various manifestations.

It is not the purpose of this book to present an exhaustive list of key terms used in discussing social justice issues, nor is it a goal of this book to unpack the many concepts associated with social justice. This is important work that I highly recommend, but it does take time, patience, study, and discussion that goes beyond the scope of this book. Happily, there are plenty of writers, theorists, and resources available that can aid anyone interested in building a complete social justice lexicon.

After much trial and error, the resource that I have found most useful is the book *Is Everyone Really Equal? An Introduction to Key Concepts in Social Justice Education*, by Ozlem Sensoy and Robin DiAngelo (2012). Think of it as a primer that provides historical perspective, simple explanations of complex sociological concepts, specialized vocabulary, suggestions for actions, ways to address possible reactions, and a comprehensive list of additional resources. There is even a glossary of terms, all of which could and should become part of the lexicon of anyone seeking to be an ally in the battle for social justice.

ELEMENTS AND ATTRIBUTES OF A SOCIALLY JUST SCHOOL

What Is Meant By a Socially Just School?

With or without an exhaustive and precise lexicon of terms related to social justice, we can use our experiences to begin to explicate what a socially just school might look like.

The activity in Figure 2.2 helps to develop a shared understanding of some of the basic elements of social justice as they play out in an educational setting. The activity builds upon a thought experiment conceived by John Rawls, an American philosopher, which was designed to determine the principles of social justice. Rawls understood that for people to be truly free to contemplate fairness and unfairness in the complex web that makes up social arrangements, they would have to liberate themselves from the threads of the web that ensnare them.

The thought experiment invited people to define justice by imagining that they were starting life from scratch without any foreknowledge of the circumstances of their birth. What kind of society, he asked, would you want to be born into if you knew nothing about your parents' religion, economic status, nationality, etc.? Rawls believed that by not knowing anything about family circumstance, people engaging in the thought experiment would be free from the ways they are currently implicated in the system. This would allow them ample room to identify those principles of justice that almost everyone would agree to and accept (Rawls, 1971).

Imagining a Socially Just School

Figure 2.2 adapts Rawls's thought experiment and applies it to the world of education. The central question of this thought experiment is to consider what kind of school you would want to enter and graduate from if you had no idea into what kind of family you might be born. This is, after all, the reality for all of us. None of us gets to choose the conditions of our birth, yet those conditions have profound ramifications that determine the teachers we have, what kind of schools we attend, what we learn, and how we are taught.

So What Is Social Justice?

There are many definitions of social justice. Clearly, *justice* implies fairness, impartiality, and integrity, concepts humans encoded into their religious and ethical teachings from early on, suggesting that a desire for justice is deep rooted. There is a systemic side to justice, too. We talk about the justice *system*, an entire and complex social organization and way of proceeding dedicated to the fair application of law (which may or may not be fair, but that is another story). The word *social*, of course, refers to groups, collectives, if you will, thereby extending the definition beyond what seems fair to any given individual.

Social justice is an interpretive lens that seeks to highlight and iron out the wrinkles in the fabric of social relationships. In other words, applying the concept of *social justice* to the multiple, myriad, and complex interactions individuals and groups have with each other provides an alternative interpretation to the narratives built to "explain" social situations. A *social justice* lens leads to crucial questions that expose the suppressed stories and further explanations of the way people act or are treated by individuals, as well as systems.

Figure 2.2 Activity: The ABCs of a Socially Just School

In this activity you will be asked to imagine a socially just school by considering this question: What kind of school would you like to enter and graduate from if you had no idea into what kind of family you would be born?

Directions Part I

- What qualities would contribute to your social, emotional, physical, and academic thriving?
- Use the chart that follows to record your ideas.

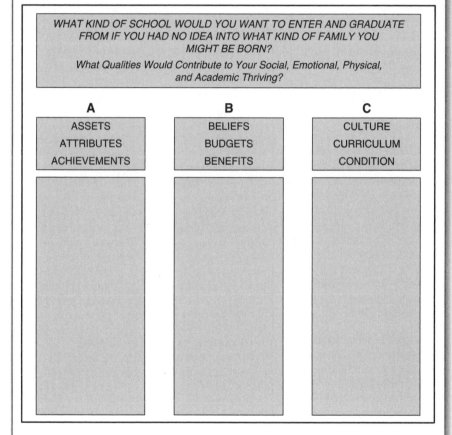

WHAT KIND OF SCHOOL WOULD YOU WANT TO ENTER AND GRADUATE FROM IF YOU HAD NO IDEA INTO WHAT KIND OF FAMILY YOU MIGHT BE BORN?

What Qualities Would Contribute to Your Social, Emotional, Physical, and Academic Thriving?

A	B	C
ASSETS	BELIEFS	CULTURE
ATTRIBUTES	BUDGETS	CURRICULUM
ACHIEVEMENTS	BENEFITS	CONDITION

Directions Part II

The second part of this activity encourages you to revisit your ideas about the characteristics of a socially just school from the perspective of a specific student.

- Based upon the first letter of your first name, you have been randomly assigned a student profile. See table below.
- Revisit the profile of a socially just school you created in Part One of this activity. What would you **add** or **enhance** based upon your profile?

(Continued)

Figure 2.2 (Continued)

First Letter of First Name A, C, D, G, I, P, U, W	E, H, J, K, M, Q, R, Y, X	B, F, L, N, O, S, T, V, Z
Profile. SA lives on the Spokane Indian Reservation with his father, mother, and five siblings. His father is a member of the Coeur d'Alene tribe and his mother is of Colville, Choctaw, Spokane, and European American ancestry. His father is an alcoholic who often leaves the house for days at a time. To support her six children, SA's mother sews quilts and works as a clerk at the Wellpinit Trading Post. SA was born with hydrocephalus, a condition that occurs when there is an abnormally large amount of cerebral fluid in the cranial cavity, and had to have brain surgery when he was six months old. He was not expected to survive. SA's surgery was successful and he survived with no mental damage, but he does suffer from other effects. SA attends school on the reservation. He is constantly teased by other kids, who have nicknamed him "The Globe" because of his larger-than-normal head size, a result of his hydrocephalus. SA suffers from seizures and bedwetting and has to take strong drugs to control them. Because of his health problems, he is excluded from many of the activities that are rites of passage for young Indian males. SA excels academically, reading everything available, including auto repair manuals.	**Profile.** MM was born in Afghanistan, where she lived with her father, mother, and two sisters. When she was a little girl, her father was killed under suspicious circumstances, leaving her mother widowed at the age of twenty-three. Under the Taliban regime, it was unsafe for a single woman to raise three daughters. MM's mother felt she had no choice but to leave. To get out of Afghanistan, MM and her family had to get through Iran, Pakistan, Kuwait, and Jordan. When MM was eleven years old, she and her remaining family arrived in Canada. Once in Canada, MM and her family lived in refugee homes and YMCA shelters, a Muslim family cared for by Christians. Now settled in a small Canadian city, MM attends school. She is the only Muslim child of color in this school and she is often teased and taunted.	**Profile.** RH is an African American boy living in a largely Black, poor part of Detroit. Before he was born, RH's parent's separated. He was taken in by a foster family who lived next door. Neither his foster family nor the Detroit ghetto where he lives offers much by way of tranquility and stability. RH's foster parents have a contentious marriage. They fight frequently and they have been known to beat RH. RH's birth mother is often on the scene attempting to win over RH's affections. As a result, he often shuttles back and forth between his birth mother and his foster family. RH is nearsighted and very slight. He is often the butt of jokes and he is frequently ostracized by his peers, who see him as nonathletic and nerdy. RH spends his free time reading. RH suffers from depression as a result of his tumultuous childhood.

Directions Part III

What is missing or needs to be enhanced?

- Based upon the profile of the marginalized student or group of students to whom you dedicated this work, what would you add or enhance? Why?

Directions Part IV

Reflection

- Based upon this exercise, reflect on the following questions:
  - How would you define a socially just school?
  - How does your school or district compare to the ideal socially just school?
  - If you could change one thing to make your school more socially just, what would that be?

Extension and Team Activities

Extension Activity: Learn more about John Rawls and his theory of justice. Go to the following link, https://www.youtube.com/watch?v=5-JQ17X6VNg, which contains a six-minute illustrated video explaining the development of John Rawls's theory of justice.

What resonated with you? How does the video inform the definition of social justice that you came up with in your reflection?

Extension Activity: Each of the three student profiles is based upon the life of a real person. Research the real life and accomplishments of the person to whom you were randomly assigned.

- SA is American poet, writer, and filmmaker Sherman Alexie.
- MM is Maryam Monse, Canadian Member of Parliament and Canada's Minister for Democratic Institutions.
- RH is African American poet Robert Hayden.

Consider: What social structures were in place to help your "student" achieve despite the circumstances of his or her life?

Team Activity: Complete the ABCs of Social Justice activity working in pairs or in small groups.

What Recess Can Teach Us About Social Justice

In the previous activity, we added the concepts *social, justice,* and a *socially just school* to our emerging lexicon of words and concepts associated with social justice. We can use another brief thought experiment to add several other terms. In the following guided thought experiment, we will endeavor to uncover significant nuances between and among the concepts of social justice, fairness, and equity.

For this thought experiment, imagine you are an elementary school teacher and your goal is to ensure that your children can go out and play during recess. It is February. What kinds of preparations would take place if your school were in Miami, average temperature of 68 degrees;

New York City, average temperature 40 degrees; or Montreal, average temperature 19 degrees, and the playground is covered with a winter's worth of accumulated ice and snow?

If you were in Miami or New York, preparation would likely include having children don jackets, light ones in Miami and more substantial ones in New York. The Montreal preparations would be the most exacting: boots, gloves, heavy jackets, and tuques (the French word for the colorful knitted beanie-like hats that adorn the heads of most Montrealers braving the outdoors in February). In other words, to give children a *fair* chance to play outdoors, preparations take into consideration the prevailing circumstances or conditions. Someone could say that it is unfair to have Montreal children spend time wrestling themselves into boots, gloves, hats, and coats, but to not do so would deny them the opportunity to spend a full, protected, glorious half hour running around outdoors.

The lesson is simple. *Socially just* does not mean *equal*. Rather, social justice means equal access through whatever means make access possible. In other words, to each according to her needs, a sentiment that has deep roots some say going back to the biblical times. This understanding implies that equal treatment is patently unjust and needs to be replaced with equitable treatment. Put another way, because of circumstances, some individuals and/or groups may have different needs in order to gain access to what is deemed of value in a society. This understanding also implies that how potential allies come to understand and think about equity is important. The next section will present three dimensions of equity in a school setting that will further refine how one might think about equity.

Dimensions of Equity

As change agents, allies need a clear vision of what equity looks like. One such vision, developed by the Bay Area Coalition for Equitable Schools, contains three critical and interrelated facets that cover a world of territory pertaining to the way schools operate. Figure 2.3 is adapted from the work of Osta and Perrow (2008) and can be viewed as a vision for equity along with a summary of the process for achieving it.

By converting these three dimensions into questions, educators can evaluate any given practice, policy, or pedagogy using a social justice yardstick; at the same time, they can begin to articulate in ever-clearer ways what a socially just school looks like, feels like, and sounds like; finally, they can make the necessary adjustments to move their school closer to the vision.

Figure 2.3 Dimensions of Equity

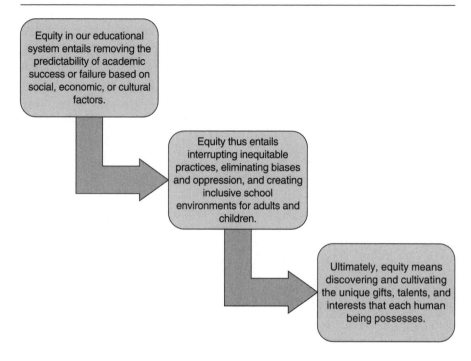

The questions are:

1. Does [insert practice, policy, or pedagogy] remove *or contribute to* the predictability of academic success or failure based on social, economic, or cultural factors? How?

2. Does [insert practice, policy, or pedagogy] interrupt *or continue* inequitable practices, eliminate *or encourage* biases and oppression, and create inclusive *or exclusive* school environments for adults and children? How?

3. Does [insert practice, policy, or pedagogy] discover and cultivate *or ignore and neglect* the unique gifts, talents, and interests that each human being possesses? How?

EMPLOYING A SOCIAL JUSTICE LENS TO "READ" HISTORICAL AND CURRENT EDUCATIONAL ISSUES

The questions above help define a social justice vision. They also reveal an important aspect of becoming literate in a discipline. Literacy goes beyond knowing isolated terms and concepts. Literacy of a discipline involves employing the discipline's way of thinking to a situation. Ways of thinking are driven by the questions the discipline asks. A scientist might look at a set of keys and ask of what they are made. A poet might ask what they symbolize. A social justice advocate might wonder who is being locked in or out, by whom, why, and by what authority. Social justice activists are engaged in efforts to uncover, critique, and challenge the taken-for-granted ways in which societies and institutions organize themselves and operate. They do this through questions.

Two pairs of questions that are extraordinarily helpful in uncovering power relationships and thus the motives behind particular ways of doing things are captured in Figure 2.4. These two pairs of questions are revelatory and often lead to further questions, uncomfortable discoveries, and deeper research.

Figure 2.4 Questions That Uncover Power Relationships

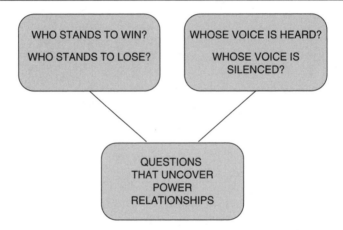

Applying Social Justice Questions to Historic and Current Educational Issues

Two examples follow to illustrate how these questions work. The first relates to the story of Christopher Columbus that is widely told in the United States. The second relates to the enactment of No Child Left Behind (NCLB) and its impact on education.

The Story of Christopher Columbus: Who Benefits? Whose Voice Is Heard?

Various individuals and groups have bravely applied the question "Who benefits?" to the story of Christopher Columbus and the "discovery of America."

American school children know the chant: In 1492, Columbus sailed the ocean blue. So far, so true, along with details that include Queen Isabelle and King Ferdinand and the famous trio of ships, the Nina, the Pinta, and the Santa Maria. True, too, is the trope that Columbus stumbled upon the

North American continent in search of a trade route to the East. For most school children, this is where the story ends. Christopher Columbus is portrayed as a hero, someone to be admired for his courage and curiosity.

Dig a little deeper and you discover that duplicitous slight of hand is responsible for this sanitized, romanticized, tender foundational myth. Christopher Columbus never set foot on what is now known as the United States. The lands in the New World that he did set foot on were—and had been for millennia before his arrival—occupied by indigenous peoples who initially welcomed the newcomers. He reciprocated by forcing many of them into unpaid labor. Others he seized, loaded into boats, and attempted to bring to Europe. Most of the people he kidnapped died in transit. In his quest for gold, Columbus grabbed land under false, forceful, and manipulating circumstances. How, then, is Christopher Columbus an American hero, entitled to a federal holiday, no less?

This story, like so many other foundational myths, is dripping in sentimentality masking brutality. Stories like the Columbus-discovered-America myth are conceived, purposely designed, and retold to "invoke lofty hopes and ideals to hide unsightly truths" (Wright, 2008). Clearly, these stories feed the national ego and benefit those in power. The sentimental story of the discovery of America that school children know so well leaves no room for the voices of those who were actually on the continent first and who were trampled upon by the European newcomers. Application of the social justice lens to the Christopher Columbus story shows that Western imperialists benefit from a story in which the cruelty and injustice of their expansionist activities are minimized, a story that amplifies the voice of the victors and silences the voice of the victimized.

But the victimized and their allies are no longer sitting on the sidelines. (They are *idle no more*, to borrow a term from a protest movement mounted by three First Nations women and one non-native ally that swept Canada in the winter of 2012–2013.) Increasingly, they are broadcasting another narrative, winning over more allies, and changing the way things are done. Thanks to these efforts, several states and many municipalities no longer celebrate Columbus Day. They have replaced Columbus Day with Indigenous Peoples' Day. These celebrations are an attempt to end the cycle of deception perpetuated by the Christopher Columbus story and instead celebrate the life and contributions of indigenous peoples.

NCLB: Who Benefits? Whose Voice Is Heard?

Asking who stands to benefit, who stands to lose; whose voice is heard, whose voice is silenced is an excellent way to peel away layers of deception that give rise to and prolong unjust situations. There is a further line of inquiry emanating from the question "Who benefits?" that gets at the root of the motivations behind stories told, policies put in place, and practices that are long accepted. The third line of inquiry is to follow the money. Doing so inevitably leads back to who stands to benefit but in an even more concrete way.

Educators with long histories remember well the days before the tsunami of testing, teaching to the test, grading the test, drilling into test data, using test-compatible materials, and ranking schools on test results existed. So, too, does the educational testing and publishing industry. Unlike the educators who long for the pre-NCLB days, the publishers are delighted with the new order. Why would they not be? *NCLB* spells *profit* for these companies. And, to my mind, it was always intended to be that way.

Cui Bono? Follow the Money. The NCLB legislation of 2001 is the brainchild of George W. Bush. The legislation, which requires annual testing of millions of school children, could only be accomplished if a huge testing infrastructure was in place to support it. Obviously, those publishing and testing companies that could get a piece of this work would be in for an enormous economic boon. If you follow the money, like writer Stephen Metcalf did as early as January 2002—little more than a year after NCLB was signed into law—you discover that the architect of the legislation, George Bush and his family, had strong and longstanding ties to the McGraw family, who just happen to be in the test and textbook publishing industry. The article provides a fascinating inside look into the ways in which cozy family relationships and the desire for increased profit margins drive policy decisions that the public is led to believe emanate from lofty, socially just fueled goals like leaving no child behind (Metcalf, 2002).

Another way to think about the Christopher Columbus story and the arrival of NCLB on the educational scene is to consider how these two ways of approaching education fit into the conception of a socially just school that you developed earlier in this chapter. Do they create the kind of school that would help you thrive academically, socially, emotionally, and physically?

Similarly, both can be filtered through the lens of the Dimensions of Equity to determine if either removes the predictability of academic success, interrupts inequitable practices, or discovers and cultivates the unique gifts, talents, and interests each human being possesses.

KEY CONSIDERATIONS FOR ALLIES

- Like all literacies, social justice literacy involves a unique vocabulary and way of questioning.

- Social justice work benefits from grounding the work in the lived reality of our marginalized students, and a relentless coming to terms with the nuances of key concepts associated with social justice.
- To work toward social justice for students, educators need to free themselves from the constraints of their particular social circumstances and come to a shared understanding of those elements that help all students thrive academically, emotionally, socially, and physically.
- **Looking Ahead**: Social justice advocates also understand deeply the topic of the next chapter: How privilege, power, and politics affect schooling.

Privilege, Power, Politics, and Schooling

Exposing the ties between the Bush and McGraw families and NCLB introduces the unsettling fact that privilege, power, and politics are rarely absent from school policy decisions. Educators who are allies in the battle for social justice know this, they go out of their way to uncover these lies, and they are diligent in broadcasting and counteracting the damage these profit-fueled, politically expedient, or otherwise misguided policies can inflict upon school children.

After considering how privilege, power, and politics work together, this chapter will make the case that power and authority are driven from two different assumptions and have two different objectives. It will conclude with several scenarios demonstrating how administrators and teachers can use their authority to create disciplinary and instructional procedures that minimize power relationships.

PRIVILEGE, POWER, AND POLITICS MATTER IN SCHOOLING

Allies benefit from clear, nuanced understanding of the ways in which privilege, power, and politics intertwine, exert influence, and play out in the lives of school children. We have already looked at the notion of privilege, the behind-the-scenes benefits and advantages that place one group above another. With privilege comes power, specifically power *over* others. That power translates into the ability to make the political decisions that ultimately affect every aspect of what schools do: how they teach, what they teach, what they value, how they are organized, who gets disciplined, who gets labeled gifted, who gets labeled "in need." The list is endless.

Figure 3.1   Factors That Drive What Happens in Schools

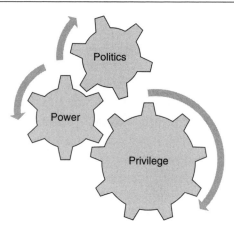

Figure 3.1 graphically represents the ways in which privilege, power, and politics work together to shape school experiences.

An example from history elucidates the ways in which privilege and power work together to affect policy. In the days of the women's suffrage movement, power resided with men, described as *captains of industry, breadwinners,* and *heads of the household*—all positional terms designed to indicate who has control over what and whom. Women, often referred to during that time as the weaker sex, "obviously" needed men's leadership, prowess, and strength in order for them to be safe and adequately provided for. In and out of the home, men were in charge. Prejudice against women fueled discriminatory practices that were encoded in fiercely defended policies. Men could vote. Women could not. Institutional power resided with men. Women felt the sting of oppression. For the institution to change, women were dependent upon those in power, men. Many men became allies to the cause. They lent their access to bastions of power, like the newspapers of the time, so that women could fight their battle for suffrage.

The *Pow* of Power

What matters to those in a dominant position is to exercise the *pow* in their power: the impact felt as the dominant one controls others, exercises personal will over others, or creates situations to demonstrate how those in control possess know-how, superiority, and merit compared to those who are on the margins, who have less power, or who are vulnerable.

Winning power and using it has reached epic heights. We see evidence of abuse of power in areas that were once civil, transparent, and open. On TV and radio talk shows, what once were *talking heads* are now *yelling heads* engaged in a pitched battle to control the conversation by outshouting, interrupting, and silencing those who think differently about an issue. At Board of Education meetings, individuals and groups come to the microphone to denigrate others, monopolize discussion, or harp on a single, narrow personal agenda item.

On a larger scale, we see how power manifests itself as an addictive drug, especially in the world of politics. Government gridlock in the United States is deemed a favorable alternative to open debate about substantive issues. Muzzling scientists and cabinet ministers was the method of control recently exerted by the Harper government in Canada.

Institutions that make power the centerpiece of their operating system produce an organization of profound distrust, rampant cynicism, sometimes overt rage. Exercising legitimate authority, on the other hand, can rebuild trust, restore optimism, and reestablish serenity.

"AUTHORING" A NEW POWER RELATIONSHIP

There is a difference between power and authority. Social institutions, like government and education, possess a legitimate authority as part of the social contract with their constituency. In a perfect world, this contract is organized to maintain order, provide services, and ensure fairness; in other words, to serve the people for the benefit of all. The people who make up social institutions like government and education would benefit from understanding the difference between power and authority. Indeed, the exercise of genuine authority could—and should—be liberating for all members of an institution, those who serve and those who are served by the institution. This happens if one understands and applies the original meaning of the word *authority*. At its root is the familiar word *author.* What do authors do? They create. They originate. They instigate. In its earliest sense, the word *author* meant "one who causes to grow," as those who write, or have been affected by the written word, know very well.

The voice of authority is separate from the voice of power. Authority and power have vastly different aims. Where power seeks domination, authority seeks growth, the common good, what is ethical (Saul, 2014). Unfortunately, over the years authority has been conflated with power. The word *authoritarian* says it all.

Those who speak from and use genuine authority, however, are ethically and morally credible. Ethical and moral behavior demands attention to others, concern about balance, application of the principles of fairness. Those who speak from and use this type of authority are allies, workers on behalf of social justice. Their goals are to dismantle manifestations of power, dominance, and narrow interests.

Educational Policy and Power

Educational policy is not neutral. It is often driven by less than noble motivation, a purposeful misreading of the human condition, and/or a desire to dominate. At the same time, there are those operating in the system who try their best to counteract the damage that adherence to official policies can inflict. The following paints a portrait of the way power and politics play out in school policy and practice. It is, admittedly, an extreme example. It also suggests the ways in which authority can be exercised to mitigate the damage done by these wrongheaded policies.

Police Presence in Math Class Does Not Add Up

As I struggled to make sense out of the 2015 video showing a police officer picking up and throwing a student across a classroom, my social justice lens reminded me to consider two things. First, bad anthropology leads to bad school policy. Second, if the only tool you have is a hammer, every problem looks like a nail. Why else would a teacher and an administrator call in a police officer to handle a routine school infraction and stand by idly watching a student being manhandled?

Bad anthropology, a belief that American school children—some of them, at least—are by nature evil and violent and need constant, robust monitoring, drove the decision to bring police officers into the South Valley High School in South Carolina, just as it has done in legions of schools throughout the nation. Not surprisingly, the darker and poorer the population, the more prevalent are heavy-handed policing, onerous metal detectors, and unforgiving disciplinary procedures.

This close relationship between law enforcement and learning is incongruent, it is closely related to the war-on-drugs and anti-violence-in-schools fervor that gave us "zero tolerance" policies, and it has been costly.

According to a study published in 2010 by the Advancement Project, American school children are now the second-most "policed" group in the United States, second only to prison inmates. A parade of disturbing data populates this report, most notably the shockingly high increases in exclusionary disciplinary actions and school arrests, often for minor infractions. According to the report, these early school encounters with the criminal justice system contribute to the increase in students leaving the school systems to become part of the prison system (Advancement Project, 2010).

In the summer of 2011, a group of high school students from the Chicago Public Schools decided to call attention to the excessive policing that the district had put into place in its schools. In analyzing Chicago's school budget, they determined that the school district allocated fourteen times more money for security and police services than for college and career counseling. If budgets are a statement of an institution's value system, then what the students uncovered is testimony to a value system sadly askew.

Values Drive Behavior

My first job after I left the classroom was dean of discipline in a suburban high school in New York State, a position I shared with a former physical education teacher and football coach. We were a strange sight: the burly football coach, affectionately known as *Big Al*, and the tiny, bookish English teacher. One of our first official tasks was to attend a full-day training session sponsored by the local police department, which was designed to teach school administrators and deans how to "take down unruly students." Really? I thought. Not on my watch. Nor was it a priority on Big Al's, as it turned out.

We used to joke that every time there was a fight in the cafeteria, Big Al was elsewhere and I was left to deal with the situation. But, as Big Al pointed out, would the situation have been handled any differently had he been present? The answer, of course, was no. Both of us possessed a repertoire of tools and skills to defuse a situation, to appeal to what we believed was the inherent goodness of our students, and to demonstrate that we understood that teenagers are tightly wound bundles of conflicting emotions who often make bewilderingly bad choices. In short, we believed in cultivating relationships and in discipline with dignity.

HOW AUTHORITY CAN COUNTERACT POWER-DRIVEN POLICIES AND PEDAGOGY

We were not alone. Over the years, I have encountered some of the most amazing educators, working in some of the most challenged communities in the United States and Canada, who possess a range of creative, dignity-preserving, and effective ways of addressing the inevitable conflicts, testing of the rules, and infractions—big and small—that take place in schools. And they remain true to their convictions, despite student handbooks, district policies, and legislation that aim to constrain their behavior to a narrow band of predetermined reactions and punishments and uneven power dynamics.

Addressing Schoolwide Discipline Using Authority, Not Power

The following examples demonstrate how several administrators have exercised authority, in the sense of authoring creative responses to the need for safe and orderly schools, as opposed to exercising power. In fact, in many instances, these responses are a direct reaction to previously harsh, oppressive measures designed to control behavior rather than shape behavior. Although these examples come from the ranks of administrators, there is direct applicability to the ways teachers can address discipline issues in their classrooms.

- Some administrators take an understated, but affirming approach, like Ms. S., who greets students referred to her for any infraction with the words, "You know, we *want* you here." Then she guides them to think through what they did and where they might have had a chance to make a different decision.
- Or take the example of the middle school principal tasked with reducing the number of incidents of weapons being brought into schools. He and two other colleagues were facing the same situation. His colleagues hired more security guards to patrol the halls. He brought in grandmothers. His school experienced the most dramatic drop in weapons-carrying infractions and violent incidents.
- And there are others, like Mr. D., who took over a middle school that was run like a prison. There were frequent lockdowns; violent encounters on and off campus; no field trips, clubs, or other activities. During his first year, two students found the decomposing body of a murder victim on school grounds. In a second incident, a gunman entered the school, threatened to kill a teacher, and robbed two employees. Undaunted, and convinced that his students were children who deserved better, Mr. D. created an island of safety in this sea of trouble. Today, the school day starts and ends with meditation to help students and teachers alleviate the high levels of stress that accompany lives lived in the unstable margins. A Community Care Team has partnered with local businesses and organizations to provide on-site counseling, before- and after-school academic support, Saturday programming, and a full range of clubs and activities.
- Finally, there is Mr. L. His school is not unlike Mr. D's in terms of the challenges present and the transformation that occurred under his watch. Mr. L. begins each day with a reminder of the school rules. There are only two. "Be safe. Be kind." For reasons of "safety," the former administration welcomed a police substation on the school grounds. Mr. L. believed that this sent the wrong message to his students, many of whom had incarcerated parents. One of his first tasks was to invite the police to leave. If only other schools would extend the same invitation.

One of the messages these vignettes have in common is that seeing people *as* problems is significantly different than recognizing that all of us *have* problems. One is a condemnation of personal merit. The other is recognition of the human condition. The first orientation often results in imposing more and more rules on behavior. The second allows for enactment of creative solutions that present positive messages about student self-worth.

Before looking specifically at power and authority from the classroom angle, the activity in Figure 3.2 will help you articulate the difference between power and authority as portrayed in the previous scenarios.

Figure 3.2   Activity: Power and Authority Reflection

Select one educator whose response resonated with you.

How did that educator's response minimize power relations?

How did the educator use his or her authority to create an alternate solution?

Addressing Classroom Discipline Using Authority, Not Power

Administrators create and sustain the school climate. Teachers create and sustain the classroom climate. How administrators and teachers choose to orient themselves to the myriad policies and required practices that circumscribe their responsibilities is, to a certain degree, a matter of discretion. In most instances, sound judgment that works to create solid relationships with students helps circumvent the need to apply draconian, one-size-fits-all disciplinary policies or stultifying approaches to learning and teaching.

A Tale of Two Classrooms

The start of the school year offers teachers a golden opportunity to coauthor classroom operating principles that lay the foundation for a socially just school.

Teachers and students know the importance of the first days of school for establishing expectations, for setting the tone, and for sizing each other up. Although rarely articulated in quite this way, teachers and students are keenly interested in figuring out the power dynamics when they meet for the first time.

Nowhere is this more evident than in how teachers go about setting expectations for behavior. Classroom management is a primary concern of teachers. Teachers can choose to emphasize and exert power as their primary means of classroom management, or they can use their positional authority to creatively address the need for safe and orderly classrooms. Whatever orientation a teacher selects is driven by different questions, sends different messages, and has different results.

To highlight how authority can be used in the service of social justice, two approaches to classroom management will be contrasted. In the first example, the teacher attempts to invite students into the process of establishing rules for behavior but unwittingly ends up emphasizing aspects of power. In the second, the teacher uses her authority to reorient the discussion away from rules for behavior, opting instead to focus on the classroom as a learning and teaching community.

Rule-Bound Classrooms Lead to Rule-Bending Students

Posters like the following can be found in many classrooms, and they contain much useful information about the teacher's approach to discipline.

Image 3.1 Classroom Poster

"Reading" the Walls: What the Poster Says

If you look closely at this poster, you may notice several things. One of the first is that students had a hand in creating it. The poster is decorated with student-drawn symbols and images. Teachers often explain that they want their students to have some "ownership" of classroom rules. Based upon the wording, one can assume that the students also had a hand in generating the rules, another nod toward "ownership" and a somewhat common practice.

Questions Raised. Despite this intention, engaging students in creating a poster such as this raises a number of issues. First, spending time on a task such as creating classroom rules as one of the first things a teacher asks students to do to start off the year highlights rules and regulations as something of major importance. Additionally, it is hard to overlook the overall message implied by the creation of a litany of ten rules. By encoding as rules things like *No Bullying, Indoor Voices, Raise Hands*, etc., the implication is that students *engage* in bullying, *do not use* indoor voices, and *do not raise* their hands. In other words, the overall approach comes from a deficit model associated with student behavior: These students do not know how to behave. They require rules to remind them how to behave. Unfortunately, over the years, this is precisely the message that some students receive and can easily internalize.

Possible Results. In addition, trying to maintain strict adherence to a litany of rules is exhausting and rarely productive. Laying down rules often results in a strong invitation to break them. Rule-bound classrooms result in rule-breaking students. Some would call this a power struggle.

Change the Conversation and You Change the Culture

How different the message would be if a different approach were taken, if a different opening-of-the-school-year task were assigned.

A Different Approach. Many teachers begin with a different approach and set of suppositions. Many assert that they and their students are part of a powerful learning-teaching community. Students are then invited to enumerate what a learning-teaching community looks like, feels like, and sounds like. The message, the implications, and the outcome change.

This approach totally shifts the conversation from an emphasis on behavior and rules to an emphasis on learning, teaching, and community. It also flattens the power dynamic. The assertion that the teacher *and* the students are both and always learners *and* teachers evens out the power dynamic normally associated with the role of the teacher and the role of the student.

Ongoing Emphasis on Learning and Teaching. The task is generative. After students—and their teacher—make their first foray into describing a powerful learning-teaching community, they can continue to add to their list throughout the year. Regularly asking students to reflect upon what they learned about themselves as a learner, as a teacher, or as a community member clarifies expectations and sends a strong message about who is in charge. The expectation is clear: Everyone is a learner, a teacher, and a community member. The message is clear: As members of the community, they are all expected to engage in a cycle of improvement and deepening understanding about what these roles mean. The message that each person is in charge of becoming a better learner, teacher, and community member can be further amplified and reinforced by asking students from time to time to make a commitment to something specific they would like to do that would enhance their contribution to their learning-teaching community.

How Is Social Justice Manifested? In the first scenario, the rule-bound classroom, the power structure is clearly evident. Students need rules to behave and reminders about how to behave. Student-generated or not, the implication is that teachers are in charge of maintaining classroom order. Rules govern what is acceptable and what is not. Students are required to follow the rules or face sanctions. (Indeed, in many classrooms these sanctions are explicitly laid out. Often, those in violation of the rules are publically called out with their names on the board and check marks placed beside their names for each infraction.) These systems perpetuate power *over* others, rather than providing opportunities for self-governance and decision making.

In the second scenario, the script is flipped. Learning, teaching, and community are central and valued, as is each individual's capacity to contribute to building a stronger learning-teaching community. In the second scenario, teachers and students exercise power *with* each other, a hallmark of a socially just school.

Figure 3.3 summarizes key points about the differences between the two approaches.

Figure 3.3 Comparison of a Socially Just Classroom and a Rule-Bound Classroom

Socially Just Classroom	Rule-Bound Classroom
❑ QUESTION: What does a learning-teaching community look like, feel like, and sound like?	❑ QUESTION: What should our classroom rules be?

(Continued)

Figure 3.3 (Continued)

Socially Just Classroom	Rule-Bound Classroom
❏ ASSUMPTION: The teacher and students are part of a learning-teaching community.	❏ ASSUMPTION: Students need rules in order to behave.
❏ MESSAGE: Our focus is on learning, teaching, and community, and students know how to contribute to all three.	❏ MESSAGE: If a rule is broken, there will be consequences.
❏ RESULT: Students "coauthor" a healthy, mutually supportive learning-teaching environment.	❏ RESULT: Students and teacher are placed in a power struggle.

Smyth et al. identified eight key characteristics associated with socially just schools. Socially just schools

- articulate their purposes;
- advance a concern for social injustice;
- continually (re)focus around learning;
- pursue a culture of innovation;
- enact democratic forms of practice;
- are community minded;
- display educative forms of leadership; and
- engage in critical literacies (as cited in Smyth, 2004, p. 19).

Figure 3.4 Activity: Key Characteristics of Socially Just Schools

Reflection

Which aspects of this description are evident in the ways in which discipline is approached in the second scenario?

Addressing Curriculum and Methods Using Authority, Not Power

Teachers have the potential to exercise power *over or with* students in matters beyond their approach to classroom management. How they orient themselves to learning and teaching sends strong messages about who is in charge and how.

Ms. P., a newly hired English teacher, took on the challenge of trying to resuscitate a senior elective, Philosophy and English, slated to be cut due to low enrollment. The semester after she took it over, additional

Figure 3.5   Pedagogy and Social Justice

> **Reflection**
>
> Grace Feuerverger (2007) defines education as "a sacred life journey, a quest toward liberation." How does the pedagogy employed by Ms. P. echo that sentiment and relate to social justice?

sections needed to be opened to accommodate the seniors who wanted to spend their last semester reading Kierkegaard and Plato, Confucius and de Beauvoir.

Her classroom was located in a dinghy afterthought of a wing that was added onto the high school during an enrollment bubble. "The Wing" was universally despised. Its hard-to-access, hard-to-heat, and dark series of classrooms was capable of destroying any enthusiasm for learning—but not in Ms. P.'s classroom.

Walk into her classroom and you would likely not be able to find her, nor would her students be sitting in rows taking notes. Instead, she would be somewhere in one of many clusters of discussion groups, prodding students to stretch their thinking, consider alternatives, account for historical context, make sense out of dense and difficult language and ideas, connect ideas to their current situation. Famously, one student was overheard saying, "I am thinking so hard my head hurts!"

Unlike other high school teachers at the time, Ms. P. did not lecture from the podium, assign but not teach, or sit at her desk reading the *New York Times* while students were engaged in silent sustained reading.

Beliefs About Power and Authority Guide Pedagogical Choices

Orientation to learning and teaching, like discipline, springs from a set of beliefs about where power resides in a classroom and how learning occurs. Paulo Freire (1985) says, "Education is a certain theory of knowledge put into practice everyday, but it is clothed in a certain aesthetic dress" (p. 17). If your theory of knowledge is that the teachers or books or curriculum guides are the power sources of knowledge, then you clothe your teaching in the aesthetic of the all-knowing expert depositing bits of knowledge into the heads of the hopelessly uninformed students.

If you believe that students bring funds of knowledge into the classroom, you believe, among other things, that people are competent and they have abundant and diverse knowledge derived from their life experiences, family, and social networks (Moll, Amanti, Neff, & Gonzalez, 1992). You might also subscribe to the notion that what people know is of value and should be shared. In other words, learning is a social enterprise. If these beliefs fuel your conception of learning and teaching, policing students and exercising power *over* them is not an aesthetic in which you need to clothe your teaching. Instead, you might see that your role is to help students shape themselves as beings. You believe that children come to school already capable of reading the world. They are passionate and curious beings. Then your role as a teacher is to fire their passions and curiosity, to help them see the world through a critical lens, one that does not shrink from the reality that places some groups in positions of dominance over others (Freire, 1985).

As educators, we do not have complete control over every aspect of what happens in a classroom. We can, however, bend the rules, skew the orientation regarding what is taught and how it is taught, and twist the political and power overlays that attempt to circumscribe and keep in check what we know in our hearts is good for our students, what fires them up, what feeds their souls, and, by the way, which does the same for us.

KEY CONSIDERATIONS FOR ALLIES

- Privilege and power are intimate bedfellows dedicated to shoring up their influence through the enactment of policies that put their interests first and the greater good second, if at all.
- Privilege, power, and politics comprise a potent stew that exerts a seemingly inescapable influence on how learning and teaching plays out.
- With careful thought, planning, and commitment, teachers and administrators can find alternative ways of conducting the business of school that smooth out uneven power dynamics created and enshrined in the politics of the privileged and powerful.
- If you change the conversation, you change the culture and the outcomes.
- **Looking Ahead:** Having established that privilege, power, and politics are potent influences upon how schools organize themselves, what they value, and how they operate, the next chapter will begin the conversation about why it is important to push back and resist, as well as how allies can prepare themselves to do so.

Dealing With Avoidance, Guilt, Feelings of Inadequacy, and Misunderstanding

So far, we have looked at three key ideas associated with becoming an ally in the battle for social justice.

- First, those in privileged positions take their privilege for granted and live in a fog that makes it difficult for them to see what is going on in the lives of those who do not share their privilege.
- Second, developing a literacy of social justice terms and concepts, which can and should be used to think through and critically question educational policy and procedures, is an extremely important step to becoming an ally.
- Third, potential allies become more and more effective once they grasp the ways in which power, politics, and schooling intersect.

All of this is pretty heavy stuff, especially if this is your first time seriously contemplating social justice issues. You may be thinking that social justice work may be more complicated and exacting than you originally thought. Maybe you are wondering whether it is even worth it to get involved. You might be persuaded to engage in the work, despite its obvious difficulties, once you get a clear picture of the landscape of resistance you are likely to encounter and once you understand the ways in which being marginalized affects our marginalized students.

The focus of this chapter is to look at ways of understanding and addressing the myriad reactions that make up the hills and valleys—and sometimes mountains—of the landscape of resistance allies are likely to encounter. Chapter 5 will make the case that this work is important and that your role in it is essential by acknowledging the social and psychological damage inflicted upon marginalized students exposed to continuous, unchallenged injustices.

As allies, we take a risk every time we challenge the status quo. Reactions are often swift and strong. Allies need to be prepared for these reactions, even though there is no foolproof formula to determine which challenge will produce which reaction. Having said that, there are a few themes, or ways of categorizing reactions, that allies could find helpful in reading resistant behaviors. Many challenges to status quo thinking derive from misinformation and lack of historical perspective. Allies have an obligation to set the record straight.

This chapter will deal with understanding and addressing strong reactions in general by considering the human dynamics that occur when the status quo is challenged. This will be done by recounting and then analyzing an incident that took place during a professional development session. Since the incident involved a teacher's strong reaction to what she viewed as politics being brought into schools, the second half of the chapter will go deeper into the topic of politics and schooling.

WHEN WE CHALLENGE THE STATUS QUO: UNDERSTANDING AND ADDRESSING REACTIONS

We will begin with a story of avoidance, which we will then analyze in order to tease out some ways in which avoidance manifests itself. In this case, both a classroom teacher and a principal manifest avoidance. They likely do so for different reasons.

"No Room for Politics in the Classroom." Really? I saved a copy of a workshop evaluation from August 2014 because of the additional comments written in by a Grade 2 special education teacher. Ms. T. wrote, "I found Dr. Love inspirational at first but offensive in conclusion. NO ROOM FOR POLITICS IN THE CLASSROOM."

The Dr. Love she is referring to is Dr. Bettina Love, whose TED Talk, *Hip Hop Grit and Academic Success* (https://www.youtube.com/watch?v=tkZqPMzgvzg) was part of a weeklong session that focused on the culturally responsive classroom. The session was requested by the principal, who felt there was a disconnect between the culture of the students, overwhelmingly children of color challenged by poverty, and the teachers, overwhelmingly White, middle-class women.

In this TED Talk, Dr. Love posited that the mainstream holds many misconceptions about Hip Hop, an integral part of the culture of many urban youth. Dr. Love maintained that, through Hip Hop, students demonstrate determination, social and emotional intelligence, and creativity, all of which, she asserted, are predictors of academic success. What's more, she had data to prove it. So far, so good. It is likely that this is what the teacher found "inspirational." About twelve minutes into the TED Talk, however, the topic shifted and the tone changed to what I believe Ms. T. meant when she referred to the "offensive conclusion."

At this juncture, Dr. Love referenced Trayvon Martin, and his killer, George Zimmerman. Teachers are not George Zimmermans, Dr. Love stated, but, she asserted, educators engage in "spirit murdering" when we tell students to stop being who they are when they enter our classrooms or when we refuse to address the racism, discrimination, bigotry, and hate that our students of color face. Strong words, possibly upsetting words to the special education teacher, a White woman.

It is interesting and important to note, however, that earlier in the day, Ms. T. passionately spoke out about the injustices the district inflicts on students by administering tests with out-of-reach cultural references. She had several examples, one of which was a reading comprehension passage that required knowledge of the specialized vocabulary and context associated with recreational sailing in order for students to answer the questions correctly. How, she pleaded, could the district expect urban students challenged by poverty to have any familiarity with recreational sailing? What can we do, how can we exert pressure, she asked, to guarantee that her students and all the students in the school would not be unfairly treated in the future?

Not knowing the teacher well, I was confused by her vehement, public, and well-articulated outrage over what she viewed as unfair treatment of students on the districtwide tests and her written comments about "the offensive conclusion" of Dr. Love's video. I felt it was my obligation to let the principal, a woman of color, know that the teacher was upset. She read the evaluation, reflected for several minutes, and then said, "I am not worried about this teacher. She always defends her students. She is one of the best student allies we have in the school."

What Lessons Can Allies Learn From This Story?

What can potential allies for social justice learn about themselves, about others, and about engaging in social justice work from the reactions of the teacher and her principal? Much, I believe, because these reactions are not uncommon. No one can know exactly what fueled each of these specific educators' responses, but there are lessons that can be learned. One lesson is that despite how fervent and passionate an ally may feel about advancing the social justice agenda, it is important to take a step back and understand the human dynamics that fuel another's desire to push back or avoid addressing inequity. Timing and relationships must be taken into consideration before movement is possible. The second lesson is that, despite what Ms. T. thinks, classrooms are jam-packed with politics and have always been so. Allies need to know how politics manifests itself in our schools, even when most of us are totally unaware of its presence, its power, and its impact. Allies will never be able to upend the pervasiveness of politics in the schoolroom until we are able to recognize it and name it.

The analysis of the vignette then will start with two human dimensions that allies benefit from understanding:

- Expect Pushback
- Expect Lost Opportunities

The analysis will continue by looking more closely at politics and the classroom to make two points:

- Politics and Partisanship Are Vastly Different
- Schools ARE Political Spaces

THE HUMAN DIMENSION: WHAT COULD ALLIES EXPECT?

Often when someone finally "gets" inequity and commits to becoming an ally to combat it, a pronounced sense of urgency to get on with the work of changing hearts, minds, and actions can overtake the new ally. After all, we understand that justice delayed is justice denied. Effective allies cultivate strategic impatience that will afford them the chance to actually change hearts, minds, and actions by timing when to push others to new understandings of how they may be contributing to injustice.

Expect Pushback

Thinking through the reactions of the Grade 2 teacher and the principal's response to that reaction reveals an important aspect of ally work: expect pushback. The case could be made that both the Grade 2 special education teacher and the principal are allies for their students, as evidenced by the teacher's plea for fair testing and the principal's desire to bring in workshops that would help teachers understand, value, and employ students' cultural references.

Neither of them, however, was ready to go beyond what, for them, was comfortable at that time. It is possible that the teacher could not envision how or why she would introduce charged concepts like "racism, discrimination, bigotry and hate" into her Grade 2 classroom. This would not be surprising. *Racism*, *discrimination*, *bigotry*, and *hate* are electrifying terms, which often engender a strong emotional pushback among White people or people in a dominant position. Another possible reason for the teacher's reaction is that most teachers have little preparation in addressing social justice efforts. These considerations may explain why the teacher reacted so strongly to Dr. Love's exhortation to bring these elements into classroom activities, discussions, and experiences.

Similarly, the principal could not envision engaging this teacher in a further discussion about her reaction. There are likely many reasons for this, some of which will be discussed in the next section. It may have been easier for the principal to just let the reaction go without discussion, without question, without challenge, rather than address it at that particular moment.

Expect Lost Opportunities

If one teacher thought some of Dr. Love's presentation was too political, it is very likely that others did, too. In some ways, this realization makes it even more of a lost opportunity that the principal decided to forego addressing it. But, she likely had some good reasons.

Many factors may have contributed to the principal's reluctance to enter into a discussion about the Grade 2 teacher's reaction. She had no specialized training in how to do so, she had no ongoing support or mentoring to help her through it, and she occupied a tenuous position. Not only was she new to the district, she was considerably younger than her staff, she was functioning as a principal for the first time, and the school was one of the lowest performing in the school district with a mandate to improve and improve fast. There had been a revolving door of administrators, and recruitment efforts to appoint two additional assistant principals were slow, resulting in opening the school year with half the number of administrators needed.

Morale was low and teacher absenteeism was high. A recent teacher survey conducted as part of a larger instructional assessment contained an open-ended question that revealed just how deeply negative the situation was. Teachers were asked to provide an adjective that best described the school's climate. Only six of the forty-four adjectives supplied were positive. Among the remaining negative ones, the two adjectives used most frequently by teachers were *frustrating* and *chaotic*. Other top negative descriptors included: *aggressive, crazy,* and *tense.* Clearly, the principal had much on her plate. One can assume that the principal had myriad reasons not to engage teachers in a discussion of the challenge posed by Dr. Love—yet.

Lost opportunity is a bitter pill for an ally to swallow, especially if you are impatient for change, if you are propelled by a sense of urgency, or if you are frustrated by lack of progress, as many allies are. In my impatience, I considered pushing the agenda with the principal, but I held back. Our relationship was new. I sensed my best option was to let this one go—for the time being only. What I could and did do was work like mad to develop the principal's confidence and trust, to determine where the principal and the staff were in their level of awareness of diversity issues, and to work with the principal to develop a strategy to push this awareness further. Timing and relationships are precursors to successful challenges to the status quo. So is patience.

The Current Reality: Where Educators Are

Many educators are not prepared to address issues as fraught with emotion as "racism, discrimination, bigotry and hate." It is not their fault. Part of the reason resides with poor-quality—or nonexistent—explicit training they receive during teacher preparation programs. Many professors in teacher training programs think of themselves as inadequately prepared to handle unsavory classroom scenarios, such as one in which a student makes a comment that offends or marginalizes another, or one in which a discussion devolves into a rant fueled by personal belief systems (Cruz, Ellerbrock, Vasquez, & Howes, 2014).

There is good news, however, when professors introduce equity issues into teacher preparation courses. First, when confronted with diversity issues, students actually engage deeply. Second, students often go through a series of somewhat predictable developmental steps as they come to understand the personal and societal implications of these issues. It is helpful for allies to understand that there is a trajectory of development. This understanding helps allies track their own development and recognize where others are on the continuum.

The framework that follows is not the only one used to map social justice awareness development. Professors who work with future teachers developed it. As such, it likely speaks to the kinds of experiences we may have or we may observe in our colleagues as we become more aware of equity issues.

Diversity Awareness and Identity Development Model

The following model identifies six developmental stages that preservice educators go through as they come to understand diversity (Cruz et al., 2014). Depending on prior experiences, they enter the discussion at various points on the continuum. Cruz et al. (2014) maintain, however, that the majority of their students enter at the first level.

The five stages of diversity awareness and identity development identified are in boldface. The more extended description of each stage reflects my understanding of people emerging from the fog of privilege.

- **Naiveté/Pre-Awareness**, which would be roughly equivalent to being encased in a fog of privilege.
- **Bombardment,** which is often the feeling those emerging from this stage feel when equity-minded instructors demand that they confront what is on the other side of the fog.
- **Dissonance and Resistance,** which arise when new information does not jive with long-held beliefs and defense mechanisms are erected. Yearning for a return to the fog of privilege is strong but not possible.
- **Adjustment and Redefinition,** which is the accommodation-making stage, the stage of attempting to incorporate new knowledge into their existing belief systems, their first real attempt at seeing beyond the fog of privilege.
- **Acceptance and Internalization,** which is the reward for those who persevere. It is the stage that moves them out of the fog of privilege so that they see more clearly and are capable of acknowledging how discriminatory practice plays out in the lives of those who do not look or act like them.

The Issue of Diversity

Although it is helpful to use a model to outline phases of becoming aware of privilege, I do have an issue with the model above being called a *Diversity Awareness and Identity Development Model.* To my way of thinking, the use of the word *diversity* in the title is a diversionary tactic, a polite substitute so that words like *race* and *privilege* can be avoided. Educators are great at politeness. How often do we see the word *culture* in all of its forms—multi*cultural, culturally* responsive teaching, *cultural* competence, *cultural* proficiency—in conference titles, articles, and professional development sessions?

All are genuine efforts to develop sensitivity and to redress wrongs. The problem is that often the terms *diversity* and *culture* and the activities used to unpack them are divorced from their roots in equity and social justice. As a result, they mask the real issues, as marginalized students will attest. During a focus group designed to assess a two-year-long Multicultural Curriculum Initiative that was the principal's effort to address the "diversity" in the school, a student who identified as Black indicated that the multicultural program was "nothing." She wanted to know when the school would start to talk about racism (Gorski & Swalwell, 2015).

Allies need to be on guard for polite substitutes that dance around real injustices. I have a particularly strong prejudice against the word *diversity*. I often think people use *diversity* to avoid having to trip over the correct way to refer to people of color, Muslims, LGBTQ, people in wheelchairs, or any other marginalized group. I have often noticed how people lower their voices if, for some reason, they cannot avoid using one of these terms.

What they do not understand is that diversity makes the world what it is. It comes with the territory of being human. Diversity is a condition, the condition of being human. Marginalization is a construct, a construct that births inequity and exclusion. There should be no discomfort and lowered voices around diversity. There should be plenty of discomfort and lots of shame around unchecked, unchallenged, unmitigated marginalization.

Orchestrate Opportunities for Conversations and Deliberation

Understanding why people demonstrate avoidance is not easy. Often, timing and circumstances contribute. Lack of adequate preparation, lack of appropriate support, and lack of a process can erect impenetrable barriers to action. One process allies can use to open up a space for consideration of social justice issues involves something people do on a regular basis: converse.

One of our roles as educators and leaders is to foster collaboration, promote a spirit of inquiry, and co-construct coherence. One of the best methods to accomplish this is through orchestrated opportunities for conversation and deliberation, for discussion and dialogue, for working through the inevitable conflicts and tensions that surface during exchanges of ideas. Conversation is a game changer. Indeed, Garmston and Wellman (2009) emphasize how important conversation is to an organization by asserting that "professional communities are born and nurtured in webs of conversation."

When done well, conversation is a purposeful craft practiced by both the facilitator and group members. Garmston and Wellman (2009) assert that carefully nurtured, deliberately practiced, and constantly reevaluated conversation can result in developing a compelling purpose, collective efficacy, collaborative culture, and communal application of practices, trust, and individual and group learning.

These results do not come easily. They require norms of collaboration, multiple discussion techniques, and methods of dealing effectively with conflict, and specific exercises and instruments (Garmston &Wellman, 2009).

The principal's reluctance to engage the faculty in a discussion of the compelling issues raised by the Grade 2 teacher may well have been fueled by not having had the training, support, or time required to develop this culture, yet.

Figure 4.1 summarizes several broad themes regarding how allies can address the very real desire to avoid confrontation, feelings of guilt once injustice is pointed out, and being swept up in a vortex of feeling overwhelmed by the enormity of injustice and its fallout.

Figure 4.1　Overcoming Avoidance, Guilt, and Feelings of Inadequacy

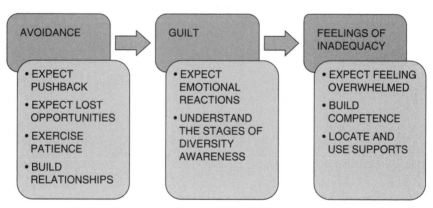

ORCHESTRATED OPPORTUNITIES FOR CONVERSATION FOSTER
COMMUNITY AND BUILD UNDERSTANDING

POLITICS AND THE CLASSROOM: SETTING THE RECORD STRAIGHT

Orchestrated opportunities for conversation and deliberation can also address misunderstandings, fill in background information, or present alternative views for consideration. An orchestrated conversation regarding the issue of politics and schools would likely cover the following broad themes:

- Politics and partisanship are vastly different.
- Schools ARE political spaces.

Ms. T.'s assertion that there is no room for politics in the classroom is not surprising. Many teachers assiduously avoid bringing politics into the classroom for many reasons. Many deny that politics is actually a part of classroom spaces. Well-prepared allies need to challenge these assertions and assumptions. Understanding that politics and partisanship are vastly different helps. So, too, does understanding that there has been—and continues to be—a history of politics influencing what happens in a classroom.

Politics and Partisanship Are Vastly Different

Teachers have many different takes on how and why politics should figure into their classrooms. Some teachers believe that they are required to maintain a neutral position in the classroom when it comes to political issues. They often interpret this to mean that they should completely avoid any discussion of political issues. This stance does a disservice to the teacher and the students, especially those who are marginalized. Often, marginalized students deeply understand the political and social landscape that contributes to their marginalization. To pretend that the political and social landscape does not exist is to ignore an essential, lived reality of many students. Honesty and authenticity demand that teachers, working with their students, fearlessly grapple with those issues that most significantly shape the lives of their students. So does a social justice lens. To negate injustice is to support the status quo.

Other teachers want to engage students in deep discussion about controversial issues in order to prepare them for their roles as members of a democratic society. Some are reluctant to state overtly their political stance on these issues, while others are quite comfortable doing so (Hesse, 2005; Hesse & McAvoy, 2015).

Still others go even further, claiming that education is, first and foremost, about political acts leading to liberation. They cry out for curriculum that acknowledges and shines a light on the ways in which the lives of marginalized students are nested in a broader cultural and sociological context. Not only do students crave this, but this acknowledgement often serves as the missing link between students and the curriculum.

In the 1960s, Sylvia Ashton-Warner discovered that her Maori children learned to read faster when their reading materials were made up of what she called students' *personal key words* (Ashton-Warner, 1963). This approach is not unlike the one Paolo Freire developed to teach Brazilian adults living in ghettos. His method involved having them learn the sounds associated with words they were familiar with and, like Ashton-Warner's list of *personal key words,* contained strong emotional overlays. In Brazil, people relegated to the lowest social and economic strata lived in ghettoes called *favelas*. The Brazilian adults who Freire worked with lived in *favelas* and were cognizant of the various injustices they lived with daily as a result of this. Learning to read the word *favela* situated learning to read in their cultural and mental context (Freire, 2008).

Stated another way, Ashton-Warner and Freire recognized that all acts of teaching are political acts because all teaching acts involve decisions about what knowledge is taught, whose knowledge it represents, and how that knowledge is organized.

Admittedly, multiple perspectives exist regarding politics in the classroom. One thing is certain, however. Politics in the classroom requires careful consideration. It is a matter of balance, requiring a steady hand. Teachers revealing their political stance on an issue is very different than outright partisanship. Partisanship is an attempt to influence students to adopt a particular position. Consideration of political issues has a place in the classroom. Partisanship does not.

Schools ARE Political Spaces

Beyond this, history demonstrates that politics has always been part of schooling.

How schools are organized, what policies govern them, what we teach, and how we teach it are all decisions driven by politics or the values of a given community, as defined by those in power. The way these values play out in school policies and practices coalesces into what has been termed "the grammar of schooling" (Tyack & Cuban, 1995), those easily recognized ways in which the business of school is carried out. The following examples demonstrate how the dominant thinking and values of the time, the politics of the period, affected the grammar of schooling in the United States.

An Example From History: Thomas Jefferson

Thomas Jefferson is often credited with being a proponent of educational opportunity. And he was. For some, at least. What he advocated was a system devoted to the study of what men of his stature valued at the time: a classical education designed for an elite. What Jefferson designed was a school system that openly promoted a progressive sifting and sorting of students so that only the best from the "residue" would be allowed to advance. He described this process as "raking a few geniuses from the rubbish." Some might argue that vestiges of the Jeffersonian model remain in today's schools.

Other examples of the ways in which politics or people's values directly influenced what happened—or not—in schools can be found in the 1830s legislation enacted by many Southern states preventing slaves from learning to read and write. In the mid-1800s, the factory model of schooling was adopted under pressure from business leaders who wanted the immigrants streaming into the country to be docile, obedient workers in their factories and other enterprises. Over the years, governance of schools in the United States see-sawed between local and regional control as the political winds swept over the land. Irish immigrants, for instance, fought pitched battles for local control when they arrived in cities like New York and Boston, because they did not want their children to be influenced by the Protestantism of the public schools of the time.

The Current Political Climate: Neoliberalism

Today, the dominant ideology governing how education is carried out derives from neoliberalism. It is a pervasive ideology that has exerted enormous influence on education. So what do allies need to know about neoliberalism, neoliberalism and education, and neoliberalism and social justice?

Neoliberalism is a political and economic theory. It is based upon the proposition that the well-being of humans is best served when humans are free to employ their entrepreneurial (business or risk-taking) skills in a setting that is free from government control. Neoliberals value strong private property rights, free markets, and free trade (Harvey, 2005).

So what does neoliberalism have to do with education? Neoliberalism seeks to enhance the role of the private sector in the economy. Historically, education has been the responsibility of the public sector. Universal free public education is a hallmark of the American system. It was considered a government responsibility and was supported by public funds. Since the 1970s, however, neoliberalism has gradually seeped into the system so that today, private individuals and private corporations play major roles in how learning and teaching play out. Think about Bill Gates, companies such as Pearson, and privately owned charter schools. These private enterprises continually grab more and more of the funds raised by state, municipal, and local communities earmarked to support education.

Not only has neoliberalism diverted public funds into private balance sheets, it has also profoundly influenced how learning and teaching occur. Neoliberals believe that what works in the private sector should work in the public sector. Among other things, the private sector values competition, enhancing the bottom line, consumerism, the use of data in decision making, and accountability with sanctions. Today, schools are in competition with each other for higher performance records. Boards of education and school leaders are consumed with the need to cut costs regardless of the ill effects of these cuts. Students consume more and more educational products sold by fewer and fewer companies who have a grip on the educational market. More and more schemes to measure the ephemeral characteristics of good teaching and deep learning are put in place by federal, state, and local communities in an attempt to hold teachers and students accountable to questionable standards and, when they do not meet these standards, to apply various types of sanctions.

What does neoliberalism have to do with social justice? During the reign of neoliberalism, the gap between rich and poor, the haves and the have nots, has reached epic proportions. Neoliberalism is built upon the notion that people are rewarded on the basis of merit. Opponents of neoliberalism point out that it takes more than individual gumption to get ahead in the world. Opportunity supported by entire social and political systems exerts an undeniable influence on who gets ahead. That is why social justice activists use the term *opportunity gap* to explain differences in student outcomes.

Neoliberalism does two things to students. On the one hand, neoliberalism encourages students to maximize their own skills and talents, to engage in self-promotion, and to seek out and develop those relationships that "get" them something. All of this individual striving leaves little room for considering the greater good. In addition, neoliberalism seeks to make students compliant, nonquestioning consumers. Where students are likely to be less compliant, heavy-handed policing has been imposed. Advocates of social justice know too well that over-policing and rigid disciplinary procedures negatively affect marginalized students more profoundly than any other group.

Neoliberalism has also given rise to a curriculum and manner of teaching that promotes the transmission of a narrowly defined knowledge, rather than developing students' ability to think critically and to question. Both of these outcomes are contrary to social justice values. The notion that knowledge is to be transmitted is anathema to social justice advocates. In the transmission, or banking model of learning, knowledge is believed to be made up of bits of information to be "deposited, repeated and memorized" (Freire, 2008). This is vastly different from learning theories that promote building from the funds of knowledge students already possess. It also begs the question, whose knowledge is being transmitted? Social justice advocates worry mightily when entire groups of students, their histories, and their ways of thinking are ignored by the school system.

Neoliberalism is no friend to social justice.

Educators often take for granted that political and social movements are of no concern to our professional lives or the lives of our students. We like to believe that policy decisions are made with pure intentions and are designed for the common good. Sadly, the opposite is often true.

Figure 4.2   Activity: Where Is Social Justice in the Neoliberal Agenda?

In this exercise, you will be asked to examine one aspect of the neoliberal agenda to determine how it plays out in school.

Directions:

- Below are three educational reforms and policies associated with the neoliberal agenda that directly affect learning and teaching:
  - High-stakes testing
  - Performance pay for teachers
  - Increased accountability
- Select one and consider your experience with this reform, some of its characteristics, and how you feel this reform advances the goal of attaining social justice, equity, and inclusion.
- In what ways does this reform impact marginalized students, including the student or students to whom you dedicated this work?

Allies in the battle for social justice run a critical eye over policy decisions in order to determine whether these decisions, as they play out in our classrooms and schools, advance or hinder attaining social justice, equity, and inclusion.

KEY CONSIDERATIONS FOR ALLIES

- Allies are often impatient to address social justice issues with others, but strategic impatience that takes into account timing and relationships often results in more efficacious results.
- Allies benefit from understanding the human dimensions, developmental stages, and amount of preparation that impact people's readiness for grappling with social justice issues.
- Allies benefit from understanding that educators have varying takes on how and when politics should be introduced into the classroom.
- Classrooms have historically enacted political agendas.
- The dominant political agenda impacting education today is neoliberalism.
- Neoliberalism is no friend to social justice.
- **Looking Ahead**: The next chapter moves away from the broader social and political considerations of social justice and focuses on students and how marginalization affects them.

Acknowledging the Social and Psychological Toll of Continued Injustice

One day, my then three-year-old granddaughter, Ida, who likes to share her observations and make jokes, decided to "play a trick on everyone" as she said, while she was being driven home from day care. "You're a boy," she told her mother. "I am?" her mother responded. "Nana, you're a boy!" she said to me via our speakerphone connection. "I am?" I said. "Cheryl's a boy," she continued, naming one of her friends. After each pronouncement she collapsed into uncontrollable giggles. Then she paused, apparently had an *aha* moment, and said, "Leo," referring to her baby brother, "is a GIRL," collapsing yet again into three-year-old uncontrollable giggles.

DIFFERENTIATION AND SOCIALIZATION

Even at the early age of three, Ida is beginning to differentiate, to notice one of the many ways in which our culture categorizes people. In other words, she is already being socialized into the norms of our culture, which places enormous stock on boys being boys and girls being girls. Her socialization to date does not allow her to contemplate babies being born with variant sex characteristics, the kind that would make the distinctions between male and female more difficult to ascertain. Having already internalized the way our culture looks at sex as being a boy-girl binary, she is able to play with it and tease the adults around her, much to her own delight.

This story illustrates that socialization begins early. It also continues throughout life. Where someone stands on the arbitrary social divisions set up by society has an enormous impact on that person's social standing and psychological well-being. Those who do not fit into what is deemed normal or acceptable experience marginalization. Marginalization manifests itself in many ways in and out of school. Acknowledging how is a way to build empathy and to strengthen an ally's ability to see and name marginalization, as well as to strengthen an ally's resolve to work to disrupt the injustices that lead to marginalization.

This chapter will look at three aspects of marginalization:

- How young people experience marginalization;
- Some of the processes, histories, and operating principles that characterize marginalization; and
- One of the big mistakes people trying to "get" marginalization can make.

HOW DO YOUNG PEOPLE EXPERIENCE MARGINALIZATION? THREE VOICES

Understanding how the world sees the marginalized and how the marginalized see the world is of great importance and the focus of the following activity in Figure 5.1.

Figure 5.1 Activity: Amplifying Voices of Marginalized Students

This activity involves three videos in which young people, all victims of marginalization, give voice to their experiences. The videos provide an opportunity for potential allies to see and hear about marginalization from the perspective of three young people, to think through responses, and to explicitly name the negative effects of being perceived to be outside cultural norms.

The experiences recounted by these three young people are not meant to represent the entire range of marginalization that occurs in the world. However, the activity does provide a template that could be used to think through personal accounts of young people from other marginalized groups.

Directions:

Complete this activity making use of the table that follows:

- Consult the first column for the title, summary, and link to each of the videos.
- Use the second column to record what resonated with you as you watched each video.
- Use the third column to record what each video reveals about the social and psychological toll of marginalization.

Video Title and Context	What resonated with you?	What does the video say about the social and psychological toll of marginalization?
A Girl Like Me In 2005, then sixteen-year-old Kiri Davis produced an award-winning documentary called *A Girl Like Me*. This seven-minute video does two things. It begins with interviews of young Black women about standards of beauty. Second, it re-creates the doll experiment conducted by Drs. Kenneth and Mamie Clark in the 1940s, which was designed to determine children's self-perception related to race. Watch the video, which can be found here: www.youtube.com/watch?v=YWyI77Yh1Gg&t=1s		
My Life With a Learning Disability Andrew Schneider is a high school student who struggles to learn. In the following video, Andrew takes us through a typical school day. He chronicles his activities, his feelings, his struggles, and his triumphs. www.youtube.com/watch?v=kiqDq0fimXk		What do Andrew's experiences add?
Bullied Jamie Nabozny, a gay student, was repeatedly harassed in middle and high school, while the school personnel upon whom he depended for protection chose to blame the victim. As an eleventh		What do Jamie's experiences add?

(Continued)

Figure 5.1 (Continued)

Video Title and Context	What resonated with you?	What does the video say about the social and psychological toll of marginalization?
grader, Jamie was the target of a particularly brutal encounter with his classmates, which landed him in the hospital. Watch the first twenty minutes of the following video, in which Jamie talks about his school experiences, the lawsuit he brought against the school, and the film that was made about it. www.youtube.com/ watch?v=EUOGtt1QEro		
How might you summarize the social and psychological impact of marginalization on the lives of those marginalized?		

Truth Be Told

Whenever I use any of these videos in a workshop, the reaction is generally the same. Viewers are moved. This is especially true of *A Girl Like Me.* Reactions are particularly strong over the doll experiment segment, which captures preschool children of color struggling to determine, among other things, which is the "nice" doll and which is the "bad" doll. Educators are genuinely troubled to see the pain and indecision on the faces of these children. They express shock and dismay that so little appears to have changed since the 1940s, when Drs. Kenneth and Mamie Clark conducted the original doll experiments. These experiments became a part of the Clarks' testimony during the 1954 *Brown v. Board of Education* case to demonstrate the extent to which self-image is shaped at an early age. How, workshop participants wonder, is this even possible? How, indeed? This is why allies are needed.

The other two videos have their own power, the power of personal narrative. Most educators know, or intuit, that life is hard for students with disabilities and students whose sexuality is considered deviant. We rarely get a chance to hear how hard it is from the mouths of those being victimized. Yet, we need to. This is called "truth-gathering."

How important it is for victims to give voice to their experiences can be seen in the unusual steps Canada took to redress the wrongs inflicted upon indigenous peoples who were part of the Indian Residential School system. For six years, Canada engaged in a dramatic and very public truth-gathering process. The Truth and Reconciliation Commission travelled the country to hear directly from Aboriginal people who had been taken from their families as children and placed in residential schools. There, the children were prevented from speaking their native languages, practicing their religion, or engaging in cultural traditions. On top of that, they were subjected to physical and sexual abuse. Truth gathering, the final report attests, is an important first step to open the door to reconciliation (Truth and Reconciliation Commission of Canada, 2015).

Some Takeaways

When these videos are shown during workshops, truth gathering takes place, eyes are opened, and some big takeaways result. Among these are the following key understandings that emerge:

- We are each authorities on our own experiences.
- Students ARE diverse.
- We need to look critically at how schools deal with difference and connection.
- Culturally transmitted understandings and assumptions are powerful and pervasive.
- Group identity and social systems work together to shape how we see ourselves.
- We come to understand who we are by who we are *not*.
- Students, even the very youngest ones, are capable of "reading" the world.
- Self-esteem is built—or not—on the basis of what others reflect back to us about who we are and where we fit in.
- How the world sees us affects how we see the world.
- Truth gathering precedes reconciliation.

WHAT PROCESSES, HISTORIES, AND OPERATING PRINCIPLES CHARACTERIZE MARGINALIZATION?

Marginalization is a complex social construct. Just how complex the web of exclusionary structures is can be illustrated by looking a little more deeply at some of the processes, histories, and operating principles that characterize marginalization and marginalizing behaviors.

A Girl Like Me

A closer look at *A Girl Like Me* reveals ways in which different types of marginalization often intersect. *Intersectionality* is a complex, overlapping array of social categorizations that interact with each other. For example, class, race, and gender can all be viewed as independent systems of discrimination with their own forms of oppression. This single-axis framework does not account for the ways in which these classifications interact simultaneously with each other on multiple levels, creating classes of people who are "multiply burdened." Furthermore, *intersectionality theory* demonstrates how, by not taking into account the interplay of multiple oppressions, the single-axis theory further marginalizes people. For example, women experience discrimination. So do people of color. Oppression of women of color is neither purely one form nor the other but rather something different. Feminist concerns can, therefore, represent and speak to experiences that are foreign to women of color, leaving them no place at the table for their unique experiences to be addressed (Crenshaw, 1989).

Racism Intersecting With Lookism

A Girl Like Me is about the racist-fueled conceptions of what is physically attractive and what kinds of people are worthy. In addition to racism, which is the predominant form of marginalization portrayed in this video, elements of lookism are also present. Lookism is less well known, often denied, but an ever-present bias. Lookism refers to the positive overlay and preferential treatment that is bestowed upon those who are deemed by society to possess physical characteristics that match cultural preferences and ideals about what is attractive. Its effects are widespread. And so is the damage it can do.

Among other things, physically attractive people are treated preferentially, are viewed more positively, are more likely to get help from strangers, and garner more leniency from the courts (Etcoff, 1999). The "beauty premium" pays well, too. A recent study linked CEO attractiveness to higher compensation for the CEO and better stock performance for shareholders (Halford & Hsu, 2014).

But there are many downsides. Adapting to cultural preferences of attractiveness leads to drastic procedures. Young girls from India bleach their faces. Korean girls are obsessed with double eyelid surgery in order to look more western. Teenage girls—and boys—starve themselves attempting to meet some internalized ideal body type. There was a time when preoccupation with appearance was a defining characteristic of teenagers. Now, that preoccupation has moved into elementary schools.

The Unsettling History of Lookism

Appearance as a basis of judgment has a long history. Beginning in the late 1860s, many municipalities in the United States passed "ugly laws," which prohibited persons with "unsightly or disgusting" disabilities to be seen in public. San Francisco was the first. Chicago was the last to repeal its ugly laws. The Chicago law prohibited the following people from being "exposed to public view": people who are "diseased, maimed, mutilated or in any way deformed," as well as those who are "unsightly or disgusting." As recently as 1971, a person with cerebral palsy was arrested and fined in a Chicago restaurant for the crime of dining out with a friend. The desire to preserve the pretty façade of communities relegates those who are differently abled, indigent, or poor to the sidelines of society.

Beauty prejudice and appearance discrimination are genuine injustices that permeate all levels of society. Societal obsession with appearances fuels lookism, an obsession that is stoked by the media, especially advertising. Is it any wonder, then, that lookism has found a place in schools? A recent study shows that schools apply the beauty premium in ways that count, specifically in the awarding of grades. Simply stated, those students rated more attractive receive higher grades (Gordon & Crosnoe, 2013).

My Life With a Disability

There is a connection between the video *My Life With a Disability*, Andrew Schneider's story of being differently abled, and the "ugly laws." Andrew Schneider and others with identified "disabilities" enjoy a range of legal protections under the Americans with Disabilities Act thanks, in part, to people's response to the injustices enshrined in the "ugly laws." Activists working on behalf of the differently abled had plenty to rail against in ugly laws that promoted discrimination based solely on appearance, laws that often targeted people suffering from crippling deformities. There are some who argue that the law has not gone far enough and that, in some instances, it is being used to promote injustice (Schweik, 2011). Even if a perfect law could be enacted, chances are Andrew and other differently abled people would not be guaranteed a discrimination-free life or be immune from the feelings of inadequacy and constant struggle that Andrew describes.

We have yet to figure out how to go against the grain of bias. We are saturated in it. And when it is applied to those who are differently abled, it goes by the name ableism. Ableism, like all *isms*, sets up an arbitrary standard upon which to measure a person's merit. In this case, the standard involves assigning lesser value to those who are differently abled physically, mentally, developmentally, emotionally, or psychiatrically. Our language reveals how the differently abled are valued. Words like *handicapped* and *disabled* are clear value markers, which is why I opt to use the term *differently abled*, which acknowledges that there are many versions and types of ability. To be *different* suggests not being the same. Differences exist in the world. Difference is a part of our human experience. Difference does not connote being *less than*.

Fighting the language battle, however, does not end with labels. Our language swarms with metaphors relating to the differently abled people that are pejorative, that possess negative connotations, that dehumanize: **Crippled** *by debt; You'd have to be* **insane** *to want to invade Syria; Only a* **moron** *would believe that* are several that Rachel Cohen-Rottenberg references (Cohen-Rottenberg, 2014). Allies work to erase these metaphors from their own speech and from language used in their schools.

Bullied

The video *Bullied* forces us to confront heterosexism. Heterosexism is the parent of homophobia. Heterosexism is based upon the belief that gender falls into two distinct categories, male and female; that heterosexuality is the only sexual norm; and, as a consequence, the only permissible form of sexual or marital relations is between people of opposite sexes. Heterosexism creates a hierarchy of sex, which in turn leads to discrimination, marginalization, and, in many cases, criminalization of those who do not fit the norm.

Jamie's story shows the many ways in which bias against students who identify outside the heterosexual binary can be treated. His story reveals the pervasive, sharp, and spirit-killing school-side weapon of choice in dealing with difference: bullying.

Countless programs, products, and personalities promote antibullying campaigns. Yet it continues. The question is why? Bullying is what injustice looks like on the interpersonal level. If this take on bullying is right, then it might be safe to conclude that as long as injustice continues, bullying will, too.

Educators know that bullying is a huge problem. It rears its ugly head on the streets, in school hallways, and on social media. Its results can be devastating. One U.S. website that maintains and tracks data regarding incidences of bullying reveals some alarming facts about bullying and its effects on young people.

- Suicide is the third leading cause of death among young people, resulting in about 4,400 deaths per year.
- For every suicide among young people, there are at least one hundred suicide attempts.
- Over 14 percent of high school students have considered suicide, and almost 7 percent have attempted it.
- Bully victims are between two and nine times more likely to consider suicide than nonvictims.
- 160,000 kids stay home from school every day because of fear of bullying (http://www.bullyingstatistics.org/content/bullying -and-suicide.html).

LGBT youth in Canada have their own problems in school despite the fact that Canada approved gay marriage in 2005. Several recent studies point to high rates of depression among LGBT youth, pronounced feelings of alienation at school, and high rates of attempted suicide. These conditions prompted one team of researchers to refer to schools as "the land time forgot" when it comes to LGBT youth.

As the Canadian research indicates, changes in legislation relating to LGBT rights do not automatically translate into improved school experiences for LGBT youth. As a social justice ally, you may well wonder is my school "a land time forgot" for LGBTQ students or is it an inclusive and welcoming school? The activity in Figure 5.2 on the pages that follow will help you determine an answer to that question.

Ensuring My School Is Not a Land Time Forgot for Any Student

Allies recognize that marginalization of any kind is deeply engrained and profoundly destructive. Their desire is to ensure that they, individually, and their school, collectively, are NOT contributing to the creation of a land time forgot for any student. This is not an easy task. For an individual or a school to be truly responsive to and welcoming of all students requires more than just a vision statement. It requires a deliberate and collaborative process in which multiple aspects of schooling are taken into consideration from attitudes and understandings to policies and pedagogy.

The following activity has been created using materials and processes developed on behalf of and with LGBTQ students, but the considerations could be—and should be—applied to all marginalized groups of students in a concerted effort to address marginalization on a systemic basis. The approaches taken by each of three groups are summarized in the

Figure 5.2 Activity: Ensuring My School Is Not a Land Time Forgot

Several excellent resources exist to help schools assess how welcoming and inclusive they are to LGBTQ students and to plan ways of making their schools even more welcoming and inclusive for them.

The chart below contains a summary of approaches taken by three organizations that can help allies assess their school's level of inclusiveness along a number of dimensions.

Directions:

- **Review** the considerations and examples in columns 1 and 2.
- **Consider the current reality.** List the specific and intentional efforts your school has made or is actively considering that relate to that dimension.
- **Consider the possibilities.** List additional ideas to enhance what your school is currently doing.

Ensuring My School Is Not a Land Time Forgot for LGBTQ Students

Creating Gender-Inclusive Schools—Points of Entry

Adapted From Gender Spectrum

https://www.genderspectrum.org/explore-topics/education/

CONSIDERATIONS	EXAMPLES	CURRENT REALITY	CONSIDER POSSIBILITIES
PERSONAL Are educators' understandings of gender issues a focus of professional development?	• The staff has targeted professional development to understand what is meant by sex and gender, the gender spectrum, the privileges associated with being "typically gendered," and their own gender journey.		

86

STRUCTURAL Are institutional policies and procedures built around gender-inclusive practices?	• The school employs a deliberate process of assessment and response to gender issues. • The school makes its values visible through policies, official documents, and forms that reflect gender inclusiveness.
INTERPERSONAL Are individual and group interactions and communications guided by inclusive language?	• Whether inside or outside the classroom, exchanges between and among students, staff, and families are guided by respect for gender issues.
INSTRUCTIONAL Is greater understanding and awareness of gender issues built into learning and teaching?	• Instructional units and individual lessons explicitly address topics such as gender awareness and bias reduction.

Checklist for a Welcoming and Inclusive School Environment

Adapted From Welcoming Schools

http://www.welcomingschools.org/pages/checklist-for-a-welcoming-and-inclusive-school-environment/

INCLUSIVE LANGUAGE Does my school take intentional steps to ensure that inclusive language is used in all formal publications and in everyday interactions?	• Official school documents have been reviewed to ensure inclusive language. • Inclusive language is modeled.

(Continued)

Figure 5.2 (Continued)

CONSIDERATIONS	EXAMPLES	CURRENT REALITY	CONSIDER POSSIBILITIES
DIVERSE BOOKS AND IMAGES Does my school have a deliberate and well-defined process for reviewing books and images through the lens of social justice?	• Students are exposed to books and images that positively reflect their lives, various family structures and gender expressions, and different races, ethnicities, and abilities.		
SPEAKING UP AGAINST MEAN WORDS AND ACTIONS Does my school have steps in place for addressing mean words and actions?	• Mean words and actions are immediately addressed. • Staff and students know how to respond to comments like, "You're gay," "A real family has a mother and a father."		
POSITIVE AND INCLUSIVE TONE FOR ALL Do plans for events and organizational procedures encourage positive school affiliations?	• Events are held that celebrate family and gender diversity. • All students have a positive relationship with an adult.		
Best Practices: Creating an LGBT-Inclusive School Climate Adapted From Teaching Tolerance http://www.tolerance.org/lgbt-best-practices			

88

BUILD INCLUSIVE ENVIRONMENT Are plans in place to ensure that every child and family feels welcome?	• Provide opportunities for members of Gay-Straight Alliance to educate others. • Review dress codes to eliminate rules that apply to only certain students. • Ensure students are addressed by their preferred pronoun.	
PREVENTING AND ADDRESSING PROBLEMS Are staff members and students aware of the negative effects of bullying and the steps necessary to address incidents of bullying?	• Designate a specially trained antibullying coordinator to prevent and respond to incidents of bullying. • Identify bullying "hot spots" and take steps to eliminate or monitor them.	

Extension Activity

- **Resource Informed List:** Each of the three websites used above contains many additional resources, including lesson plans, position papers, and policy statements that could help craft a blueprint for a more inclusive school. Consult one or more of them for additional ideas. Two additional resources are Gay, Lesbian & Straight Education Network (GLSEN.org) and the Gay-Straight Alliance (www.gsanetwork.org).

Team Activity

- Create work groups tasked with applying the same considerations and processes to all forms of marginalization: racism, classism, ableism, lookism, etc.

accompanying chart. The three approaches are, in many ways, different ways of organizing the same key considerations.

Gender Spectrum organizes considerations into four entry points: personal, structural, interpersonal, and instructional. Welcoming Schools has a checklist schools can use to determine their level of inclusiveness by considering four categories: inclusive language, diverse books and images, speaking up against mean words and actions, and inclusive tone. Teaching Tolerance divides the considerations into two categories: building an inclusive environment, and preventing and addressing bullying. Although there is overlap in some areas, going through each of the ways in which the considerations have been organized and reading the variety of examples provided is a way for allies to consider a number of manifestations of injustice.

Marginalization, Microaggressions, and Stereotype Threats

There are several other manifestations of marginalization that allies need to take into account as they engage in specific activities designed to interrupt unjust practices and their effects on students. These facets include coming to understand microaggressions and stereotype threats.

Microaggressions

A discussion of the social and psychological toll marginalization takes on those marginalized would not be complete without thinking about and through the ways microaggressions work on the spirit.

Chester M. Pierce coined the term *microaggression*. The term refers to the casual, off-handed, stereotype-fueled comments that subtly put down a marginalized group. For instance, the teacher who tells a wheelchair-bound student, "Your paper was surprisingly good," suggests that the teacher is "surprised" that those who are differently abled physically could do quality academic work. The stranger who says to a Black person, "You speak so well," is implying that most Black people do not.

African American writer Jacqueline Woodson, author of the award-winning book, *Brown Girl Dreaming*, captures in vivid terms how a moment of glory can be turned on its head by a microaggression. As she tells the story, she was on her way back to her seat amid warm applause and a standing ovation after having just received the National Book Award. The master of ceremonies, a friend, shattered the moment. During a dinner at his home the previous summer, Jacqueline did not eat the watermelon soup that was served, explaining that she was allergic to watermelon. Apparently remembering this event, the master of ceremonies decided to quip, "Jackie's allergic to watermelon." And then added, "Just let that sink in." The impact of his words was startling. As Jacqueline Woodson put it,

"In a few short words, the audience and I were asked to take a step back from everything I've ever written, a step back from the power and meaning of the National Book Award, lest we forget, lest I forget, where I came from" (Woodson, 2014).

In the past, microaggressions were silently, if not happily, tolerated. As a result, it was difficult to assess how widespread they were. Two Columbia University students put an end to suffering in silence and to the mystery behind the prevalence of microaggressions by putting up a blog called *The Microaggressions Project*. In a four-year period, the blog attracted 15,000 submissions and received 2.5 million page views in forty countries (Vega, 2014).

Stereotype Threats

There is another type of psychological/emotional toll that comes into play that is especially damaging for many of our marginalized students. It is called *stereotype threat*.

Stereotype threats are the often unstated but very real pressures that come over us in situations where we are likely to confirm a negative cultural stereotype about a group to which we belong. For example, women, who are stereotyped as being weak in math and science, could feel it when taking math or science tests. Their sense is that if they do poorly, their performance will not only affect how people judge them individually, it will also confirm the stereotype that women are not good in math and science.

Psychologist Claude Steele (2010) indicates that identity and performance are intertwined. His research shows that even subtle or indirect reminders of a negative stereotype can affect minority group performance negatively. The opposite is also true. When students engage in values affirming activities that boost their identity, performance is enhanced.

GETTING IT WRONG WHEN TRYING TO "GET" MARGINALIZATION

Allies who are members of a dominant group often go out of their way to try to walk a mile in other people's shoes, to try to see the world from other's perspectives. One of the ways they do this is to take a personal experience in which they may have been left out or momentarily in the position of being a minority and use it to claim this experience provides them with what they need to know to understand lifelong, pernicious, pervasive oppression. And they can do so even when they should know better, which is exactly what I did.

I am embarrassed to admit that a first draft of this book included a thirteen-paragraph, almost 1,200-word personal anecdote in which

I recounted my after-retirement move from New York to Montreal; my coming to understand the language-fueled, rocky relationship between Anglophones and Francophones in Quebec; my desire to integrate into both worlds; and my real discomfort one day when the director of the French choir I had joined to help improve my French asked us to sing a traditional French song as a warm-up exercise. As a result, my normal supports were missing: no music and no words, which left me feeling isolated and different. I concluded this reflection with the following, very problematic words:

In the space of several minutes, I knew what it felt like to be on the margins, to not see myself reflected in common activities, to be the other.

Responding to This Story. When I initially wrote this anecdote, I was very pleased with it. Unnoticed by me, the fog of privilege crept in and led me to believe that my story was important. Upon reflection, however, I saw it for what it really was.

- This was not a story of marginalization and oppression. How many times did I use the word *I*? Clearly, I and my concerns were at the center of this story; I and my concerns were far from the margins.
- This is the story of a dominant body doing what dominant bodies expect to do: be heard. As a member of a dominant group, I unconsciously have come to expect that my experiences matter, that others are actually interested in them, and that some universal truths or important insights are part of my story. Why else would this anecdote be filled with details about where I live, what I read, my opinions about Montreal, and so on?
- This is the story of a dominant body expecting to occupy the familiar position of expert. Oppressed people know more about being oppressed than anyone occupying a more privileged position. They own the experience; they own the rights to the story.
- This is the story of a dominant body being disingenuous. Dominant bodies are best able to tell stories about their experiences of being privileged, since privilege is the world we occupy.
- This is the old story of the volume being turned up on the experiences of the dominant group and turned down on the experiences of the marginalized.
- This story overlooks, dismisses, minimizes, underrepresents, ignores, and sanitizes the real toll that oppression takes. Oppression is not a trifling matter. Its consequences are real. *Isms* may be social constructs. Their effects are real.

- This story takes away space and time and resources from stories of oppression told by people who actually experience oppression.
- This story prevents me from shutting up and listening, perhaps the first and most important lesson any potential ally needs to learn.

In short, my choir story, and others like it, reinforces the status quo, provides little by way of genuine understanding of how oppression is experienced, and adds little to a much-needed conversation on how to dismantle oppressive systems. Beyond that, it reeks of unearned privileges, none of which are acknowledged as such.

Good intentions aside, to take up the I-know-what-it-feels-like-to-be-oppressed stance is wrong. It is hurtful. It is actually violent. It is to be avoided.

The toll of marginalization is enormous. There are those who maintain that the effect of long-term marginalization is nothing short of a form of trauma. Indeed, psychologist Kenneth Handy (2013) maintains that racial marginalization and the oppression that characterizes it is "a traumatic form of interpersonal violence which can lacerate the spirit, scar the soul, and puncture the psyche."

KEY CONSIDERATIONS FOR ALLIES

There are many facets to marginalization. So far we have looked at the following:

- Marginalization is often experienced as multiple oppressions (intersectionality).
- Lookism promotes unfair advantages for those who are perceived to fit an appearance norm and exerts undo pressures on those who perceive themselves as not fitting that norm.
- "Ugly laws" contributed to ableism.
- Despite forward-thinking legislation, schools sometimes do not do enough to protect their vulnerable LGBT and other marginalized students.
- Ensuring your school is NOT a land time forgot takes a systemic, rather than patchwork, approach that addresses multiple aspects of what happens in schools.
- Microaggressions and stereotype threats have negative psychological, social, academic, and physical ramifications for those who suffer from them.

- A fleeting experience of being a momentary minority does not entitle a person in a dominant position to claim to know what it feels like to be marginalized.
- No matter how well-intentioned, well-read, or committed you are to social justice issues, you can be temporarily swamped by the fog of privilege.
- **Looking Ahead:** Once the fog of privilege lifts, even briefly, it reveals what is on the other side, a revelation that leads allies to wonder, "What else might be out there?" The next chapter will present ways allies can "read" unjust situations.

You Can't
"Un-See" What
You Have Seen

6

The previous chapters have been an attempt to pierce through the fog of privilege that envelops the lives of those in dominant positions in order to reveal realities beyond the dense cocoon of that privileged fog. For some, you may now see more clearly aspects of society that you previously saw but dimly: social justice, privilege, power, politics, and marginalization. For others, you may be seeing these elements for the first time. Whether more clearly focused or seen for the first time, these elements are now part of the way you see the world. As one teacher said, "You can't un-see what you have seen."

You could, of course, resolutely avoid what you now know is beyond the fog. Chances are that will not happen. What is more likely to occur is that you will "see" things that others do not. Once you do, you will have to figure out how to address the situation. Deepening your grasp of key social justice theories and sharpening your ability to use a social justice lens to "read" what is happening in your school that may be promoting injustice are two ways allies can prepare themselves to help others "see." Both take practice and both will be addressed in this chapter.

USING SOCIAL JUSTICE THEORIES
TO "READ" UNJUST SITUATIONS

In the last chapter, we watched three videos in which young people give their take on the experience of marginalization. By looking a little more closely at their experiences, we uncovered some of the processes, histories, and operating principles that characterize marginalization. Clearly, marginalization is a term that potential allies need to spend time thinking through. Unfortunately, many well-meaning people have an emotional reaction to the idea of marginalization. Allies counteract emotion with understanding, reason, and insight based upon a firm theoretical foundation.

Getting Past Emotional Responses

One of the ways we try to make sense of new information is by comparing it to things that are familiar. Indeed, a good teaching practice we engage in is to encourage students to make text-to-self comparisons. When it comes to some White people coming to terms with Black marginalization, however, this text-to-self process can backfire, resulting in tearful and angry responses.

One day during a break in a professional development session that was being led by a team of African American scholars with earned doctorates, a White teacher approached me and asked if we could speak privately. She was clearly agitated and almost immediately burst into tears saying that she was "sick and tired of having all those Black people refer to themselves as Doctor this and Doctor that." She went on to say that she, too, suffered as a child. She was raised in an unheated house, where every winter morning getting out of bed involved putting her blanket-warm feet on cold wooden planks. She continued saying that she now has many degrees but she doesn't "lord it over others." She ended by asking, "Why do all of the Black presenters have to lord it over the rest of us?"

Along the same lines was a conversation I had with a White colleague who said she was tired of hearing about the trials and tribulations of Black people. As a Jew and a woman, she said, her people and she have also suffered. She concluded by saying maybe people should just get on with their lives.

No one can deny that because of our multiple identities it is likely that we have experienced marginalization and reduced opportunity. It would be equally foolish to deny, however, that for certain groups the system is assembled in such a way as to make the ill-effects of marginalization a permanent and prominent feature of their existence.

Gary Howard (1999) summarizes four theories that allies could use to respond to comments like these from a sociological and historical perspective. See Figure 6.1.

If I could respond to the teacher and my colleague today, the three more deeply shaded theories might help me to acknowledge that yes, of course, they and their social and cultural groups have felt the sting of society's obsession with classification. These theories suggest that a propensity to categorize and value different groups appears to be part of the

Figure 6.1 Various Perspectives on Social Dominance

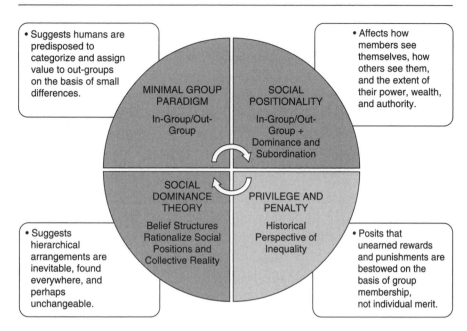

Adapted from Gary Howard (1999).

human condition. Along with the categorization comes discrimination. As a result, they, individually, and their cultural groups, collectively, may have been penalized because of where they have been placed in the social hierarchy. Understanding the concept of privilege and penalty a little more deeply, however, demonstrates that certain groups have historically suffered from an overabundance of penalty and a paucity of privilege.

Having the ability to articulate the theoretical stances that others have developed to explain privilege and dominance supplies the potential ally with a firm foundational vocabulary and a particular conceptual language in which to deconstruct and challenge emotionally held perspectives.

"SEEING" WHAT THE WALLS ARE SAYING

A fitting end to the concepts and ideas developed in Part One of the book might be to practice applying a social justice lens to an actual situation as a means of guiding you through a process you could apply to situations you may face in your school or classroom. The anecdote involves "seeing" what the walls are saying.

The Story

The Context. How many times have we heard the expression "If the walls could talk"? The truth is that they do—and they speak volumes. Take, for example, the boardroom of a school district. Like many others located near a large urban center, the school district is undergoing a major demographic shift, as more children challenged by poverty, more immigrants, more Black and brown children move in at the same time former residents of a previously all-White enclave move out. Fortunately, the superintendent is forward thinking and socially aware, centered and compassionate, persuasive and persistent.

Accomplishments to Date. Under his leadership, the school district has adopted a vision squarely focused on equity. Purposeful hiring practices have populated leadership and teaching positions with faces that reflect the changing student body. Professional development has centered upon issues of equity. Board sessions have included book studies on social justice issues, including conversations with authors. Policies and practices that marginalize certain students have been questioned, reviewed, and revised.

The Challenge. These efforts have gone on for several years and they are bearing fruit. Yet, if you walk into their boardroom, you might be shocked. I have conducted several professional development sessions in this room over a number of years. All had to do with leadership for equity and social justice in some manner, shape, or form. Participants included district and school leaders, instructional coaches, equity officers, and teacher leaders. The room, a well-equipped, technologically sophisticated site, contains only two wall displays. Both are football jerseys encased in glass enclosures and neatly framed.

As we got to know and trust each other over time, I felt I was ready to call participants' attention to the display. I asked them to "read" the room and to think about the message delivered by this display.

Reading the Room. Reading the room is a quick and effective way to come to understand power structures as they unintentionally play out in social and institutional settings. All it takes to "read" a room are observational and interpretational skills. In any given setting, observe who is present and who is missing. Who gets to talk and is listened to? Who is silenced or ignored? What messages are given off by the physical arrangement or room decorations? Taken as a whole, the answers to these questions reveal who and what are valued.

Figure 6.2 Activity: If the Walls Could Talk

In the following activity, you will be asked to apply your observational and interpretive skills to the boardroom display of football jerseys by applying the same questions I asked the group of workshop participants to consider. The questions should have a familiar ring and they will allow you an opportunity to apply a social justice lens to what the walls are saying.

Football Jersey Displays Consider the messages delivered by exclusively adorning the walls of the board of education meeting room with football jerseys.	
What aspect of school life is recognized as having value?	What aspects are left out?
Who is represented?	Who is not?
Recall the marginalized student or students to whom you have dedicated your work. In what ways are the life, interests, culture, strengths of your student or students reflected in the display?	Recall the marginalized student or students to whom you have dedicated your work. In what ways are the life, interests, culture, strengths of your student or students NOT reflected in the display?

The Reactions

Some Conclusions. I am certain that you, like the group I was with, immediately recognized that the display of football jerseys provided a strong, if unintentional message, that athletics, and only one type of athletics, was of value. The list of those aspects of school life that are omitted is huge. So is student representation. In this case, able-bodied, athletic males capable of making the football team are portrayed as having value. Everyone else is left out. If there were a marginalization scale, this display would be prize worthy. Where is equity in such a scenario? Where are the values of the district vision statement?

Some Arguments. When something like this is pointed out, people can become defensive and offer counterarguments. One might argue that the school district has a long tradition of being a football powerhouse, so the display was merely a nod to this proud history. One might argue that nowadays the majority of players are Black, and therefore the display could not be marginalizing. One might argue that football teaches many valuable life lessons. But these arguments miss the point. When the list of those being left out exceeds the list of those being included, equity is not being served. When vast numbers of students do not see themselves reflected in the items chosen to adorn the walls of the district board of education meeting room, then a major disservice is being done and marginalization flourishes.

An Ally's Response

Make no mistake about it. It was not easy—nor was it a quick journey—that got me to the point of being able to identify the issues with the football jersey display and then to find the courage—and the "right" words—to say something about it. A burden of being attuned to social justice issues is that you notice more. A gift of being an ally is that you can work to counteract the negative fallout of seemingly innocuous decisions like how the board of education meeting room is decorated.

Some Takeaways

An important takeaway from this exercise is that the walls do talk. Once participants "saw" what the boardroom walls said, they were prompted to take action. What, they wondered, were the walls really saying in their classrooms and in their buildings? In order to be true to their vision for equity, they decided they needed to find out. They agreed to conduct an equity audit of classroom and hallway displays, stationery and website logos, and other images to find out what the walls were actually saying. The goal was to ferret out those displays that "spoke" to only a few of the students and to find alternatives that would be more inclusive.

Not a bad impulse, and certainly one that was in line with the leadership institutes a colleague and I had been conducting with them on fearless leadership. One of the protocols we use includes a three-step process: affirmation, inspiration, and mediation. We use the acronym AIM to delineate these steps. By affirmation, we mean acknowledging the current reality. By inspiration, we mean envisioning what reality could be. By mediation, we mean the specific actions taken to get from the current reality to the vision (Jackson & McDermott, 2009; Jackson & McDermott, 2012).

Needless to say, I was delighted that the group wanted to put a deliberate process in place in order to effect change. There was a problem, though, from a social justice perspective.

Moving to the Next Level of Practice

Allies accept a supporting role in liberation. They are NOT liberators. Having a group of administrators and teacher leaders, representatives of the power structure, conduct the equity audit leaves out of the process those with less power and the likely recipients of any slight that may emanate from school displays. The people left out, the people most directly affected, are the students.

By virtue of their roles, administrators and teachers occupy a position of privilege in the power structure that makes up schools. Who decides to conduct an equity audit, who ultimately conducts it, who controls how it will be conducted, who determines what will be done with the information collected are all matters of great import. True allies would shy away from taking on the responsibility of conducting an equity audit. They would see such an action as a manifestation of administrators and teachers using their privileged position to take over a matter that rightfully belongs to those most directly affected, in this case, the students. Often the fog of privilege masks the myriad ways in which privilege is a "power over" tactic. It swoops in, encircles, and overtakes situations.

Additionally, eliminating students from the process significantly diminishes the process. Anne Bishop reminds us that members of the dominant group cannot see what is going on as clearly as members of the oppressed group (Bishop, 2002). Therefore, students would likely see much that adults might miss.

Beyond that, having students conduct an equity audit is an authentic learning experience that has multiple academic benefits, as well as the potential to effect genuine change in the school culture. Concepts of equity and fairness are important to students. Reading, writing, and thinking about equity would be relevant and meaningful to them. Figuring out how to conduct the audit—what to look for, how to code findings, how to ensure interrated reliability—would engage them in thinking through complex processes. Analyzing the data would necessarily involve them in summarizing and synthesizing. Determining how to best present the data would tap into their creativity and technical skills. Making recommendations would involve them in problem solving.

Intention and Attention

So were the adult workshop participants wrong in deciding they wanted to conduct an equity audit? Not at all. Their response was perfectly understandable given where they were in their quest to be allies. One of the goals of this book in general, and the telling and analyzing of this anecdote in particular, is to demonstrate that the trajectory for becoming an ally is one of continuous improvement. Allies work toward moving to the next level of practice and understanding. Allies are clear about their *intention* in order to assess to what they need to pay *attention*. If our intention is to be allies in a concerted effort to move the equity needle, we could, and should, be asking questions. Good questions to start with are the question pairs previously provided: *Who stands to win? Who stands to lose? Whose voices are heard? Whose voices are silenced?* By thinking through these questions, other possibilities often emerge, which can bring allies

Figure 6.3   Activity: Awareness Test

There is a fifty-five-second public service announcement that connects to the theme of this chapter. Watch the video. Consider the ways in which the message of the video connects to the theme of the chapter, "You Can't Un-see What You Have Seen." The video may be found at the following website: https://www.youtube.com/watch?v=Ahg6qcgoay4

closer to the intended goal, which helps lift the fog that encases their thinking, and which assists them in labeling and responding to what they previously did not see.

KEY CONSIDERATIONS FOR ALLIES

- You can't un-see what you have seen.
- Effectively applying a social justice lens to actual experiences benefits from a conceptual understanding of social justice theory and a well-defined, but generative, process.
- Becoming an ally is an ongoing, recursive process, not a one-time conversion experience.
- **Looking Ahead**: Once allies begin to see things that do not fit into their world view, a certain amount of dissonance sets in. Addressing this dissonance needs to be tackled before allies are ready to dismantle the questionable stories that keep injustice intact.

Part II

Exposing the Flaws in the Dominant Narrative

FINDING YOUR WAY OUT OF THE FOG OF PRIVILEGE

Fogs are interesting phenomena. They have personalities, character, and peculiarities. Some are dense, somber, and seemingly impenetrable, a gauzy iron wall separating those inside the fog from the world on the other side. Others are ephemeral, fluid, and fickle, swirling hither and yon guided by a puff of wind or altered by a change in elevation or transformed by a shift in direction.

They come and go at will, they cannot be avoided, and they can be dangerous. Ask hikers, skiers, and drivers who have ever been caught in a fog. Fogs can blind us, disorient us, and hold us in place. The fog of privilege can do the same. But, there are ways to navigate out of a fog, to get to the other side where vistas become visible, where the landscape becomes clear.

Fogs render old, comfortable ways of navigating useless. No map will get you out of a dense fog. Specialized tools and skills are called for. A compass, for instance, is essential. In the case of the fog of privilege, a finely tuned, social-justice compass can help point the way to equity and bring clarity to anti-oppression work. Carefully applied, well-thought-out questions are part of the social justice compass, like the ones we have already used: *Who stands to win? Who stands to lose? Whose voice is heard? Whose voice is silenced? In what ways would the marginalized students or students to whom I have dedicated my work be helped or hindered, feel belonging or alienation, thrive or whither as a result of this event, story, action, etc.?*

So, too, is accuracy. The terrain of injustice is fraught with twists and turns and efforts to knock allies off track. Knowing and being able to articulate the facts, the history, and the political agendas behind policies and practices is a powerful tool that can pierce through the fog of deception that encases many of the ways of doing things that we take for granted.

Attention is also needed. One misstep navigating a fog could land you in a ditch, bruised, bloodied, and dazed. Being alert at all times, reading the room, ferreting out messages behind what appears to be innocuous wall decorations, paying attention to language, challenging interpretations of taken-for-granted ways of doing business have the power to lift the fog of privilege layer by layer.

The good news is that these tools—questioning, accuracy, and attention—become second nature and easier to do the more times they are put to use, which is what we will do in the next section. Our focus will be on exposing the flaws in the dominant narrative.

PART TWO OPENING ANECDOTE:
THE DANGER OF A SINGLE STORY

Recently, a group of teachers, administrators, counselors, and professors gathered in a large southern state to consider learning, teaching, and poverty. Present, too, were state officials, including the president of the state board of education and state secretary of education. I could not have been more impressed with their orientation and grasp of the issues, their desire to improve opportunities for students challenged by poverty, and their dedication to the cause. Obviously, they were people who could be considered potentially strong, well-informed allies in the battle for social justice.

As one of the keynote speakers, I tried to figure out how we could work together to push our thinking to another level. I suggested we consider the difference between avoiding stereotyping and understanding what Nigerian novelist Chimamanda Ngozi Adichie calls the danger of a single story (Adichie, 2009). What came out was very informative.

In discussing stereotyping, several key points emerged. "Don't stereotype" is one of the rules many of us live by, and for good reason. Stereotyping is judgmental. It simplifies. It denies individuality and diminishes the members of a group whom we perceive to be different from us to a single conception or image often fraught with special meaning, generally not complimentary. In other words, stereotyping tells a single story about a complex group of people. It is also dismissive. "What can you expect from _____?" You fill in the blank: *Blacks, immigrants, poor people*. Worse yet, it leads to many harmful results, racial profiling being one that has finally caught Americans' attention big time.

During the session, most agreed that those who choose not to stereotype understand the ways in which stereotyping diminishes those being stereotyped. What they often do not see are the ways in which choosing not to stereotype, laudable as it is, is not enough in the battle for social justice. One can choose not to stereotype and remain complicit in the institutions and structures that privilege one group over another. Intentional action to counteract the pernicious effects of stereotyping is necessary to shatter the status quo.

But the conversation went further. What those of us who choose not to stereotype do not necessarily understand, we discovered, is that simply choosing not to stereotype and leaving it at that diminishes **us**. We can purposefully, high-mindedly, altruistically choose not to stereotype and still remain separate and largely uninformed about groups different than the ones to which we belong. Chimamanda Adichie, a Nigerian writer, addresses this nuance in her TED Talk, *The Danger of a Single Story*, which we watched as a discussion stimulator. In it, Chimamanda Adichie provides multiple examples of the danger of a single story from two perspectives, that of being a victim of stereotyping and that of being a perpetrator. She knows and retells in sharp detail the kinds of assumptions people made about her when she came to the United States to attend university. Her recounting of the single story ascribed to her because of her African background reveals the ways in which ignorance fuels the details of a single story. She also tells a story in which she falls prey to stereotyping. Her TED Talk makes it clear that those who limit themselves to a single story miss out on a lot.

For example, she tells what she missed as an eight-year-old because she had a single story about Fide, her middle-class family's houseboy. The only thing she knew about Fide was that he was poor. It wasn't until her family visited his family in their home in a rural part of Nigeria did she realize there was more to Fide than his poverty. His mother showed them a "beautifully patterned" basket that his brother had made. As she says, it had not occurred to her that anyone from Fide's family could make something beautiful. The single story of his poverty—and the pity she felt for him and his family—blinded her to other possibilities. By succumbing to a single story, she was diminished. The danger of a single story is that it is doubly diminishing. It paints a distorted and dismissive portrait of those being stereotyped and prevents those adhering to the story to engage fully with others, to see possibilities, and to be mutually enriched by this engagement and vision.

Embracing Dissonance

7

When Chimamanda Adichie came face-to-face with another aspect of the reality of Fide's life, she came face-to-face with dissonance. By embracing the incongruity created by the story of Fide's poverty and the richness of his life, she filled out the dimensions of Fide's life and story and was enriched at the same time. Fully articulated, deeply nuanced stories do that to us. They help us read between the lines, even if doing so is uncomfortable. Embracing dissonance requires one to seek the truth, to be open-minded, and to willingly admit to and publically trumpet other possibilities.

This chapter will consider the role dissonance plays in social justice work. It will also provide alternative readings of the stories of three marginalized groups: people challenged by poverty, Muslims, and North American native peoples. These alternative readings will provide examples of how myths are built upon inaccurate information, unchallenged assumptions, and lack of historical context. In addition, these alternative readings will provide several examples of dedicated dissonance makers and how they go about the business of challenging preconceived notions.

THE ROLE OF DISSONANCE IN SOCIAL JUSTICE WORK

In the world of social justice work, embracing dissonance is critical, uncomfortable, and challenging. In fact, activist-educator Paul Gorski (2009) indicates that in his social justice workshops he actively and purposely creates cognitive dissonance. Cognitive dissonance is that moment when new information clashes with established, comfortable, heretofore unchallenged current understandings. In the world of social justice work, dismantling long-held, unquestioned beliefs and assumptions constitutes the core of the work. Gorski calls these moments "critical crossroads of learning" (p. 54), ones he explicitly uses as a pedagogical tool, often providing learners with a cognitive-dissonance warning label: "What you are about to experience may ignite cognitive dissonance," he might say. Warning issued, he plunges in and takes his audience with him. These moments are messy but essential. Unless we engage cognitive dissonance, we will be condemned to the contours of a single story.

To a lesser or greater degree, we have internalized stories about groups of people that get in the way of our seeing them for who they really are. As allies, one of our first tasks, then, is to seek the truth about marginalized groups, to fill in the gaping holes that exist in the rendering of a single story. This is the jumping-off point for the eventual dismantling of the myths that "explain" marginalized groups' behavior. And the full story will likely create dissonance.

COUNTERNARRATIVES CHALLENGE PREVAILING NOTIONS

Unfortunately, the history of the human race provides a startlingly wide array of examples of groups of people demonizing others through the powerful weapon of stories built upon innuendo, half-truths, and blatant lies. These distorted stories have one aim in mind: to keep both the powerful and the less powerful in their different places. With every retelling, with every additional example of a group's "laziness" or "deviant behavior" or "intellectual deficiency" added to the narrative, with every story of failed efforts to "fix" the group's problems, these manufactured tales develop an aura of truth. Potential allies are not immune to having been taken in by many of these narratives of group failure. Even the most big-hearted, potential allies may have difficulty embracing the dissonance created when confronted for the first time with alternate readings of a group's character, accomplishments, and potential. Serious allies work through this. They embrace the dissonance and, once awakened to the idea that the long-told narrative about one group in a less dominant position may not be true, they learn to poke holes in the tightly woven web of lies applied to other marginalized groups.

Where can an ally in the battle for social justice go to locate information that challenges prevailing cultural understandings and fills in the truth gaps? Fortunately, there are abundant sources and numerous researchers that can help. This section seeks to introduce some of the many people who, in pursuit of dismantling myths associated with marginalized groups, have relentlessly created dissonance in the form of counternarratives.

It would be impossible to demonstrate ways to embrace dissonance using examples from every marginalized community. Instead, for purposes of illustrating how a counternarrative can be crafted from the fiber of facts, I have selected three groups who have well-regarded champions working on their behalf. The groups include people challenged by poverty, Muslims, and Native Americans.

This section will demonstrate how myths associated with these three groups play out in their group and individual consciousness. It will provide a historical context for how and why the myths have been fashioned. It will demonstrate the importance of creating a counternarrative using facts and figures, statistics rather than sentiments, and defensible research rather than innuendo. It will introduce some of the people who are actively engaged in promoting counternarratives.

Dismantling the Myths About People Challenged by Poverty

In addition to providing a historical context for the roots of many of the myths about people living in poverty, Paul Gorski (2008) provides alternative narratives to many of these myths. Among the myths he corrects are the myths about the motivation and work ethic of those living in poverty, their involvement in their children's learning, their level of language, and their use of drugs and alcohol compared to those who do not live in poverty. The facts create dissonance. Once the truth is revealed, such as the fact that 83 percent of children from low-income families have at least one parent employed, the myth about motivation and work ethic is shattered. Those of us who are involved with children living in poverty know only too well that many of the working poor hold multiple jobs, have unstable work schedules, and can be let go if they take time off to tend to the needs of their sick children or other family emergencies (Slaughter, 2015). Is it any wonder, then, that they are often not able to attend school events?

It is not only the dominant class that holds unfounded beliefs about marginalized groups of people. A survey conducted in 2001 by NPR, the Kaiser Foundation, and Harvard University reported that 50 percent of more affluent people believed that people challenged by poverty were not doing enough to help themselves. Not surprising in a nation married to the belief that all it takes to be financially secure is a strong will and a stronger work ethic, a trope that implies that more assets is a sign of moral superiority. It is in the best interest of the more affluent, then, to buy, unquestioned, the story that the less affluent are too lazy to pull themselves out of poverty. What is surprising is that 39 percent of people challenged by poverty believed the same thing. When victims begin believing the story that others have created to explain the victims' situation, there is a problem.

The belief that poverty is the result of personal failure or moral turpitude is deeply engrained in the American psyche, despite the fact that it is pure make-believe. Faced with these obvious inconsistencies, allies ask questions. Two of the most powerful questions for uncovering other possible explanations are "How did this single story emerge?" and "Who benefits from it?"

Americans' attitudes toward poverty have been shaped by the beliefs of those who first colonized North America. The shadows of double predestination and individualism cover the contemporary landscape, seeping into the beliefs and attitudes of those who have and those who do not have. These outdated ideas persist because there is great benefit to some in believing that the poor are poor because of their own failings. This belief makes it easier to construct policies that punish the poor and, in the process, push them deeper into poverty. The alternative is very distasteful to many. The alternative requires admitting some unsavory truths and accepting responsibility for changing the status quo.

The truth is that there are systemic and institutional structures that drive people into poverty and keep them there. One of the most obvious to me as I traveled the country providing professional learning experiences in schools located in areas challenged by poverty is the lack of resources in these communities. Time after time, the scene was the same. The schools I visited were once beacons of pride, imposing structures at the heart of vibrant communities, where homes and factories coexisted, where cities had nicknames like "The Garden City," where community centers and churches and stores and services flourished.

Now the schools are run-down and overlook dilapidated homes and boarded-up factories surrounded by barbed wire. No factories mean no work. Community centers and churches struggle to stay open and find the funds to repair leaking roofs, to replace antiquated heating systems, and to otherwise deal with the ravages of time and lack of resources. In the meantime, outsized, well-equipped, modern police stations are being built. Surveillance by hostile outsiders means more arrests and incarceration. In one community, I saw a large, handmade sign indicating that the store carried greeting cards for the incarcerated. The advertisement literally took my breath away. What public transportation and stores that do exist are limited. Buses run infrequently. Grocery stores are small, devoid of fresh fruit and vegetables, and expensive. In one city, the staff of a local community center conducted a services inventory, which pointed out that within their catchment area there were no food stores; no drug stores; no dentists, health clinics, or doctors within walking distance. There was, however, a veterinarian.

For many, it is easier to blame poor people for the demise of their communities instead of recognizing that there are precious few options for those living in poverty to find jobs and services within their own communities that those of us who live in other parts of town take for granted. In many communities, policies were put into place to ensure that high concentrations of people challenged by poverty would be forced to live in certain sectors of town. This was accomplished by limiting affordable housing to these areas. At the same time, opportunities to work locally were undermined by moving factories and other workplaces to locations inaccessible to those without cars. Policies need to change to reverse this situation.

Figure 7.1   Activity: Challenging the Dominant Narrative of People Living in Poverty

---

Reflection 1: What aspects of the counternarrative about the lives of people living in poverty were most surprising to you?

Reflection 2: Self-published author Ruby Payne has introduced countless educators to the highly problematic concept of a "culture of poverty." She has done this through her book, *A Framework for Understanding Poverty*, which sold more than 800,000 copies between 1998 and 2005, as well as through the many workshops and other businesses that have grown up around the claims made in her book. Many scholars have criticized her work on numerous fronts. For those touched by Payne's framework, this alternate reading could create dissonance, a dissonance that is incumbent upon allies to embrace and work through.

In this reflection, consider the conclusion drawn by a group of researchers and published in 2008. What aspects of this conclusion are dissonant with what you may have previously thought about Payne's work, her framework, her characterization of people challenged by poverty, or the impact of her work on children categorized as living in poverty?

"Our critical analysis of Payne's characterizations of people living in poverty indicates that her work represents a classic example of what has been identified as deficit thinking. We found that her truth claims, offered without any supporting evidence, are contradicted by anthropological, sociological and other research on poverty. We have demonstrated through our analysis that teachers may be misinformed by Payne's claims. As a consequence of low teacher expectations, poor students are more likely to be in lower tracks or lower ability groups and their educational experience is more often dominated by rote drill and practice" (Bomer, Dworin, May, & Semingson, 2008).

Extension Activity

Read the entire report from which the above conclusion was drawn, which can be retrieved from http://www.tcrecord.org/Content.asp?ContentId=14591. What additional dissonances arise?

The Single Story About Muslims Debunked

It is not only our perception of people challenged by poverty that is fueled by inaccurate information, unchallenged assumptions, and lack of historical context. Another group victimized and misrepresented by the bulldozer of a single story is Muslims.

In September 2015, social media went into high outrage when a fourteen-year-old Muslim student, Ahmed Mohamed, was arrested at his Texas high school for bringing a homemade clock to school. This incident raises a number of issues relating to the prevailing narrative about Muslims circulating in North America, some of which will be discussed in this section.

As educators, we are particularly moved by injustices inflicted upon children. More and more, innocent Muslim children, like Ahmed, who could easily be students in our schools, are the victims of the virulent and relentless Islamophobia that has had a stranglehold on Western attitudes toward Muslims, particularly since 9/11. Why else would an intelligent, well-spoken fourteen-year-old fond of tinkering with electronics be suspected of making a bomb, subsequently arrested, and suspended from school? There is no school code of conduct that I know of which prohibits an eager, insatiably curious, and ingenious student who wants to show off his latest invention to one of his teachers from doing so. Of course, when the invention is a homemade clock and the student's name is Ahmed Mohamed, other *codes* take over. Ahmed's goal is to go to MIT. Instead, during the first days of his first year of high school, he went to the police station in handcuffs.

Within days of fourteen-year-old Ahmed Mohamed's arrest for bringing to school a clock he invented, then Republican presidential candidate Ben Carson shattered the dreams of thousands of Muslim Americans who aspire to a life in politics. His aspiration-dampening comment, "I would not advocate we put a Muslim in charge of this nation," hurts the many Muslim students who, like seventeen-year-old Aya Beydoun, really DO want to become president of the United States. Aya is politically active and works hard to maintain the straight-A average needed to get into a competitive university (Laughland & Ackerman, 2015).

Teenagers work hard at developing their identities. Adults who care about students deliberately nurture positive behaviors among teenagers, mine for their strengths, and work to develop potential. Certainly as educators this is what we strive to do, which is why we find attitudes like Ben Carson's to be more than hurtful, limiting, and counterproductive. Giving voice to sentiments such as these is an act of psychological violence.

Both of these incidents are instructive on many levels. They reveal the deeply ingrained, unsavory side of prejudice and the depths to which people can sink as subscribers of a single story. They are deeply unsettling. Because they are upsetting, they might have the potential to get us to stop and raise questions. These questions can propel us into the joy of coming to a more nuanced understanding of what it means to be Muslim, which, in turn, will enhance us.

To fill in the contours of the story of Muslims in the West, one could begin by finding out more information about their history. The Southern Poverty Law Center's Teaching Tolerance website has an excellent publication titled "What Is the Truth About American Muslims? Questions and Answers" (http://www.tolerance.org/publication/law-religious-freedom). The publication provides easily understood, well-researched summaries of such topics as the law of religious freedom and sharia law. One section directly addresses the topic of American Muslims in the United States. Organized in question-answer format, it reveals many interesting facts about Muslims, including the fact that far from being newcomers, the first Muslims arrived in the Americas 400 years ago. It sets straight questions uninformed people may have about Muslims, questions that help fill in the contours of what it means to be a Muslim in a non-Muslim part of the world. For instance, what is the role of mosques in Muslim American life? Do American Muslim leaders support freedom of expression and religious liberty? The answers to the numerous questions that appear on the website could easily be converted into an anticipation guide before having students verify their answers.

The Teaching Tolerance website also includes lesson plans and other resources, including one lesson for middle-school students on stereotyping called "Debunking Stereotypes About Muslims and Islam" (http://www.tolerance.org/lesson/debunking-stereotypes-about-muslims-and-islam).

Figure 7.2   Activity: Counteracting the Dominant Narrative About American Muslims

---

Reflection: Consult the section of the Teaching Tolerance website called "What Is the Truth About American Muslims?" (http://www.tolerance.org/publication/law-religious-freedom). What information about American Muslims did you find to be the most surprising?

Out of Sight, Out of Mind, Out of the Way: The Twisted Tale of the Inconvenient "Indian"

Countering what the media says about people challenged by poverty and Muslims with facts creates healthy dissonance that allies embrace and promulgate in order to shine a light on the narrowness of a single story. The same is true regarding the received narrative about North American natives.

The United States and Canada share a troubling history and troubled ongoing relationships with North American natives, histories that dominant Americans and Canadians would just as soon forget. However, as allies in the service of social justice, we are obliged to mine the depths of these histories to uncover the stories conveniently minimized, twisted, or suppressed.

Normally complacent Canadians received a jolt in January 2015 when *Maclean's,* the Canadian equivalent of *Time,* appeared on the newsstands. A feature article proclaimed, "Canada's race problem? It's even worse than America's" (Gilmore, 2015). The article was accompanied by a table that compared the Canadian Aboriginal population to the African American population in terms of quality of life indicators such as infant mortality, education, and life expectancy. The conclusion: "By every measurable indicator, Canada's Aboriginal population suffers a worse fate and more hardship than the African-American population in the United States." To be sure, the writer was quick to point out that there are many, Aboriginal and non-Aboriginal alike to be blamed for this sad state of affairs. The justice system, police forces, band councils, federal officials, the school system are all cited, as well as other institutions and groups. The author makes it clear, however, that his purpose is not to shame and blame but to encourage change, and that the first step in combating the problem is for Canadians to admit publically and loudly that a problem exists.

Similarly, American Canadian novelist Thomas King is on a quest for uncovering truth about the relationship between North America's native and nonnative populations. His 2012 book *The Inconvenient Indian: A Curious Account of Native People in North America* uncovers much. King, who is part Cherokee, unashamedly posits that from the beginning of White settlement in North America, settlers found the original inhabitants of the continent to be "inconvenient." Hence, the long list of treaties, removals, massacres, and schemes, such as residential schools, designed to make way for the White way. The case he makes is impressive and expansive. It is full of facts, its scope is broad, and its alternate way of understanding the plight of native peoples is eye opening (King, 2012). It is not a pretty story, but it is one that needed to be told and it bears repeating. If we are honest, nonnatives have long desired that native populations remain out of sight, out of mind, and out of their way.

Figure 7.3   Activity: Reflecting Upon Myths

In the following, I reflect upon an experience I had with a school that uncritically believed the myth that families challenged by poverty do not value education.

Directions:

Read the reflection that follows, looking for what the faculty originally believed, what they came to understand, and how that new understanding altered the way the school did business with the community.

My reflection: Every time I think about the ways in which our uncritical acceptance of myths drives our behavior, I think about a school where I directed a project for several years. The principal and faculty were well meaning, extremely dedicated educators who strove to do what was right for their students, most of whom were struggling. When asked why they thought their students were not doing so well despite their best efforts, they blamed students' poor performance on lack of parent participation in school.

The context: The profile of the school includes the following. The school is a neighborhood school, located in what is obviously a diverse suburban setting. The majority of parents work as domestics or kitchen staff in the private homes of other residents of the town or in the many hotels and restaurants that attract visitors to the area. The school serves 411 students, K–4, most of whom identify as Hispanic (43 percent). Another 22 percent of the population is African American. More than three-fourths of the students qualify for free or reduced lunch.

In an effort to provide a high-quality learning facility for the children, the district recently built a new school. The faculty is justly proud of the building. Among its features are high ceilings, wide hallways, airy classrooms with window walls, stonework, a cafeteria with a large stage and built-in sound system, smart boards in all classrooms, and a hiking trail that wends its way through the surrounding woods. What I noticed the first day I arrived is that there is not a house visible anywhere near the school nor is the school visible from the road. It sits atop a hill that can only be accessed by a long, winding road.

The analysis: To the minds of the faculty and administration, the school is a lovely, inviting building, and it is. But it is completely inaccessible to families who do not have cars. Rather than acknowledge the truth of the life circumstances of their families, rather than address the symbolic and literal distance between the school-on-the hill and the community it serves, the faculty and administration chose to bemoan the ingratitude of their students' families. They uncritically accepted the trope that families living in poverty do not value education without considering other scenarios.

Rethinking the situation: Once they came to grips with the fact that most families do not have cars, their work schedules are variable, and their hold on employment is tenuous, they chose to hold school events in the part of town where the majority of the families live. They also began conversations with the community to find out other ways that they could be more accessible.

Extension Activity

- Reflect upon an experience you may have had or a story you know in which a myth about a marginalized group of people was uncritically accepted. Give the context. What myth was being perpetuated? Analyze the situation. How was the situation resolved? Share your story in writing or orally.

WHOSE LIVES MATTER? PERCEPTIONS AND TRUTH

In September 2016, after two more incidents of Black men being killed by police officers, a Google search of Black Lives Matter resulted in over 81 million hits in forty-one seconds. Clearly, Black Lives Matter is a monumental movement, a movement that taps into visceral emotions, a movement that highlights profound fault lines in the ways in which different members of the same society view issues of policing, protest, and race.

Allies in the battle for social justice cannot ignore this movement. They absolutely need to engage. The question is how?

The answer is pretty straightforward. Allies need to separate twisted portrayals from truth, media manipulation from reality, frenzied fantasies from facts.

The best ways to do this is to go to the source. Consult the Black Lives Matter website. Find out who they are, what they stand for, and why they feel compelled to create and sustain this movement. Compare what *they* say to what is said *about* them. Consider the source of the portrayals. Ask yourself who stands to win, who stands to lose. Consider whose voice is heard and amplified, and whose voice is diminished and silenced when otherwise well-meaning people want the focus to be on all lives matter, rather than Black lives matter.

Be prepared for a certain amount of dissonance. Be prepared for some shocks. Be prepared to know how to set the record straight. Be prepared to take action.

At a minimum, be prepared to know how to address your Black students and colleagues the next time the news roils with the all-too-familiar horror of another senseless loss of a Black life. It is wrong to have these moments pass unacknowledged. A White educator recently admitted that she was surprised to find a post on a Black colleague's social media page in which the Black colleague said how hurt she felt that none of her White colleagues acknowledged the two September 2016 shootings. The White colleague felt terrible. She admitted, "I was just not sure what to say." Saying nothing diminishes the real pain the Black community feels in these horrific moments. Saying nothing reinforces that certain lives matter more than others. Worse still, saying nothing changes nothing.

TRUTH AND MYTH

On June 11, 1962, in his address to the graduates of Yale University, President John F. Kennedy put truth and myth into perspective when he said,

The great enemy of truth is very often not the lie—deliberate, contrived and dishonest—but the myth—persistent, persuasive and unrealistic. Too often we hold fast to the clichés of our forebears. We subject all facts to a prefabricated set of interpretations. We enjoy the comfort of opinion without the discomfort of thought.

One of our first tasks as allies in the battle for social justice, then, is to seek out the truth through relentless pursuit of the facts, to embrace the dissonance created by these facts, to expect and to learn from the discomfort experienced by thinking through these facts, and then to stand up and counter others when they insist on perpetuating myths.

KEY CONSIDERATIONS FOR ALLIES

- Initial contact with information that goes against the grain of prevailing beliefs often causes dissonance.
- Dissonance, although messy, can be healthy. It can lead to the dismantling of harmful myths.
- Prevailing myths about marginalized groups have deep and self-serving historical and cultural tentacles.
- Allies in the battle for social justice have several tasks to accomplish when it comes to challenging the single stories associated with marginalized groups. They need to
  - seek out the truth about marginalized groups through relentless pursuit of facts,
  - embrace the dissonance created by these facts,
  - learn from the discomfort experienced by thinking through these facts, and
  - stand up and counter others when they insist on perpetuating myths.
- **Looking Ahead**: In addition to embracing the dissonance that results when truth challenges myths, another task that potential allies have is to consider deeply the insidious and pervasive tactics of deception that those in power often use to retain power and sustain myths.

Tactics of Deception and Flawed Theories

So how do the bankrupt, single-sided stories come to be and persist? This chapter will explore the many ways in which those who benefit from these stories continually breathe new life into bankrupt lies, which translate into bankrupt policies that most often end up hurting our most vulnerable students.

Just as allies benefit from embracing the dissonance caused by discovering that many of the narratives about marginalized people are fabrications, allies also benefit from embracing the dissonance that results as allies grow in awareness regarding what fuels some educational policies.

Among the bankrupt lies and flawed theories that drive educational policy are two of particular note. The first is that educational outcomes will be better if schools adopt principles borrowed from the business world, including an emphasis on competition. The second is that the purpose of an education is to learn facts and that the most efficient ways of doing so are ranking students by performance level, publishing these results, and publicly shaming schools and students who do not meet standards.

This chapter will begin with a brief discussion regarding why bankrupt lies and flawed theories survive. This will be followed by stories of the ways in which the business model has taken over educational spaces. The chapter will end with stories that demonstrate some of the flawed theories about human nature and learning that have infiltrated and dramatically altered the learning-teaching environment.

WHY BANKRUPT LIES AND POLICIES
SURVIVE—AND THRIVE

The discussion around satisfaction with public schools is a curious one. Time and again, surveys indicate that most families are more than pleased with their local public schools at the same time headlines scream about the overall failure of the public education system.

To be fair, there are schools that are unsafe, low performing, far from satisfactory. But there is a counternarrative to this prevailing story. These schools, some have asserted, are doing exactly what they were designed to do. They fail because the conditions have been designed and aligned to make it impossible for them to do anything *but* fail (Duncan-Andrade & Morrell, 2008). Ensuring that some schools are located in communities with concentrated poverty, high crime rates, and lack of access to quality health care or fresh, affordable food and then withholding resources and services that might have a slight chance of mitigating some of these factors that are out of the control of the school is nothing more than a purposely designed and implemented scheme to condemn certain schools and students to failure.

Why is it important for the American public to believe that their public schools are failing? Follow the money. According to the National Center for Education Statistics, local, state, and federal funding of public elementary and secondary schools amounted to $621 billion in 2011–2012. By having the public believe that public education is failing, the door is left open for private, for-profit enterprises to cash in, and that is exactly what they have been doing. For-profit enterprises are using tax-raised revenues to plump up their bottom lines to address what Berliner and Biddle call a "manufactured crisis" (Berliner & Biddle, 1995).

Those poised to gain mightily by this manufactured crisis employ methods that are calculated and calculating. They hone in on and trumpet the very values that resonate with people (Apple, 2006). For example, who among us would be opposed to *school choice?* Choice, after all, is one of the values of our democratic way of life. What self-respecting citizen would want to deny other citizens the right to *choose* a good school for their children? Of course, the harsh reality is that with few exceptions, choosing to dismantle public schools in favor of privately-owned schools offers little by way of real choice in the communities most challenged by debilitating social conditions—lack of jobs and lack of opportunity among them—for the simple reason that those in power have not made the choice to address these larger social conditions in purposeful and effective ways. Choice may work, but the choices need to be viable ones.

Cultivating Fact Resistance

One of the tactics those who stand to gain by diverting public funds to private business cultivate is to be resistant to facts. It benefits them to promulgate the narrative that the public education system, once considered the great equalizer and the seedbed for American creativity and inventiveness, is in a state of free fall. Their fact resistant message is that public education in America is ill conceived, ill managed, and ill prepared to address the nation's educational needs.

The litany of myths and lies that they use to support their version of the state of public education covers a wide swath of territory. Here are a handful.

- Myths and lies abound about which countries and which types of schools are the "best." (*It turns out that American school children perform as well as or even better than their counterparts in other countries when results are disaggregated by economic status. In fact, children in schools where family poverty rates were less than 50 percent outperformed Finnish children in math and science in both the Grade 4 and 8 as measured by the 2011 international math and science assessment, TIMSS.*)

- Myths and lies abound about how much influence teachers really have in the learning-teaching relationship, about which pay schemes produce the best results, about the quality of those teachers who serve students challenged by poverty, and about union responsibility for low performance of students. (*Teachers do have influence on student outcomes, but this is often outweighed by social factors, such as poverty, that are out of the control of teachers. Pay schemes based upon merit and competition do not work. Although it is true that many teachers in urban schools are poorly prepared to teach due in some part to alternative certification programs, many argue that those who choose to stay in urban assignments are there because they feel they have a "duty" to serve urban students and that they indeed may be more committed and talented than their suburban counterparts. A familiar cry is that unions impede student progress, when the opposite is true. It turns out that low student performance is most closely associated with those states that do not have binding contracts for teachers.*)

- Myths and lies abound about how to make our schools better. (*Retention and tracking do not work, and, yes, class size does matter. Here is a summary of the class size issue: Smaller class sizes result in higher performance; larger class sizes result in lower costs.*)

- Myths and lies abound about school funding, including the extent to which tuition tax credits and education savings accounts benefit children living in poverty. *They do not* (Berliner & Glass, 2014).

The list goes on in an uninterrupted, unchallenged, relentless invocation of myths, hoaxes, and outright lies. These twisted versions of reality are pervasive, and because of the wide play they get from the media and politicians, they begin to have a ring of truth and authority about them. It is no wonder that some allies, who have not been primed to challenge these narratives, often find themselves in the awkward position of being shocked by alternate versions of what they have been led to believe. Educators who embrace this dissonance, who are willing to challenge prevailing notions, cross an important threshold on the journey to becoming an ally.

THE BUSINESS MODEL IS GOOD FOR EDUCATION: AN ALTERNATE VIEW

One of the most powerful and pervasive myths that has been promulgated is that the business model is good for education. A closer look at how this has played out in schools will likely challenge this belief.

There are many insidious ways in which the more harmful aspects of the business model have been applied to schools. The results have not been pretty. I begin this section with an anecdote that does two things. It tells of my discomfort attending an educational conference in which the normal lexicon of educational terms was hijacked by the language of business. The anecdote also reveals the way in which I may have unconsciously borrowed concepts from the business model and used them to craft my presentation. This section ends with a cautionary note about the business model and education. No Child Left Behind (NCLB) imposed the business model on education in a very big way. Since the Every Student Succeeds Act has recently replaced NCLB, many people could be lulled into thinking that the business approach promulgated by NCLB will evaporate. I would like to argue otherwise.

The World of Business Has No Business in Schools

After I retired and left Long Island, I was invited to give a workshop on how fearless leadership—that is to say, leadership that springs from reconceptualizing leaders as architects, soul friends, muses, and ministers—can transform high- and varying-needs schools into oases of success

(Jackson & McDermott, 2012). I took away several vivid memories and critical insights from that event.

The session took place in what was once familiar territory to me, a place where I, too, attended many workshops and conferences. The format was equally familiar. State education representatives were on hand to give an update on state initiatives and to answer beginning-of-the-year questions about these initiatives. This is where the similarities to my preretirement days ended.

Since the educational community on Long Island is relatively small and I had served as an educator there for many years, I expected to see lots of familiar faces among the 400 or so attendees, mostly administrators and teacher-leaders. Instead, I saw precious few people I knew. Those who could leave their positions had done so. They left the system to escape what was becoming an increasingly harsh educational environment of regulations, impossible-to-achieve goals, and increasingly punitive repercussions. No surprise, then, that the vast majority of participants were brand new to their positions. They were young, and they were scared.

In the old days, state education officials used to dread addressing an audience of Long Island administrators and teachers. We had a reputation for being cynical, confrontational, and challenging. Not so with this new crop of administrators. The desire to keep their jobs in a time of heightened accountability was stronger than any outrage they felt, an impulse I completely understood, but one that, nonetheless, troubled me.

The topic the state representatives were there to elucidate was NCLB and testing requirements. It was October and the state had yet to provide schools with much guidance and certainly no examples of what the newest crop of high-stakes testing would look like. For two hours, one official after another addressed this group of educators, explaining in rich detail the process of finding, contracting with, and working with vendors who would be designing the new tests to be administered in the spring. If I were to do a word cloud on the most frequently used words during the session, they would be *vendor, testing,* and *accountability. Student, learning,* and *teaching* were rarely, if ever, mentioned.

I was horrified. The lexicon of education had clearly been co-opted by the business model. The presenters, all of whom were young, articulate, and snatched from the *best* universities and most prestigious businesses (accounting and law being the top two) to *fix* the New York State educational system, had never taught a day their lives. Now I look back and realize that they represented what Michael Apple refers to as the new professional and managerial middle class, who forge new identities as society's auditors and insurers of accountability (Apple, 2006).

How I Was Hijacked

I also look back with chagrin on the focus of my presentation. The workshop was intended to provide a shot in the arm to those schools and school districts euphemistically called *high needs*, a label concocted by the state to classify schools by demographics. The title, I am embarrassed to say, was *School as an Oases of Success*. By advocating for schools to become oases of *success*, I became complicit in promoting, on some level, the values of the business model.

The business model is designed to put schools in competition with each other in order to delineate between *successful* schools and *failing* schools. The competition is put into place without a nuanced discussion about what success could or should look like outside the confines of the narrow band of testing instruments and schemes promulgated by for-profit enterprises and misguided policy makers. Nor does this emphasis on competition consider the systemic and societal issues that might lead to one school's success and another's failure. If I could rewrite the title and redo the presentation, I would.

Competition and the Soul

Promoting competition, the heart of the business model, is a bankrupt construct when it comes to learning and teaching. Competition creates three things:

- winners, of which there are few;
- losers, of which there are many; and
- cheaters, of which there are too many.

Competition for more and more profits enabled businesses to engage in ruinous methods that nearly drove the economy into collapse in 2008. Is that the model we want to promulgate in our schools?

The toxic mix of competition, public shaming, and impossible-to-achieve goals resulted in educational scandals, too. Most of us are familiar with the unfortunate educators who succumbed to cheating in order to avoid having their class or school or district labeled a failure. When people are put in difficult situations and when their livelihood depends upon performance that they cannot control, some people do desperate things. Many of these educators are serving time as a result of the decisions they made, decisions I do not in any way condone. What I also do not condone is allowing policy makers to implement wrong-headed and harmful practices that drive people to consider, and sometimes choose, illegal and immoral actions.

Why is success so important? Why does education have to be a *race to the top?* Does no one remember Lance Armstrong and doping scandals? Fear of failure drives people to do unethical, harmful things.

Success at all costs in highly competitive environments is a noxious combination that generates fear. Fear kills the spirit. How different the dialogue would be if educators were free to abandon the competition/success/failure trope and strove, instead, to focus on cultivating, thriving, and flourishing. How would students be treated? How would students feel? In particular, how would marginalized students be treated and feel? How would teachers be treated and feel? How would the learning-teaching dynamic change? I venture to guess the changes would be palpable, certainly more humane, and infinitely more achievable than NCLB or its much-touted 2015 replacement, Every Student Succeeds Act (ESSA).

The Underbelly of ESSA

If you were not a supporter of NCLB, do not jump up and down in joy over the passage of its replacement. At least two things are wrong with its replacement, Every Student Succeeds Act (ESSA). First, ESSA is still a law based upon a business perspective and controlling mantra: competition, success, and failure. Second, although it diminishes the role of the federal government in education (a good thing) and scales back federally mandated testing (another good thing), educators need to be cautious. State governments and state education departments are now fully peopled with supporters of the competition/success/failure approach that fueled NCLB with all of its emphasis on accountability and sanctions.

Allies need to be vigilant. While we were not watching, NCLB was signed into law. While we were not watching, the conversation about education was co-opted by powerful forces that stood to gain by becoming major players in educational policy decisions. Since the beginning of

Figure 8.1   Success Versus Thriving

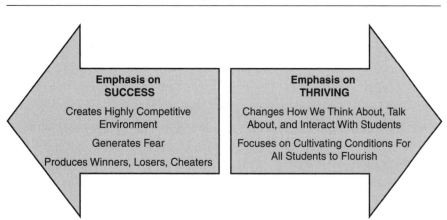

NCLB, they have become deeply entrenched in state government and state departments of education. They are well funded. They lobby. They influence policy. They pay for and obtain research that supports their off-base, counterproductive practices. Most importantly, they have gained a major portion of U.S. taxpayer funds for education. They are not likely to walk away from this lucrative market, and with ESSA, they have no reason to walk away.

ESSA: Read the Small Print

There is one other troubling aspect of the new ESSA that cries out to be addressed by allies. Deep in the recesses of the 391-page legislation is a section that appears, on the surface, to address issues that would benefit students. Section IV, titled "21st Century Schools," includes provisions for "student support and academic enrichment grants." Dig a little deeper, though, and you discover that this portion of the legislation is about providing huge grants for schools to bolster the use of technology in education (EdTech).

Again, on the surface, providing more opportunities to train teachers in new technologies or investing in technology innovations or filling the gaps in technology accessibility for students all sound like good ideas. But dig deeper still and the loaded language becomes evident. What could technology-based, *personalized* learning really mean? Fewer teachers? Questionable pedagogy centered around discrete bits of knowledge neatly organized into learning modules that can be quickly and impersonally assessed? Dependence upon coolly calculated algorithms to determine next steps for learners instead of teachers who have developed personal relationships and bonds with their students? I suppose EdTech could mean other things, but I doubt it. The only articles I could find that extol the virtues of this emphasis on EdTech and praise the funding stream supporting it came from companies in the business of providing technology to schools. Nowhere in these slickly produced, self-serving articles did I see mention of the well-documented, staggeringly high number of students who drop out of cyberschools, their abysmal graduation rates, and their heartbreakingly low achievement rates (Berliner & Glass, 2014).

Who stands to gain? Who stands to lose? It is pretty clear to me that the campaign for *personalized* education is a not-so-thinly veiled attempt to reduce the teaching force, union bust, cut costs, and line the pockets of private companies that are in the business of producing all manner of tech-based educational and assessment packages, whether they are good for students or not.

HOW BAD ANTHROPOLOGY PRODUCES BAD POLICY

The policy decisions that brought NCLB, ESSA, and a host of other educational *reform* measures into American schools are based upon flawed and insupportable theories about the human condition and how learning actually occurs. Allies in the battle for social justice need to regularly and robustly practice the discipline of questioning the anthropology—the understanding of human nature—that drives policy decisions. Over the years, I have done exactly that. I would like to share three theories that, in the end, are different manifestations of the same flawed thinking about how children learn. The first one is drawn from fiction but resonates loud and clear with today's educational climate. Sadly, the other two are drawn from contemporary and influential actors in the educational reform movement.

Flawed Theory 1: The Only Side of the Human Condition That Needs to Be Developed Is the Rational Side

Two characters stand out in Charles Dickens's novel *Hard Times*. One is a teacher, Mr. Gradgrind. The second is a government officer, a school inspector of some kind, called Mr. M'Choakumchild. Yes, say these names out loud. Dickens is purposely using their names to provide insight into their character and their educational philosophy. He does not leave it there, though.

Mr. Gradgrind, we are told, is "a man of realities . . . a man of facts and calculations . . . with a rule and a pair of scales . . . ready to measure any parcel of human nature, and to tell you exactly what it comes to." This description reminds me of the measuring and testing madness that has been part of learning and teaching since 2001 when NCLB was signed into law. Mr. Gradgrind refers to his students by number and demands students regurgitate facts rather than generate questions. "Girl number twenty," he famously ordered, "give me your definition of a horse."

Neither "girl number twenty" nor readers are told why it is necessary to know—on demand—the definition of a horse, in much the same way today's educators are sometimes held responsible for demanding questionable or meaningless information from students. By having the teacher call on a student with the cold and distancing appellation, "girl number twenty," Dickens is continuing to comment on the heartless educational practices of his era and, surprisingly, of ours, too. At the time Dickens was writing, he never could have envisioned the pre-slugged, automated response sheets children would consume by the thousands in yearly testing schemes that transformed their personal names to lifeless identification numbers. Or, maybe he did have a crystal ball. He certainly nailed the impulse, though. For some in the educational community, children are nothing more than numbers with coded names, racial, language, sexual, and economic identities. I prefer to think of each one as an individual with important histories and boundless potential.

Not surprisingly, Mr. M'Choakumchild, the visiting government official, shares Mr. Gradgrind's focus on facts and measurement. As a government official, he may well have been one of the architects of the policy governing what the curriculum should look like. When girl number twenty is unable to define a horse, he is upset. Girl number twenty is creative and inventive. She is not interested in defining a horse. She is curious about what would happen if she papered the entire room with pictures of horses, for no other reason than she "fancies" horses.

"You are not to do anything of the kind," declares Mr. M'Choakumchild. "Fact, fact, fact," he continues. "You are to be in all things regulated and governed by fact. We hope to have, before long, a board of fact, composed of commissioners of fact, who will force the people to be a people of fact, and of nothing but fact. You must discard the word *fancy* altogether."

For many students, school today is as dismal as it was in Dickens's fictional classroom. Relentless attention on passing tests has stifled the more fanciful aspects of learning and teaching and has choked out any chance of flights of imagination, the stuff of which children are made.

Dickens's fictional school may have been "regulated and governed by facts," while today's schools—especially underperforming ones largely populated by marginalized students—are regulated and governed by tests and measurement schemes, including number-based teacher evaluation systems that take hundreds of pages to explain, enormous amounts of time to implement, and end up saying very little about what good learning and teaching looks like. Ask anyone to describe a teacher who has influenced his or her life and that description will look nothing like the lifeless state and district mandated descriptors. Instead, the description will likely focus on connections and relationships: how the teacher connected with and related to the student on a personal level, how the teacher connected and related classroom learning to life's big issues, how the teacher connected and related apparently unconnected ideas into a cohesive theory. Influential teachers know that connections and relations are the heart of teaching. Influential teachers know what James Comer succinctly stated: "No significant learning occurs without a significant relationship." Put another way, influential teachers tune in carefully to the question many marginalized students ask: "How can you teach me if you don't know me?" George Yancy (2012) asks that question with regard to White teachers addressing racism. By *knowing*, George Yancy means several things, including teachers being willing to hear—really hear—authentic voices of their students relating uncomfortable stories about racism, to avoid filtering these stores through their lens of privilege, and to risk looking inwardly in order to know themselves.

Influential teachers know that without the connection-relationship dynamic we lose students. In Dickens's anecdote, "girl number twenty" acquiesced to the soul-diminishing and intellectual suffocation imposed upon her with a curtsy and a polite, "Yes, sir." In today's schools, some cave in, choosing compliance over challenge or complaisance over disobedience. Others flee. So do many of their teachers.

We need to rethink the high drop-out rates and high teacher attrition rates that plague many of our schools and communities to understand that those who leave are no longer able to exist and grow where they belong. In other words, they are exiled, forced to leave. Students and teachers belong in schools where students reap the joy of self-discovery, uncover the mysteries of the universe, and engage in the pursuit of intellectual promise, while teachers experience the excitement, stimulation, and satisfaction that comes from learning and teaching in a supportive, expansive, and emotionally healthy environment (Jackson & McDermott, 2012).

Flawed Theory 2: Praise and Trophies Are Harmful to Children's Development

School policies based upon questionable theories and practices did not die during the Dickensian era. They are alive and well and being promulgated in the 21st century.

Several years ago, I heard a commentary on NPR's Marketplace in which a well-known educator posited that America is losing its competitive edge economically and that part of the blame falls on educators who are "obsessed with making kids feel good about themselves." By way of example, she cites the conflict she faces when she feels compelled to tell her daughters that, despite the many soccer trophies they possess, "their soccer skills are lacking." Indeed, she goes one step further, exhorting the United States to borrow from her country where students are ranked one through forty in their class and "everyone knows where they stand."

There are many troubling aspects of this opinion, not the least of which is that it could only have been made by a person whose values are deeply rooted in a suburban, White-flight mentality, complete with its references to soccer and competition. One could forgive the author, except for the fact that she is not an ordinary soccer mom who need not worry about "other people's children" (Delpit, 1995). Instead, she is a woman previously charged with leading one of the most challenged school districts in the nation, the Washington, DC, schools. The commentator, educator, and mother was none other than Michelle Rhee.

Clearly, Michelle Rhee and others like her are intent upon maintaining a system in which competition reigns, where there are a handful of winners—a thin layer of people at the top—and everyone else on the bottom. Michelle Rhee should know better than to impose her set of cultural norms on other groups of people.

Flawed Theory 3: Public Shaming Is Motivating

Eva Moskowitz is CEO of Success Academy Charter Schools, a publically funded, privately operated chain of charter schools in New York City. Her 2011–2012 salary was reportedly $475,299, more than that of the then New York City School Chancellor. In April 2015, the number of charter schools she had established in New York City was about to exceed the total number of schools in Buffalo, NY, the second-largest city in New York State.

Ms. Moskowitz has been a polarizing figure in New York City. Her schools, which serve predominantly Black and Hispanic children challenged by poverty, have been called successful by some and relentless test-prep machines by others. Teacher turnover matches the high stress level that comes from an uncompromising focus on results, military school style behavior regiments that must be adhered to precisely, constant monitoring, competition for ever better results, and eleven-hour days.

For many teachers who leave, the worst part is the treatment of students. Public shaming is part of the regiment. Student scores on practice tests are published for the entire class to see. Those who do not make the grade are sent to the "effort academy," described as part study hall, part detention. Children well beyond the age of wetting themselves have been reported to do so with some frequency during practice tests, a result of the pressure to do well. One teacher reported that a school leader sent out an internal memo in which teachers were exhorted to make those students who did not do well feel "misery." One teacher reported crying every night because of the way she was told to treat her students (Taylor, 2015).

An incident involving a Success Academy first grader having her test paper torn up in front of her while being berated by her teacher for poor test performance was caught on video, was widely circulated in 2016, and resulted in the girl's mother removing her child from the school. Eva Moskowitz claimed the incident was a one off, an anomaly. Others suggested otherwise. Shocking, unacceptable, malpractice, and abuse are some of the sentiments expressed by others throughout the world. Seeing a White teacher belittle a Black child is reminiscent of the treatment Black enslaved people received at the hands of their White masters after a long, hard day in the fields. If they returned with less than the amount of cotton expected, they received forty lashes (Baptist, 2014).

When I read about the modern-day versions of Mr. Gradgrind and Mr. M'Choakumchild, I cannot help but wonder how they see children, how they understand the purpose of education, and how they could be so oblivious to what we know about how the brain functions. Fear and stress are roadblocks to learning. There will always be those students who excel in a harsh, competitive, single-focus learning environment. Because some do, however, it does not mean that the anthropology and the policies and pedagogical approaches that emanate from it are sound, worthwhile, or acceptable.

What motivates people is not strict controls on what they are allowed to do, ranking them and shaming them. Instead, what motivates people is the desire to be self-directed, the desire to get better, and the desire to do something meaningful. Punishments and rewards work on those activities that require little thinking, little creativity, and have a single answer (Pink, 2011). In addition to destroying the potential for learning, punishment and rewards are ways of manipulating behavior (Kohn, 1993). Manipulation is a power move. It is a form of control rather than a formula for the development of self-control.

Beliefs About Human Nature Drive Policy and Affect Outcomes

Schools and classrooms operate within a complex web of policies and practices that often have unintended, unexamined, or untenable consequences. They impact all students, but especially those who are the most vulnerable.

These polices are expansive. They cover everything from discipline to diploma granting, from sharpening pencils to using the bathroom, from the content of the curriculum to the food served in the cafeteria.

Every policy and practice derives from an anthropological bias that either understands the multifaceted nature of human beings or does not. Policies springing from an understanding that human beings are complex, nuanced beings provide wiggle room, take into account the ways in which children develop, and reflect the conditions that we know support motivation, engagement, and the way the brain processes information.

Beliefs, practice, structures, and outcomes are intricately intertwined. They feed into and out of each other. It is often possible to start anywhere on the cycle above and backfill the other elements. For example, it is possible to look at an outcome and backfill the beliefs, practices, and structures that made the outcome likely. (See Figure 8.2 on page 130.)

Figure 8.2   Beliefs, Practices, Structures, and Outcomes

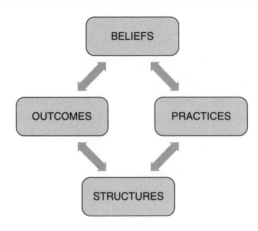

Figure 8.3   Activity: Interrogating Beliefs About Human Nature and Policy
Decisions

Directions:

Choose one of the policies and practices listed below, all of which are based upon actual events. Think through the anthropology—the understanding of the human condition—that is likely driving the policy or practice. Does it spring from an understanding of the complex nature of the human condition or does it derive from a single, possibly flawed understanding of how to effectively motivate, deeply engage, and positively affect learning?

Using the continuum reproduced below, indicate where you feel the policy or practice is located along the continuum. Is it leaning more toward a nuanced understanding of the human condition or a less nuanced understanding?

- Why did you choose to locate the policy or practice where you did?
- What effect do you think the policy or practice has on helping students to thrive?

Less Nuanced   More Nuanced

Policies and Practices

- Zero Tolerance Policy, which results in suspending a kindergartner for saying on the playground, "I'm going to shoot you."
- Publically displaying students' grades.
- Handing out math tests and saying to students who did not pass, "I guess you will be working at McDonald's."
- Having a group of students identified as special needs stand in front of the class and say, "I am stupid. I am stupid. I am stupid."
- Using external rewards for behavior and good grades.

- During Black history month assigning several students to research Denzel Washington because the teacher "could not find Black people who were not violent."
- Posting the following poster in a kindergarten classroom:

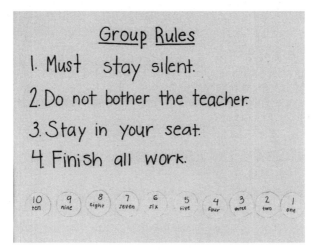

- Sending the following note home to the families of preschool children:

11-14-13

URGENT NOTICE!!!

Please Read

Several children in Pre-K ages 3-4 are coming to school (sometimes daily) with soiled, stained, or dirty clothes. Some give off unpleasant smells and some appear unclean and unkempt.

Parents please take care of this matter. It is a health and safety concern. It also makes it difficult for me to be close to them or even want to touch them.
    Enough said

Please sign and return so I know you've read this.
            Thank you
            Ms Smith

I have read the notice _____ parent
                        _____ child

(Continued)

Figure 8.3 (Continued)

> **Reflection:**
> Consider the policy or practice as it pertains to marginalized students.
> - What effect does this policy or practice have on marginalized students?
> - Is it the same or different than the effect on nonmarginalized students?
>
> Maximizing Positive Effects
> - How might this policy or practice be modified so that it gets closer to being based upon a more nuanced understanding of human nature?

KEY CONSIDERATIONS FOR ALLIES

- Educational policy is fueled by myths, lies, and flawed theories.
- One of the most potent tactics of deception used by those who want to deceive is to ignore and to twist the facts, resulting in a litany of lies and myths to support flawed and harmful policies.
- People are NOT problems. They HAVE problems (often created and supported by systems and processes out of their control).
- The business model has no business in schools.
- Bad anthropology leads to bad educational policy.
- **Looking Ahead**: Allies who embrace the dissonance created by coming into contact with information that challenges existing beliefs are ready to move into the next level of addressing dominant narratives, that of confronting them to reveal their fault lines.

Troubling the Dominant Narrative 9

As discussed in the last chapter, the story of the failure of public education is a strong narrative thread in today's culture. Cultures thrive—and survive—on the stories they tell. Rarely are these stories neutral. They are told to reinforce specific values, ways of viewing the world, and ways of being in the world. When told and retold by a dominant group, they can be extremely self-serving, designed as they are to keep power relations intact in order to serve dominant interests. As such, they are imbued with ideology. Sociologists call this type of story the dominant narrative.

Most of us today laugh at representations of women as the weaker sex, inferior to men, incapable of rational thought, but for many years this was the dominant narrative perpetuated by those who held real power: men. Despite evidence to the contrary, including the armies of women, often women of color, who worked long hours, doing physically demanding work, public policy was based on this narrative. Women were not allowed to go to university, to vote, or to hold public office. It took a dedicated band of women and men to question, challenge, and present evidence to the contrary before the dominant narrative was crushed and kicked to the side.

This chapter will address ways allies can learn to counter, or trouble, the dominant narrative. It will begin with an account of how easy it is to succumb to the dominant narrative, along with one way to overcome it. The second part of the chapter will address what troubling the dominant narrative means, followed by a number of strategies and resources that can help allies improve their ability to do so.

CONFRONTING THE DOMINANT NARRATIVE

I was in my mid-sixties the first time I spoke to a veiled Muslim woman. We were taking a French conversation course together. Her name was Sawsan, which means *lily of the valley* in Arabic, but she went by the name Suzanne 2. The professor said her Syrian name was too difficult to pronounce. The number indicated that, by coincidence, there was a previously registered student with the same Syrian name. Upon the arrival of my friend Sawsan, she became Suzanne 2. Not only did the teacher violate her identity by changing her name, he also relegated her to second-class stature by making her number 2.

Sawsan is not the only immigrant whose name was judged too difficult to pronounce and then changed. Sadly, the immigrant experience is full of similar stories, as are stories from the period of enslavement or from the history of the residential schools. By stripping people of their names, those in power stripped them of an important, fundamental element of their identity.

So yes, names matter. In my view, however, what really smarted was the way in which Sawsan accepted this brutal erasure of her identity by a person in power. What I did not realize until later was that I, too, was involved in minimizing and judging her identity. My awareness of this occurred by happenstance, but I learned a very real lesson that improved my ability to be an effective ally. Here is how it happened and what I learned.

Conversation as a Bridge to Understanding

Until I met Sawsan, I was not immune to clucking my oh-so-liberated tongue in dismay at hijab-wearing women. You can only imagine what I thought of those sporting a niqab. At first, Sawsan appeared reluctant to engage with me. Perhaps my manner of dress and bearing put her off.

Despite the perceived gaps between our upbringings, cultures, and religions, it took no more than two classes before Sawsan and I realized how much we had in common.

Conversation, in the true meaning of that word, will do that. In the middle ages, the word *conversation* meant *living together, having dealings with others.* (It literally means to *turn about with* from the Latin *com + vertere.*) Sawsan and I managed to *deal with each other*—we were open to *turn about **with** each other*—despite our preconceived notions. We achieved this bridging of a huge cultural and experiential divide through conversation, a conversation that was mediated by a language we were both trying hard to master, French. We lovingly laughed at each other's mistakes. We joyfully supplied missing words when one of us got stuck. We eagerly awaited the breaks in class so we could catch up on each other's doings and delve deeper into the circumstances of our lives that brought us together in Montreal in the historically cold winter of 2015.

Until I had conversations with Sawsan, I had a single story of Muslim women as oppressed. *Pointe finale,* as they say in French. I never looked beyond their manner of dress to peak under their veils and headscarves in order to find out who they were as individuals. In other words, I was comfortably complacent. I saw no need to trouble the dominant narrative about Muslim women. As a result, I believed the story that all Muslim women are oppressed. I received this reading as the whole story. It was not until I met a Muslim woman and got to know her through conversation that I found out how similar we were in attitudes, interests, and many values, if not in dress.

The Aftermath. Perhaps that is why I responded vehemently during the 2015 Canadian federal elections when then Prime Minister Stephen Harper mounted a campaign to ban Muslim women from wearing the niqab during their citizenship ceremony. The niqab is the Muslim dress that keeps a woman's face out of view. The courts had ruled that as long as niqab wearers had otherwise met all of the requirements to become citizens and had revealed their faces in private to a female immigration officer, they should not be banned from taking their oath with covered faces. Despite this ruling, the Prime Minister mounted a hate-filled effort to prohibit women wearing niqabs to participate in the swearing-in ceremony.

What makes this particular brand of Islamophobia even more offensive was Harper's simultaneous announcement that he was prepared to create a law enforcement tip line where Canadians could report "barbaric cultural practices." Thank goodness non-Muslim allies live in Canada. Many opted to go to the polls on October 19, 2015, wearing makeshift head and face coverings. Still others spread the word that Canadians should call the barbaric practices cultural tip line the next time there was a fight during a hockey game. Obviously, Canadians have a sense of humor. They also have a sense of justice. Stephen Harper's ill-advised policies never came to fruition. Canadians voted his party out of office.

How the Dominant Narrative
Morphs Into the Received Narrative

During this very troubling time, I heard and read many accounts of Muslim women in Canada vehemently resisting the portrayal of them as subservient, oppressed women. But resistance is not always what happens when a group is subjugated and stories about their deficiencies are widespread. Some dominant narratives have been told for so long that the very people whose lives are distorted by these narratives begin to believe them, they are shaped by them, and they interfere mightily with their ability to perform outside of the narrative, or stereotype, that has been promulgated about them. When the dominant narrative is internalized, it takes another form: It becomes the received, or accepted, narrative. There is a way to fight back, however, and it has a name. It is called *troubling the dominant narrative.*

TROUBLING THE DOMINANT NARRATIVE: WHAT IT MEANS

To *trouble* the dominant narrative means to disturb, disrupt, or unhinge what has been perpetuated by those in power as the single rendition or *true narrative* that makes up the story of different groups of people. Those committed to troubling the dominant narrative do so with the intention of interfering with the dominant narrative in order to expose the myths perpetuated in these stories to fact checking, to truth seeking, to alternative interpretations, to the bright light of the whole story. In other words, to trouble the dominant narrative is to flush out the flaws in the dominant narrative. The dominant narrative can exist without the complicity of those whose stories are being distorted, and it often does.

TROUBLING THE DOMINANT NARRATIVE: WHAT IT TAKES

The narratives we receive about "others" around us are potent. Allies in the fight for social justice hone their skills as myth busters. We earn a reputation as repudiators of dominant narratives that reek of half-truths and missing details. We are more than mildly cynical when the stories we are told about others are singularly simple. We learn to trouble the dominant narrative looking for flaws, oversights, lies, anything that will cast doubt about the legitimacy of the story being told. We search for information from reliable sources, the most reliable being those who are victims of pernicious tales. We approach them, get to know them, converse with them. Then we make up our own minds about what is true and what is false regarding the tales told about "others."

Allies in the battle for social justice work on their own attitudes, beliefs, and knowledge before they begin working with others. Initially, they devote a lot of time dismantling in their own minds the assumptions and false perceptions they have been fed over the years. Fortunately for those of us who are anxious to become better at troubling the dominant narrative, there are specific steps that can be taken and several resources we can tap into that will sharpen our ability to trouble the dominant narrative. Allies who are good at troubling the dominant narrative

- Ask Questions Using a Social Justice Lens
- Exercise Fearless Leadership
- Create Identity-Safe Schools and Classrooms
- Scour the Media for Alternate Viewpoints
- Step Out of the Zone of Comfort

Each of these steps is described in more detail in the section that follows.

Ask Questions Using a Social Justice Lens

In Chapter 2, we looked at two pairs of questions that help develop these insights and foster social justice literacy:

- Who stands to gain? Who stands to lose?
- Whose voice is heard? Whose voice is silenced?

By adding *How?* after each question, potential allies can delve even deeper into what is likely driving the dominant narrative, thus providing more fuel to support the work of challenging the dominant narrative. By following the money to find out who is likely to gain financially from unquestioned belief in the tales being promulgated, allies often come up with surprising answers that help them see the situation in a new light. The Internet is a quick and accessible resource for this type of questioning.

Exercise Fearless Leadership

Often, educators fall prey to the prevailing narrative about a group of students, in which case they need to consciously take steps to reorient themselves. This is difficult enough to do on an individual basis. On a schoolwide or systemwide basis, it requires fearless leadership. Fearless leadership has multiple facets, but one of the most critical is how leaders—and allies are leaders—orient themselves toward their work. They deliberately push back against the dominant narrative. They are incrementally more effective when they see themselves and function as an architect, soul friend, muse, and minister.

- Allies understand that they can create the architecture, or structural elements, that enable attitudinal and cultural shifts to occur. This architecture could be something as simple as organizing and hosting study and discussion groups that present alternative views.

- Like a soul friend who understands you better than you under-stand yourself, allies possess deep insight into themselves, their students, their colleagues, and their schools, and they are not afraid to affirm what they see. They honestly portray the current reality and they intentionally find ways to highlight the often-overlooked virtues students possess. Affirmation activities can be deliberately inserted into lessons and can take many forms: student to self, student to student, and teacher to student. For example, lesson reflections that ask students to indicate what they observed, what they wondered about, and what they learned about themselves as learners imply and affirm that they are obser-vant, curious students.

- Allies who exercise fearless leadership are also muses. They inspire others. They possess a clear vision for equity and, like the muses of old, they prod and prompt and push others to work toward that vision.

- Fearless leaders are also ministers. The root of the word *admin-istrator* is *minister*. Ministers are go-betweens, putting resources where needed. Whether an ally has the title of administrator or not, allies can still *administer* to the needs of others by finding resources, lending support, doing all they can do to bridge—or mediate—the divide between the current reality and the vision (Jackson & McDermott, 2012).

Figure 9.1 graphically represents the relationship between fearless leading and the role of architect, soul friend, muse, and minister. It also provides guiding questions that emanate from these roles.

Create Identity-Safe Classrooms and Schools

Affirming, inspiring, and mediating activities can be crafted. So can identity-safe classrooms. In identity-safe classrooms, students' identi-ties—linguistic, cultural, ethnic, physical, etc.—are treated as assets. Because they are viewed as assets, students' identities become the perfect jumping-off point for providing students with what they crave, a chal-lenging curriculum replete with the supports that allow them to effec-tively and deeply engage in meaningful learning activities. Identity-safe classrooms encourage students to bring their identities to the classroom and to use and build upon them in the normal course of learning and teaching. In identity-safe classrooms, the central message is that the stu-dents and teachers care deeply about each other's experiences (Steele & Cohn-Vargas, 2013).

Figure 9.1 Leadership for Equity: Guiding Questions

LEADERSHIP FOR EQUITY
GUIDING QUESTIONS

FEARLESS LEADING → ARCHITECT

SOUL FRIEND AFFIRMATION

Whose voice is heard?
Whose is silenced?
Who is represented?
Who is missing?
Who stands to benefit?
Who stands to lose?
What assumptions fuel
this policy, action,
pedagogy?

MUSE INSPIRATION

How does this policy,
action, pedagogy align
with the vision?

MINISTER MEDIATION

What policies, action or
pedagogy might be
implemented to move to
the next level of equity
practice?

Scour the Media for Alternate Viewpoints

Allies often wonder where they can go to obtain information that challenges the dominant narrative.

- *Start With Accessible Mainstream Publications.* Many mainstream news outlets exist that present alternate and subtly nuanced views on topics of current interest. Some reliable sources are *The Huffington Post* and *The Guardian.* Frequently, their news reports provide information not found in other sources—nor are the perspectives of their opinion writers. Reading them on a regular basis helps allies open their eyes to other possibilities. Be patient, though. Moving through dissonance to a somewhat cohesive new way of looking at things is anxiety producing and difficult.

- *Maintain a List of Dependable Writers and Commentators Committed to Social Justice.* Maintaining a list of go-to writers and commentators who can be depended upon to bring a fresh and comprehensible perspective to thorny issues helps. Some of my favorites are Paul Krugman for economic information, Charles Blow for commentary about race relations, and Robert Fisk for information about the Middle East. Many, like Frank Bruni, often base their opinion pieces on outside sources. By seeking out and consulting the sources cited, you will likely discover many other interesting thinkers and uncover more in-depth understanding of the points being made in these opinion pieces.

- *Maintain Criticality.* Being critical requires caution. Allies do not uncritically accept everything they read in alternative renderings of news events or in the columns of their favorite writers any more than they uncritically accept the prevailing narrative. Indeed, the mark of an ally who has developed a particularly sharp critical eye and social justice sensibility is the one who can find the flaws in the narratives on both sides of an issue. And they do exist.

Step Out of the Zone of Comfort

Given a choice, most of us associate with those who look like, think like, and act like us. The choice is understandable. The familiar is comfortable and comforting. But, allies cannot afford to stay in a cocoon of comfort or their work will be stymied.

To purposefully step out of your comfort zone takes courage, strength of character, and openness, but the rewards are staggering. Teachers Jennifer Obidah and Karen Teel stepped out of their comfort zones to work together on a research project designed to come to understand the racial and cultural divide that exists between Black students and White teachers. In the process, they confronted the racial and cultural divide that existed between them.

Jennifer, who identifies as African American, and Karen, who identifies as White, worked together over a three-year period on this project. Along the way, both seriously contemplated abandoning the project because of the pronounced and difficult racial tensions that developed between them. In the end, they persevered and happily report that the experience deepened their relationship, altered their understanding of how race plays out in school, and changed their lives. Their book, as well as the analysis by Lisa Delpit at the end of the book, provides tremendous insight into the inherent challenges in trying to bridge to another's racial and cultural world (Obidah & Teel, 2001).

Among the issues they needed to confront with regard to students were their different perceptions of African American students, conflicting communication styles, dissimilar expectations regarding student behavior, and divergent understandings of teacher authority. On a personal level, they both took many risks and had much work to do. For example, Jennifer says she worked hard to trust a White person, while Karen admits she had to face the possibility that she might be a racist.

In the end, they concluded that their story was a story of success against many odds. They speak openly of the difficulties inherent in battling preconceived notions, prejudices, and expectations. They also talk about coming out the other side convinced that their relationship and teaching are stronger. Most importantly, they are allies united in the belief that what they experienced is vital for teachers to effectively educate all students, especially those who are most distant from them in terms of race and culture.

None of this work was easy. Bridging cultural and experiential divides never is. But without this bridging, disrupting inequity will remain a stagnant, unfulfilled, and broken dream. Figure 9.2 summarizes the ways in which the dominant narrative can be challenged.

Practice in Troubling the Dominant Narrative

The Center for Racial Justice Innovation maintains an excellent website that advances racial justice through research, media, and practice. The website is called Race Forward. The purpose of Race Forward is to "build awareness, solutions and leadership for racial justice by generating transformative ideas, information, and experiences" (https://www .raceforward.org).

One of their documents speaks directly to the issue of troubling the dominant narrative. "Moving the Race Conversation Forward" is a two-part report that aims to reshape and reform the way race and racism are discussed. Part 1 chronicles and quantifies the many ways in which the media fails to accurately discuss and report on race, especially the way the media ignores systemic racism. It also includes a list of seven harmful racial discourse practices that reinforce the idea that racism is a problem

Figure 9.2   Ways to Trouble the Dominant Narrative

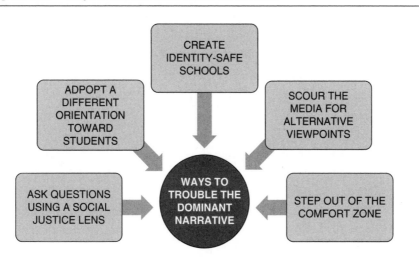

situated in rare individuals who display isolated acts of racially insensitive actions and attitudes.

Part 2 of the report, "Racial Discourse Change in Practice," provides several case studies and profiles of recent efforts to trouble the dominant narrative. Each one provides a window into successful campaigns to challenge, or trouble, the dominant narrative.

Use the activity in Figure 9.3 to practice troubling the dominant narrative.

Figure 9.3   Activity: Troubling the Dominant Narrative

Directions

- Watch the video that summarizes the report "Moving the Race Conversation Forward": https://www.raceforward.org/research/reports/moving-race-conversation-forward.
- What does the video say about how and why the media gets race and racism wrong?
- In what ways does the media's failure to be systemically aware contribute to maintaining the dominant narrative?

Extension and Team Activities

Directions

- Download Part 2 of the report "Moving the Race Conversation Forward," which presents two case studies and three profiles documenting ways in which the dominant narrative was challenged by individuals and groups of individuals.
- Select one of these case studies or profiles. With a partner consider the following:
  - o What was the dominant narrative that the individual or group challenged?
  - o What did the individual or group do to challenge the dominant narrative?
  - o Where and how do you see allies at work in the case study or profile?
  - o What did you take away from this case study or profile that you might be able to use in your own work of becoming an ally in the battle for social justice?

KEY CONSIDERATIONS FOR ALLIES

- The dominant narrative about "others" is a carefully crafted construct built to perpetuate lies, often to stoke fear, and most often authored by those in dominant positions who stand to gain by diminishing or demonizing others.
- Told long enough and proclaimed loudly enough, the dominant narrative can morph into the received narrative, believed by the oppressor and oppressed alike.

- There are multiple ways to refute, challenge, disrupt, or otherwise "trouble" the dominant narrative.
- **Looking Ahead**: Once allies have embraced dissonance, once they understand how the dominant narrative functions, they are often ready to begin the work of openly challenging unjust systems and oppressive individual actions. At this juncture, silence is not an option, but adequate preparation is a necessity. These are two major themes of the next chapter.

Silence Is Not an Option   10

Sadly, examples of patently unfair dominant narratives are all around us. How to react when confronted by one is a matter of choice. For allies, silence is not an option.

I stumbled upon my first opportunity to speak out about racism. I was surfing the website of a very highly regarded educational publishing company when I clicked on a video accompanying a newly published book for teachers that interested me. Then my jaw dropped. As I watched the video, I saw the author, a White woman (and again highly regarded), interacting with two different middle school students, both girls, one clearly a child of color, the other noticeably fair skinned. The difference in the teacher's approach to these two students, and the commentary accompanying it, were vastly different. The child of color was described as a student who was easily distracted and who "bothered" other students during reading time. As the teacher "conferred" with this student—a conference in which the teacher did all the talking—the teacher handed the student a book and suggested that the student might want to read it because it was "easy and had lots of pictures."

With the second, fair-skinned student, the teacher took a different tack. The second student was described by the teacher as a focused learner, an avid reader, and an all-around good student. The teacher approached the second student gingerly, excused herself for interrupting her reading, and, in hushed, almost reverential tones, she asked the student how her reading was going, whether she had selected another book to read, and if she wanted any suggestions.

I am well aware that some students come to school prepared to meet school expectations and others not so much. What upset me about the video, however, is that it perpetuated the myth that students of color are not to be trusted (hence the teacher did all the talking), are deficient (hence the suggestion of an "easy book with lots of pictures"), and are incapable of knowing what they should select as their next book (otherwise why would she have brought a preselected book to the reading conference). Plus, her description of the student of color as easily distracted and who "bothers" other students feeds into the destructive trope that students of color are problems in the classroom, are troublemakers, and are not "good" students, however "good" is defined.

Since I have a relationship with this publisher, since everyone I showed the video to gasped in disbelief, and since the video clearly perpetuated and reinforced the notion that children of color are deficient, I decided silence was not an option. I needed to be an ally on behalf of students of color, using my relationship with the publisher, my growing awareness of the insidiousness of racism, and my emerging voice to speak out about the injustices inherent in dissemination of a video such as this.

Frankly, I was very scared. I prepared my points carefully and wrote them down. I rehearsed what I was going to say. I did all I could to control the trembling that wanted to force its way into my voice when the publisher and I spoke. I reminded him of my relationship with his organization and my high regard for the excellent contributions he and his writers make to the world of education. It is because of this influence and my high regard, I said, that I decided I needed to let him know how I—and others—saw the video.

At first, he was silent, then a bit defensive. He was certain, he said, that no harm was intended. I was prepared for that defense, indicating that intention and interpretation are two different things and that in today's world, publishers have an obligation to step back and ask how others *might* interpret the ways in which students and teachers are portrayed. I went further. I said I believed it was our obligation to ensure that products are screened for harmful stereotypes. I even said I knew some people who could help in this regard. He coolly thanked me and said he would get back to me. Surprisingly, he did.

Several weeks later, I received an e-mail from the publisher indicating that he had discussed the incident with the author, that she insisted she meant no harm, and that, in fact, the fairer-skinned student was of Hispanic background. To my mind, that comment was pure defensiveness. The publisher also indicated that the video was pulled from the website and that he was sending me a free copy of the book. The video was, indeed, pulled from the website, which I count as a victory. I did receive the book, which I chose not to read. And I never heard from the publisher again, which I see as the price you sometimes have to pay when you choose to be true to your values and act as an ally for others. For many reasons, I wish the publisher would have chosen to continue to have someone else with a social justice lens review and comment on manuscripts and promotional materials, but he clearly was not ready to take that step.

BREAKING THE SILENCE—WHAT IT TAKES

If silence is not an option for educators who are allies in the battle for social justice, what do allies need in order speak out, in order to break the silence of complicity? As much as I hate reducing complex work to lists, for the sake of clarity, I am going to delineate what I see as three interrelated elements that allies need to understand and to cultivate in order to break the silence.

Allies Need Allies and a Period of Silence

This may sound counterintuitive in a chapter about breaking the silence, but my first recommendation is to be silent. By being silent, you can hear the voices of others; you can observe carefully and closely; you can read body language and eye movements. This silent period of observation will enable you to identify potential allies who can ground, support, and instruct you, and who are willing to do so. Without finding other allies, your work could be severely hampered.

When I first got involved in antiracism work, I was very used to having my voice heard, my opinions validated, my recommendations followed. In the White world in which I formerly functioned, what I had to say had a lot of currency by virtue of my color, my reputation, and my position. It was hard to dismiss what the superintendent of schools said. It was very unsettling, frustrating, and anger provoking for me to find myself in a new setting in which I was routinely ignored, silenced, or passed over by some of my Black colleagues.

After several of these less-than-satisfactory meetings, I decided to remain quiet and observe the dynamics; to "read the room"; to figure out who got to speak, whose opinions were endorsed, and who held sway. More importantly, my silence allowed me to locate those in the group whose attitudes were more tolerant; who seemed genuinely interested in supporting the ideas of White colleagues; who appeared willing to help White colleagues understand the incredibly intricate web of racial positioning, power, and politics.

My silence enabled me to find allies inclined to help me deepen my understanding of race and racial issues. This silence was eventually followed by long discussions, recommended readings, more long discussions, time spent debriefing meetings and clarifying positions, and lots of questions. These led to many *aha* moments, strong bonds, and the insight to see where and how my current skill set could be most useful. More importantly, with the help of allies, I was eventually able to present myself as someone who was developing a more nuanced understanding of marginalization and racism. Once I reached this point, I was trusted more and more to join the battle for social justice. I also learned to wait in silence until I was asked.

Allies Need Courage and a Thick Skin

There is no question in my mind that social justice work takes courage and a thick skin. Prior to my making the call to the publisher about the video I found on the company's website, I went to several allies to get their reactions, to confirm my read on the situation, and to discuss strategies for engaging the publisher in a discussion about the video. In the end, I took all of this information, analyzed it, and synthesized it with who I am, what I felt comfortable saying, and how I felt I could handle the situation. It took all of these steps for me to muster the courage to actually place the call.

Not only did I rehearse what I was going to say, I mapped out several possible response scenarios. I knew how I was going to react if the editor was hostile, how I would push the agenda if he appeared momentarily taken aback, how I would up the ante if he appeared chastened and willing to listen to a detailed analysis of my take on the situation.

Anticipating possible reactions, including total dismissal and hostility, and thinking through my possible responses to the range of possible reactions provided the courage and thick skin I needed to make the call. I was prepared for total rejection. I had discussed this possibility with my ally friends. I knew that no matter what happened, I would have the intestinal fortitude and arsenal of arguments to engage in a purposeful and respectful counterattack. Preparation also removed the personal aspect. I was prepared with a full array of arguments with which to counter an equally full array of responses. As a result, I approached the call with much more objectivity than I otherwise would have been able to muster.

Allies Need to Believe in the Work

It was extremely difficult for me to point out to an editor of an important book company that some of the material used to promote one of the company's publications was racially insensitive. It is no less difficult, and some might say even more so, to correct friends who tell a racially insensitive joke or who use expressions that depend upon maligning differently abled people or who comment with a wink and a knowing glance on a colleague or student's sexuality.

Figure 10.1   Activity: Silence Is Not an Option

Directions:

Consider the words of Elie Wiesel, which clearly ask allies to turn their backs on neutrality and silence:

We must always take sides. Neutrality helps the oppressor, never the victim. Silence encourages the tormentor, never the tormented.

Based upon what you have been reading and thinking about so far, on what are you now prepared to take sides? About what are you now considering to speak out?

When I want to avoid confrontation, when I want to hide behind a shield of silence, when I want to preserve relationships more than point out injustices, I often think of the words of the 1986 Nobel Peace Prize winner and concentration camp survivor Elie Wiesel. "We must always take sides. Neutrality helps the oppressor, never the oppressed. Silence encourages the tormentor, never the tormented."

MARGINALIZATION, SOCIALIZATION, AND SILENCE

How children are prepared to understand race, ability, sexuality, and any of the ways in which people are categorized runs the gamut from total silence to a proactive approach.

When Silence Is the Default Position

When they are uncomfortable, adult caregivers and teachers alike often opt for silence and avoidance rather than engagement. I vividly remember my parents' and teachers' admonitions to not stare at anyone who was "different": the homeless person; the man with the severely burned face; or the Hasidic Jew wearing a beard, long dark coat, and heavy hat. I, like many other children, was taught to avert my eyes; to bury my questions; to bypass, step over, or flee from anyone who did not fit the "norm." Not staring was the first part of a one-two punch on openness, understanding, and respect. The second part is not talking about race, ability, or sexuality.

Danger lurks in silence. Quiet as it is, silence delivers loud messages. Polite people do not talk about these topics is one such message. So is the message that polite people do not *need* to talk about these topics. By not engaging and by choosing to remain silent, polite people erase entire life stories, real human beings, and rich and vibrant cultures. By not engaging, polite people do not adequately prepare their children to understand the difference between race and racism, ability and ableism, sex and sexism. As a result, children grow up thinking there is something wrong with talking about these topics, and, if given the chance to engage in a conversation about any of them, they find themselves tripping over terms and concepts. Shame and inadequacy are the legacies of silence.

Opening Up Spaces for Discussion

Allies take steps to dismantle the legacy of shame and inadequacy that silence reinforces. Educators who are allies in the battle for social justice are uniquely placed to dismantle this legacy. They open up spaces for healthy discussions about difference and social systems; about individual biases and systemic injustice; about how race, ability, and sex are essential parts of identity; how media perpetuates stereotypes. In short, they proactively push against the ways children have been socialized.

What White Children Need to Know About Racism

Ali Michael and Eleonora Bartoli (2014) address the issue of adult silence and children's understanding of race. Their studies show that the preferred ways in which White parents socialize their children about race—that is to say, telling them not to be racist, not to talk about race, not to use the word *Black*, and not to notice racial differences—inadequately prepare their children to resist racial stereotypes, to comprehend systemic racism, or to recognize the difference between racial and racist.

If what is happening in the home, the primary locus of racial socialization, is not adequately preparing children to understand race, schools need to step in. Although Michael and Bartoli focus their attention on racism and their recommendations are aimed at the independent school system, their analysis can be more broadly applied to all "isms" and their recommendations to all schools. Many schools, private or public, are de facto sites of diversity, and many schools and districts have committed to visions that include statements about equity and anti-oppression.

Michael and Bartoli divide their recommendations into three categories, including messages, content knowledge, and skills.

- One of the key messages they believe students should receive is that talking about race is NOT racist. Indeed it is important and okay. The same is true about talking about other "isms."

- Students benefit from understanding race as a social construct and how antiracism works. This content knowledge is helpful in anti-oppression work in general.
- Finally, students benefit from developing specific skills, such as how to critically analyze the media, what to do when they witness racism, and how to connect with peers of different races. These skills can easily be applied more generally to cover other oppressed groups and contribute to the development of more socially aware students and more socially just schools.

SILENCE, LOST OPPORTUNITY, AND LOST LIVES

Keeping silent in the face of injustice can have horrific results, as the following story about the murder of Marcelo Lucero, a thirty-seven-year old Ecuadorian immigrant, illustrates.

This is a story that I wish I did not have to tell.

In 2008, three years after I retired and moved from Long Island to Montreal, I was surprised to hear a Long Island voice on the radio, and I was bowled over by shock at the story being recounted.

I heard the voice of Paul Pontieri, mayor of the Village of Patchogue, the same town where I had served as a school administrator for twenty years until my retirement. Mayor Pontieri was discussing the horrific and shocking incident in which a group of seven Patchogue-Medford High School students set off to "get a Mexican" one Saturday night. By the end of that night, Marcelo Lucero was surrounded and taunted by the group and ultimately fatally stabbed by one of them.

The mayor was visibly moved, completely outraged, and totally perplexed by the behavior of these young men.

So was I. During my tenure in the district from 1985 until 2005, English Language Learners, predominantly from Central and South America, represented the fastest growing segment of the school district population. The district's commitment to English literacy among the newly arrived was well known and well regarded. Indeed, the district's adult education office had one of the largest adult English as a Second Language (ESL) programs in the area and even provided satellite services throughout Long Island.

One of the highlights of the school year for me was attending the adult education graduation in June in which hundreds of students, accompanied by family and friends, came to receive their high school equivalency diplomas and ESL certificates. These celebratory graduation nights were in stark contrast to that Saturday night killing of Marcelo Lucero, who had lived in Patchogue for sixteen years, and, for all I know, may have attended the adult education program. What had happened?

There are no simple answers. However, one likely contributing factor is the reluctance of some Long Islanders to directly and courageously address the immigration trends taking place at the time and the growing anti-Hispanic sentiment that accompanied it.

A few years before the killing of Mr. Lucero, the neighboring town of Farmingville was in the news because some residents protested the presence of "illegal aliens." These residents were vocal in their displeasure at the large numbers of Spanish-speaking men who gathered on street corners each morning waiting to be picked up as day laborers and who gathered in large numbers at night in overcrowded rented homes. Each morning as I drove to work, I would see members of the Farmingville community protesting vehemently over the presence of these "illegal immigrants" in their town. They marched. They picketed. They petitioned. Then it got really ugly.

In 2001, two Mexican day workers were lured into an abandoned basement on the pretext of being hired for the day. They were brutally beaten, stabbed, and left for dead. Israel Pérez and Magdaleno Escamilla did not die, nor did their story. Two filmmakers spent nine months making a documentary about the town. The film, *Farmingville*, chronicles the fractious and contentious events that often occur when a small town unexpectedly receives an influx of immigrants and anti-immigrant sentiment is allowed to flourish.

An Unheeded Wake-Up Call

What happened in Farmingville was a wake-up call that went unheeded. It was an opportunity for the neighboring town of Patchogue to think through the sources of anti-immigration sentiment, to proactively welcome and celebrate the Spanish-speaking community, to make cross-cultural connections, to de-demonize the day laborers who came to the United States in search of the same better life that scores of U.S. immigrants before them had searched out. Instead, Patchogue chose to ignore what happened next door. Like a foul odor, anti-immigration sentiment seeped across town borders; grew in intensity; overtook a second community; and ended up with teenage boys being tried for assault, harassment, and murder.

Many among the community in Patchogue indicated that the murder of Marcelo Lucero, or something like it, was inevitable. High school friends of the boys who attacked Marcelo Lucero admitted it was not uncommon to hear talk of kids planning to go on mugging raids on the weekends.

Members of the Hispanic community reported that verbal and physical harassment had long been a part of their experience living in Patchogue. Broken windows in their homes, bottles being thrown at them on the street, racial epithets being hurled at them in school corridors made up some of the harassment they dealt with regularly and suffered silently. Many Latino and Latina victims indicated that filing a complaint was not considered a viable option. Some who were in the country legally felt their complaints would go unheard and unheeded. Those who were undocumented indicated that they did not trust the system and feared that they would be deported if they called attention to themselves by registering a complaint.

How an Ally Responded

After the murder of Marcelo Lucero, which took place two blocks from where Patchogue Village Mayor Paul Pontieri grew up, the mayor chose to speak out, spurring him to action and eloquence. He reached out to the Hispanic community and worked with them to craft a response.

As a result, open discussions about racism took place in the community. One of the middle schools hosted an outdoor exhibit of banners painted by local artists called *Embracing Our Differences*. Teachers were encouraged to lead discussions with students about the banners. Community members were encouraged to visit the exhibit and join the conversation. The Board of Trustees renamed the street where the murder occurred. It is now called *Unity Place*. The town board also passed a resolution opposing anti-immigration rhetoric. The resolution encourages "thoughtful discourse" in an environment "free from hatred and vilification." Anti-immigrant rhetoric, the resolution brilliantly states, not only hurts targeted groups, it also harms "our entire social fabric."

Building Bridges of Trust and Understanding

In September 2011, the story of the murder of Marcelo Lucero and the efforts of the Village of Patchogue to come together after the violence of this event was told in a one-hour PBS documentary, *Light in the Darkness*. The film follows key players in the healing process: the mayor, the victim's brother, a local police officer, and a local librarian. All are committed to building bridges of trust and understanding between and among different community groups, governmental agencies, and law enforcement.

The nagging question for the community of Patchogue is this: Would the murder of Marcelo Lucero have been avoided if steps were taken early on to build the bridges of trust and understanding that every community needs?

Would the murder have been avoided if they looked to their neighbors in Farmingville and seriously considered to what unchecked hatred, unwillingness to adapt, and refusal to accommodate can lead? These are the very questions that communities across the United States and Canada need to be asking now as the newest waves of immigrants come streaming across our borders.

Responding to Anti-Immigration Sentiment

Carlos Sandoval, one of the filmmakers of *Farmingville*, says that one of the reasons he makes documentaries is because "a country without documentaries is like a family without a photo album." Documentaries and photo albums allow families to look at themselves as they are or as they once were. There is an immediacy, honesty, and subtlety to a well-made documentary that few other forms of expression can capture.

This activity will give potential allies an opportunity to peak into the "family albums" of two neighboring communities. The activity will challenge potential allies to think through the ways in which silence in the face of hate speech can result in tragedy, as well as ways several allies bravely opted to break the silence and counteract hate speech with a more positive message.

Figure 10.2   Activity: Responding to Anti-Immigration Sentiment

Directions:

- Watch the video *Farmingville*. What does the video capture about the Farmingville "family" that resonates with you? What social justice issues are raised? How are Hispanic Americans or Latino Americans talked about, treated, and understood? Who function as allies in the story of this "family"?
- Watch the video *Light in the Darkness*. What does the video capture about the Patchogue "family" that resonates with you? What social justice issues are raised? How are Hispanic Americans or Latino Americans talked about, treated, and understood? Who function as allies in the story of this "family"?
- What are the similarities and differences in the way the "families" in each of the videos are portrayed? You may want to capture these comparisons using a Venn Diagram or, alternatively, a Double Bubble Map (Hyerle, 2004). The Double Bubble Map is another Thinking Map. The Double Bubble Map is designed to demonstrate the thinking process of comparison and contrast. It differs from a Venn Diagram in that it is more generative. Venn Diagrams confine answers to the amount of space encircled, whereas with the Double Bubble Map, items can continually be added simply by adding more connecting lines and bubbles.

(Continued)

Figure 10.2 (Continued)

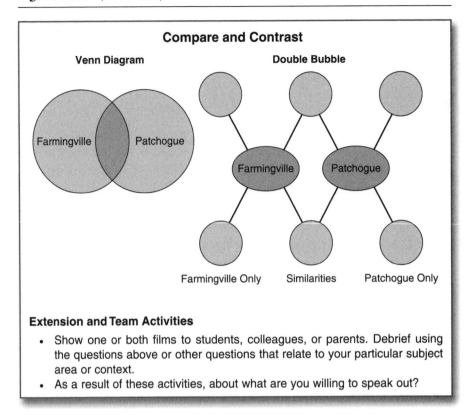

Extension and Team Activities

- Show one or both films to students, colleagues, or parents. Debrief using the questions above or other questions that relate to your particular subject area or context.
- As a result of these activities, about what are you willing to speak out?

KEY CONSIDERATIONS FOR ALLIES

- Allies need to be prepared to speak up when they encounter injustice.
- Counterintuitively, that preparation may include a period of silence.
- Adults send powerful harmful messages to children when they elect not to engage in discussions regarding difference.
- Schools can take a number of proactive steps to encourage and support healthy discussions about racism and other "isms."
- Silently accepting hate speech can result in tragedy.
- **Looking Ahead:** If silence is not an option, how can allies not only break the silence, but do so in a specific, culture-changing way? Culture-changing conversations are the subject of the next chapter.

Change the Culture? Change the Conversation

11

For allies, silence is not an option. Talk, especially culture-changing talk, is a necessity.

Culture-changing talk means purposeful and carefully chosen words, themes, and stories designed to fill in the contours of the story of the lives of our marginalized students with the stories rarely told about them, the stories that paint a portrait of possibilities. There are at least three ways allies can paint a portrait of possibilities. The first is to be deliberate when choosing what school stories to share outside the school. The second is to identify and activate student strengths. The third is to orchestrate opportunities for culture-changing dialogue.

CHOOSE WHICH STORIES TO TELL

Teachers talk. Indeed, they talk a lot—in and out of school—and what they say matters.

All schools are filled with stories, and these stories make up an important part of the culture of the school. In many ways, these stories sculpt how the community inside and outside the school responds to the school, its students, and its teachers.

Storytellers have a choice. They can feed into the dominant, received narrative, replete with stereotypes and reeking in negativity, or they can tell the untold, overlooked, more complete story of who our marginalized students are, what they are made of, and how forces outside their control have shaped how the world sees them and how they see the world. Allies opt for the second approach and they are willing to challenge those who persist in repeating a litany of lies and half-truths. I had the chance to employ the second option. The following anecdote will tell how and why.

I was meeting with a new principal and his leadership team for the first time. All were eager to "do something" to improve learning and teaching outcomes for their students, the vast majority of whom identified as Black and 100% of whom qualified for free or reduced lunch. The principal and his leadership team were all White. The leadership team was all female, as was the majority of the staff. In telling me about their school, located in an inner city of a once thriving northeastern city, they mentioned proudly that the majority of the teachers take the long drive in from the suburbs daily because they "love" their kids, they are committed to them, and they want to change things for them. Not an uncommon story, but one that often leaves me with more questions than answers and gobs of suspicion.

During a break, one of the teacher-leaders, making small talk, told the group how she was at a party over the weekend and she just had to recount to her neighbors an incident that took place in school that "shocked" her. According to her, she was trying to encourage a group of her remedial reading students to work harder at school so that they could get into college and get a good job. I chose not to comment on this part of her story, thinking it might be way too soon to bring up the institutional and structural impediments that make access to college and good jobs difficult for entire swaths of the population.

She then went on to say that one of the students, whom she identified as a Black boy, leaned back in his chair and pronounced that he did not need to work hard because when he grew up he was going to go on welfare like his parents. "Can you imagine?" she asked, shocked and outraged. "Those people have no motivation," she said, tsking and shaking her head in disbelief, disgust, and disdain. Worse yet, the other leadership team members were nodding in agreement.

Silence is not an option, I reminded myself. So, I decided to push back, to ask a few questions, borrowing some of her words to do so. "Do you know any children of color who are working incredibly hard because they *want* to go to college and get a good job?" "Plenty," she said.

"Do you know any White kids who do not want to go to college and get a good job, preferring instead to be on welfare like their parents?" Once again, she said yes, she has met several over the years.

This time, I decided to challenge her. "Why, then, did you choose to tell *this* story?" Of course, she had no answer.

I could have remained silent and not challenged this teacher and her head-nodding colleagues, but here was a perfect teachable moment, so I asked the questions I did and explained why I felt I needed to do so.

I indicated that stories like this one trouble me, because as teachers in the mix, our friends and neighbors look to us as authorities, as ones who have the inside scoop on the lives and values of the children we teach. How we represent our students to those who do not know them is a matter of great import. We can continue to feed into the negative, single story about inner-city children of color challenged by poverty as shiftless and unmotivated. Or, we can be truthful and we can trumpet and celebrate the brilliance, the perseverance, the integrity of the countless inner-city children who come from loving, supportive families, albeit families who, for various reasons, are challenged by poverty. Or we could tell yet another story, the one about those of our children who are victims of the circumstances of their birth, and who, despite extraordinarily trying circumstances, come to school daily, do their work, and often take on adult responsibilities at home.

The choice is ours. If we choose not to remain silent, then we need to also choose to be deliberate and responsible about what we say. Educators have the authority and the obligation to change the conversation.

IDENTIFY AND ACTIVATE STUDENT STRENGTHS

In addition to choosing which stories to tell, allies change the conversation about marginalized students when they intentionally identify and activate their strengths. This section will begin with a discussion of how linguistically diverse students are currently viewed and how this view hurts them. It will end with a demonstration of the power of an alternate reading fueled by intentionally mining for these students' strengths.

Seeing Linguistically Diverse Students as "Problems"

Teachers are part of mainstream culture, and they often adopt the attitudes of mainstream culture toward their students. This can be seen in the ways in which linguistically diverse people are treated and talked about in the culture at large and the ways in which their children are treated and talked about in schools.

Linguistically diverse students are a growing reality in American and Canadian schools. Both countries have long been considered lands of opportunity; sanctuaries for immigrants seeking a better life; political safe havens for many fleeing oppressive, dangerous governments. According to the U.S. Department of Education, during the 2012–2013 school year, English Language Learners (ELL) constituted almost 10 percent of U.S. public school enrollment. In California, almost a quarter of the student population is designated ELL. The new Liberal government in Canada promised to bring 25,000 Syrian refugees into Canada during 2016. These 25,000 refugees are in addition to the 240,000 to 265,000 other immigrants Canada historically accepts yearly.

In both the United States and Canada, the majority of these immigrants do not speak the official language or languages of their adopted countries: English in the United States; or French or English in the case of Canada. Schools in both countries are tasked with educating children of immigrants in the ways and values of their adopted home, as well as in the acquisition of another language.

Societal attitudes about linguistically diverse students are particularly negative in the United States, where several states have held referendums and campaigns banning bilingual education (despite research indicating its benefits for all learners) or reducing the amount of ELL instruction linguistically diverse students are allowed to receive. Not only is the number of linguistically diverse students entering U.S. schools increasing, they are moving into less-populated communities with little experience in integrating people from different cultural and linguistic backgrounds. At the same time, federal and state legislation has increased teacher accountability for the academic progress of linguistically diverse students. It is not surprising, then, to find out that some mainstream teachers demonstrate negative attitudes toward children whose cultures and languages are different from their own. Simply put, many teachers feel ill prepared to cope with what they view as the challenges linguistically diverse students represent (Walker, Shafer, & Iiams, 2004).

As a result, linguistically diverse students are viewed as simultaneously different and deficient. In the stories told about them, they and their status are often portrayed as problems. Being considered a problem, or being "problematized," often leads to negative attitudes that are acted out in overt and subtle ways. Teachers who feel overwhelmed and underprepared prefer to hide their own deficiencies by highlighting and/or manufacturing the deficiencies of their students.

How the Current Conversation Affects Linguistically Diverse Students

Not only is a different approach to linguistically diverse students possible and preferable, it is crucial for their academic, mental, emotional, and social development. The first experiences of linguistically diverse students in school also affect their eventual integration into the larger communities around them. Experiencing personal and structural discrimination, then, has significant negative repercussions for young children of immigrants and society at large (Adair, 2015).

Changing how school personnel think about, talk about, and interact with linguistically diverse students, or any other group of marginalized students, is a critical first step in assuring that these students thrive in our schools. Two commonly held viewpoints that harm linguistically diverse—and other marginalized—students are the deficit viewpoint and the viewpoint that difference is bad.

Figure 11.1 Activity: The Problem With Problematizing

In this activity, you will have an opportunity to think through how problematizing can manifest itself in a school setting.

The following letter was given to me years ago by an ELL teacher who was totally at a loss as to how to address this student's Grade 5 mainstream teacher about her attitudes toward Johanna, a recently arrived ELL student.

Directions:

Read the letter, looking for ways in which the mainstream teacher has made Johanna into a problem.

First Quarter Report

Johanna entered Main Street School in September from Ecuador. She understands only a few English words.

At this point, Johanna has very little understanding of basic commands in English and is unable to comprehend academics or interact with the teacher or fellow students.

Due to the lack of foundation in English fluency, this child has barely made any academic progress in reading, social studies, science, language, and spelling. In math, she is functioning at the third grade level. She has not mastered her basic addition and subtraction facts and is reluctant to work on multiplication facts. She frequently "loses" her work to avoid doing it. I am concerned that Johanna is not making progress and seems to require more time with an ESL teacher in a small group setting.

Sincerely,
Ms. G.

Reflections:

- In what ways has Ms. G. problematized Johanna?
- As an ally, how might you, in your current capacity, address this situation?
- Think of the marginalized student or students to whom you have dedicated your work. In what way or ways are your marginalized student or students problematized?

The deficit viewpoint is what we see in Figure 11.1 in the letter about Johanna, a relentless focus on what Johanna could not do—yet.

No wonder Johanna frequently "loses" her work. Johanna may not yet be capable of reading English, but I suspect she could expertly read her teacher's attitude toward her.

Although not explicitly stated, the letter suggests lack of tolerance for difference. Clearly, Johanna, as a newcomer, IS different from those students born and raised in the United States, for whom English is their first language and for whom American culture is deeply rooted. Those differences need to be acknowledged and made visible but from a positive frame of reference. Difference need not be synonymous with deficit, and students should not be asked to jettison their differences as soon as they cross the threshold of their new schools. Instead, schools have a responsibility to make provisions for all learners through pedagogy that incorporates students' lives and strengths.

Identifying and Activating Student Strengths in Practice

One of the seven high operational practices of the Pedagogy of Confidence is identifying and activating strengths, a practice routinely used with those students deemed *gifted* but conspicuously absent from the educational approaches for most other students, especially those labeled low performers. Yet, the cognitive and psychological benefits for students and teachers are enormous when teachers flip the script, stop drilling down for deficits, and instead intentionally identify and activate student strengths (Jackson, 2011). Abandoning the deficit model in favor of one that starts from strengths is a low-cost, highly effective strategy for changing the conversation about students otherwise thought of as problems (Jackson & McDermott, 2015).

Identifying Student Strengths. During a recent conference addressing the education of English Language Learners, participants responded to a simple prompt: What are the strengths of your English Language Learners? To record their ideas graphically, participants were asked to use a Bubble Map. A Bubble Map is a Thinking Map designed for the process of describing attributes, qualities, traits, and characteristics (Hyerle, 2004).

As you can see from Figure 11.2, the center circle contains what is being described: in this case, the strengths of English Language Learners. Fanning out from the center circle are some of the adjectives used by one group to describe the strengths of English Language Learners. Among the strengths this group recorded are trusting, compassionate, mature, and capable. In addition to recording one adjective in each bubble, participants were asked to indicate "as evidenced by . . ." Having to provide an example or proof of each quality listed requires deeper analysis. When the group that created the Bubble Map below shared their responses, the other groups were particularly taken by several of their responses, notably their assertion that a strength of their ELL students is that they are "loving, as evidenced by the hugs every day."

Figure 11.2   Strengths of English Language Learners

Figure 11.3   Activity: Application: Identifying Student Strengths

Directions:

- Consider the strengths of the marginalized student or students to whom you have dedicated this work.
- Record adjectives that describe their strengths using a Bubble Map.
- For each strength recorded, indicate "as evidenced by…"

Reflection:

- What did you discover about your marginalized student or students?
- How might the strengths that you identified contribute to mastering school content?

Activating Student Strengths. Although identifying student strengths is a crucial step in changing the conversation about marginalized students, the real power of this exercise comes from putting the identified strengths into action. There are many ways to activate student strengths. For the participants of the workshop on educating English Language Learners, we turned to four assets identified by WIDA. (WIDA is an organization devoted to the academic achievement of linguistically diverse students.)

According to WIDA, the assets that linguistically diverse students possess fall into four categories: linguistic, cultural, experiential, and social and emotional assets. The question the workshop participants considered was how might these assets or strengths of English Language Learners be incorporated into learning and teaching?

Figure 11.4 shows some of their responses.

Figure 11.4   Activating the Strengths of English Language Learners

Asset	How to Incorporate Strengths Into Learning and Teaching
Linguistic	Pair students strategically Celebrate a different home country each month Use students' home language to build confidence Do projects in home language Incorporate books in students' home language
Cultural	Use art from home countries Incorporate sports from home countries Conduct multicultural nights Tap into country-specific background knowledge
Experiential	Compare and contrast ways of thinking, ways of doing things Make connections between language, culture, and academic methods
Social/Emotional	Use students as ambassadors for new students Acknowledge differences and similarities Designate them "experts" when reading about their countries

When teachers have a chance to explicitly think through and name the strengths of students who are commonly thought of as deficient in some way, attitudes and actions change. When teachers deliberately activate those strengths, students feel welcome and perform better. When deliberate attempts to identify and activate strengths are coupled with opportunities to consider where these deficit mindsets spring from and the damage they do, culture shifts can occur. The final section of this chapter will provide some suggestions on how to foster culture-changing conversations.

CHANGE THE CONVERSATION: ORCHESTRATE TIME AND SPACE FOR DIALOGUE

Educators can paint a portrait of possibilities by selectively editing what stories they tell about their marginalized students and by intentionally identifying and activating student strengths. Educators can also paint a portrait of possibilities by intentionally allocating the time and space needed to conduct the kinds of activities that contribute to a cultural shift in a school. One of the most powerful ways of doing this is to open up a space for text-based discussions in already existing venues, such as faculty meetings, grade-level meetings, book studies, and professional learning sessions.

Reading carefully selected texts and using carefully selected protocols to discuss the texts make up a powerful two-step strategy to begin shifting the conversation about marginalized students, a precursor to changing the culture.

Select Appropriate Texts

Fortunately for allies willing to shift the conversation, there are many individuals and organizations that present a different take on the causes and results of marginalization that can easily be used as discussion starters. These texts take many forms: articles, videos, multi-media presentations, etc. Several are included in this book, many of which are powerful conversation-changing texts. This list is in no way exhaustive. Once you begin searching for materials on a particular aspect of marginalization and inequity, you will find that the resources are deeper and more extensive than you might have imagined. One of your biggest challenges will be to figure out which texts to use. The following guidelines may be helpful.

- Use excerpts or short works. Short works that can be read or viewed during a class or meeting work better than longer ones. This is especially true when a group of participants is new to this kind of work.
- Go slowly. Select materials that elucidate a single, important concept rather than multiple ideas. Depth is important. Breadth can be built over time.
- Use material that is presented in accessible language. Scholarship is vitally important to understanding the complex nature of social justice and those forces that work against it. Scholarly texts, on the other hand, can become an impediment to enticing reluctant participants into the conversation.

○ Look for someone saying the same thing in a simpler way.

○ Where necessary, simplify the language yourself. (Produce one-pagers summarizing critical aspects of key scholars' thinking. Remember to credit their work by citing the original and indicating that you have summarized it.)

- Spend a session unpacking a single critical social justice concept or term. Some terms are multifaceted and therefore capture nuances better than circumlocutions.

- In addition to addressing an extremely important topic directed at educators from both a theoretical and practical perspective, *Everyday Antiracism: Getting Real About Race in School* (Pollock, 2008) is organized in a way that employs each of the elements described above. The book is made up of over sixty short essays divided into six umbrella topics. Each essay can be read and discussed in a single session. Each umbrella topic can be unpacked gradually, deepening understanding along the way. The material is highly accessible. It is written by teachers for teachers and includes practical actions educators can take to work against, thwart, and otherwise neutralize institutionalized inequity and marginalizing practices that are sewn into the fabric of school life.

There is much to be gained by building colleagues' social justice literacy through these methods. The same suggestions work for teachers willing to engage students in social justice conversations. Having teachers and students work together is a third, and extremely productive, way of addressing social justice issues. When teachers and students are co-learners, both begin to see each other differently, barriers tumble, and culture-changing conversations take place. Adding family and community members to the mix is a fourth approach that results in powerful cross-group conversations.

Use Protocols

Protocols are powerful. They prevent the two most common and destructive problems with open-ended discussion: monopolization and its counterpart, avoidance. We have all participated in classes or meetings in which one or two voices monopolize the conversation, often in a negative and counterproductive manner. I have little tolerance for those who so blatantly want to derail the conversation. I am equally frustrated by those who refuse to speak up at a meeting, sometimes out of passive-aggression, sometimes out of fear of being bullied by the stronger personalities in the room.

Avoidance and disrespectful behavior can also undermine a meeting. I once had a staff member who brought his copy of the *New York Times* to department meetings. I was shocked the first time this happened. He walked in, sat down, opened up the paper with great fanfare, then proceeded to read it, noisily turning the pages and obviously disassociating himself from the proceedings. I had no choice but to address the issue. As a result, he only did that once. Another diversionary tactic students and adults use when they want to disengage is the private, off-topic conversation.

To avoid monopolization and various forms of avoidance strategies, use discussion protocols that foster participation.

- Most text-based discussion protocols are open ended and delve into individual interpretations of text, which is often enough to encourage participation. Something as simple as the prompt "What resonated with you?" is a great discussion starter.
- Some are more formal, like Final Word Protocol, which spells out how, when, and for how long participants are to speak.
- Most are organized around small groups working together, followed by whole group sharing, thus optimizing opportunities for all voices to be heard.
- Opportunities for small and large groups to synthesize ideas and organize them around major themes are also helpful for processing.
- Converting these ideas into some form of visual display or a mime or a tableau—anything that gets participants to stretch their thinking and represent their ideas in nontraditional ways—is helpful on many levels.
- Creating a nonverbal representation of a complex understanding taps into the diverse and often underemployed skill sets that any group of people possesses.
- Creation and display of the products encourages camaraderie, lots of laughs, and totally unpredictable results.

In addition to text-based discussion protocols, there are many protocols that can be used to increase group cohesiveness and ability to collaborate, to develop discussion and sharing skills, and to increase a group's conflict-resolution skills. Two well-regarded resources are *The Adaptive School: A Sourcebook for Developing Collaborative Groups*, by Robert Garmston and Bruce Wellman, and *The Power of Protocols: An Educator's Guide to Better Practice*, by Joseph McDonald, Nancy Mohr, Alan Dichter, and Elizabeth McDonald. In addition to making meetings more efficient, focused, and democratic, most of the protocols can be easily adapted for use in classroom settings.

The critical issue is that the open exchange of ideas facilitated by deep and honest conversation is the most potent tool an organization can use to change its culture. Allies are born, nurtured, and supported in ongoing cross-power group conversations about the myriad manifestations of inequity and how to adequately respond to inequity institutionally.

Acknowledge That by Changing Nothing, Nothing Changes

Some claim that the purpose of an institution is to perpetuate itself. This principle is in operation in what has come to be termed institutional inertia or institutional resistance to change. Perhaps the most glaring example educators have regarding institutional inertia is the way learning and teaching, the way we "do'"' school, has remained largely unchanged over the last several hundred years. Further, these hard-wired ways have stayed in place despite several waves of reform, the influx of new and different learning and teaching technologies, and the proliferation of research on everything from brain-based learning to 21st century skill development.

There are many reasons, including psychological resistance to change, that keep our schools looking and feeling very similar to our counterparts of years gone by and, in some instances, adopting previously abandoned pedagogical methods.

Figure 11.5   Activity: Start a Culture-Changing Conversation

---

In the following anecdote, I report on a district practice that I inherited and eventually changed by changing the conversation.

Directions:
- After reading the anecdote, consider a longstanding practice that has far-reaching negative results for certain students.
- Describe the practice, why you think it is harmful, and speculate on how it might be changed or replaced.
- What types of conversations might be needed to change the culture that created and cemented the tradition in the first place?

The Speech and Recitation Competition. When I became the Director of English and Reading in another school district, I inherited a much-talked-about Speech and Recitation Competition. Every fourth- through eighth-grade student throughout the district participated in this event in which students memorized and recited short pieces written by others. To be a classroom winner was quite an accomplishment, but to be a building grade-level winner was even more so. The event culminated in a districtwide competition in which grade-level winners met their counterparts and did their presentations in front of an audience of family members, their classroom teachers who were relieved of teaching duties that day, their principals, and a panel of invited judges, usually notable people from the community.

I was responsible for coordinating the series of events, which virtually dominated classroom time from January until mid-March. I was responsible for sending out the memos about the competition, complete with rules and reminders, deadlines, and dates. When the districtwide competition day arrived in March, I was truly excited to meet the students, their families, their principals, and teachers.

Excitement, however, was not on the agenda that day. Anxiety was, and I could feel it and the tension anxiety produces. In this case, it produces a room full of young children with no sounds of joy, no playground jostling and jumping, no glow in the eye, no smile on the face, nothing childlike and carefree. Instead, the anxiety grew as the room filled up and the time for the competition got closer.

But it got worse. The judges were introduced. The competitors, audience, and judges were all reminded about the task for the Grade 4 students and the rules of the competition, and the scoring sheets were then distributed. The first contestant was called to the front of the room. The competition began. One by one, all seven fourth graders, called up in alphabetical order based upon the name of their school, stood in front of their family members, principals, and teachers and performed for the benefit of a panel of strangers. Judges' evaluation sheets were collected, tabulated, verified, and the winner was determined.

The hardest part was yet to come. All students were praised for their wonderful accomplishments and performances, a message no one wanted to hear. The only thing they wanted to know was who the winner was. When I announced the winner, the room suddenly burst into a cacophony of noise and movement. Cries of joy from the winner, her family, principal, and teacher (girls almost always won) mixed with cries of disbelief and bitter disappointment from the six "losers," some of whom had to be taken out of the room to be consoled.

I decided then and there that I would never again allow such heartbreak to be part of the school experience of the children for whom I was responsible. Their anguish and tears gave me the courage to challenge the thinking behind a district tradition that I believed to be pedagogically unsound (reciting from memory the words others had written), psychologically damaging (I once read that people fear speaking in public more than they fear dying), grossly unfair (some teachers were so heavily invested in this competition that they lobbied principals for students they thought had the potential to be next year's winners to be placed in their classes), and emotionally scarring (to bring joy to one winner, each grade level had approximately 700 other students who were "losers").

Changing the Conversation. I knew it would be risky to tackle a deeply rooted institutional tradition, but I felt I had no choice if I were to be an ally for the children I served. I needed to use my position to support the vast majority of students. I also knew that it was likely that raising this issue would require some convincing talk and strong allies. I marshaled my arguments, found allies, and formed a committee. In the end, we prevailed. The competition was downgraded to a festival, the tasks students were asked to do involved reading and writing original texts of varying kinds over various grade levels, and the grade-level representatives were randomly selected instead of competing for a place of honor.

Once allies are motivated to act, they can exert a powerful positive force in a school setting by taking deliberate steps to change the conversation about the school's most vulnerable students. When they work in conjunction with colleagues, they can work together to uncover the specific injustices perpetuated in their school, then craft the deliberate processes that will lead to systemic change. Systemic change grows out of unified commitment to a vision and personalized responses to particular contexts.

KEY CONSIDERATIONS FOR ALLIES

- Allies in the battle for social justice have three major tools that paint a portrait of possibilities about their marginalized students:
  - Consider the whole story before contributing another negative chapter to the dominant narrative about marginalized students.
  - Deliberately identify and activate the strengths of marginalized students.
  - Orchestrate time and space for having culture-changing conversations.
- **Looking Ahead**: Part III moves to a discussion about what it means to be an ally.

Part III

Embracing "Allyhood"

WHEN THE FOG LIFTS

Fogs disappear in curious ways. Sometimes a single sunray appears to laser its way through a weak opening in the fog. Other times the fog dissipates slowly in wispy, willowy swirls of evaporating gossamer threads. Sometimes it appears that a thick border separates the foggy from the fogless. Cross the line and you are suddenly in the clear.

Sometimes, and this is important, when it comes to social justice work, the fog returns, unheralded, unwanted, and unexpected. Frustrating as it is, fogs do return. Allies make mistakes. Social justice efforts take a step backward.

The reality of becoming an ally is that it is ongoing work, fraught with setbacks to be sure, but, like coming out of a thick fog, it is dizzily rewarding. For this reason, becoming an ally is work that needs to be embraced fully. It is work that can be aided by knowing what lies ahead, by recognizing the importance of the work, and by walking in the footsteps of those allies who came before. Knowing how they got through the fog emboldens us to find our way through it, too.

PART THREE OPENING ANECDOTE: CHICAGO FIFTH GRADERS TELL *THEIR* CHICAGO STORY

Before Michael Brown, an unarmed Black youth, was shot on the streets of Ferguson, Missouri, on August 9, 2014, the June media frenzy was feeding off stories of multiple killings in the South Side of Chicago. These killings led some inventive reporters to rename Chicago "Terror Town" and others to dub the Windy City "Chi-raq." A group of perceptive fifth-grade students was troubled by the way their neighborhood was being portrayed

169

by the media. They decided to fight back. Under the guidance of their teacher, Linsey Rose, they collectively wrote an opinion piece—a counternarrative—that appeared in the *Chicago Tribune* that set the record straight on several counts. At first read, their letter appears to be addressed to the media, who came into their neighborhood, took a quick look around, and wrote a portrayal of a community they never bothered to get to know. On a grander scale, the students' piece is addressed to anyone who has ever tried to narrate the lives of others without benefit of being a part of the community. There is much wisdom in what they wrote.

This is us, they began their piece. The assertion that they will tell others who they are is boldly placed at the beginning of the piece, and, as if to make the point even clearer, it is the only sentence in the first paragraph. This assertion leaves no doubt that these students will be narrating *their* version of who they are.

They tell why this is necessary in the next paragraph. "We saw your news trucks and cameras here recently and we read your articles, *Six Shot in South Shore Laundromat*." The students pull no punches. You reporters in "fancy suits," who spent less than twenty-four hours in the neighborhood "Don't really know us," they assert.

The piece also vividly recounts how "those who do not know us" see their community. You see "abandoned buildings everywhere, wood covered doors, police on the corner" and you think "all we are about is drugs and violence." We are "uneducated, jobless and thieves." That is why, they say, when outsiders see us coming, "You run into your cars, lock your doors" and "speed through these streets at 60 mph like you are on the highway."

In the next section, they contrast what outsiders see to their lived experience. They talk about the man on the corner who works at the store and gives them free Lemonheads. They introduce us to Precious, Aniya, and Nivia. They want outsiders to learn their names, to personalize them, to *see* the girls jumping rope on the corner. Then they correct a misconception. The people wearing suits are going to church, they explain. They are *not* going to a funeral. And that "creepy" dog is not to be feared. He is Saianis, Lamaur's dog.

They want the world to know who they are. "We are the kids who find crates, so we can shoot hoops." When the sun shines, "It is not God saying he wants to burn us; he sees us all with bright futures." Those who know the neighborhood children, they continue, choose to see the ones who are planning to go to college, not the dropouts.

Finally, they ask outsiders to really listen, to really observe. Listen, they counsel, and you will hear the laughter and chattering of "a group of girls who are best friends who really care about each other." "Look," they advise, "and you will see the smile on the cashier's face, when the kids walk in." Why? they ask rhetorically. Because, they end, "this neighborhood is filled with love."

Learning From Students

Students often teach us the most important lessons about life, and, thanks to these courageous, perceptive South Side Chicago fifth graders, educators who want to become allies in the battle for social justice can learn a lot about what embracing allyhood is not, along with what it is.

Allies do not appropriate other people's narratives. The students in Linsey Rose's class begin their editorial with three extremely crucial, highly charged, unequivocal words. "This is us." These words are more than just a simple introduction to the piece or a mild assertion of identity.

"This is us" are line-in-the-sand words, indicating that the media has crossed the line into territory that does not belong to visitors in "fancy suits."

"This is us" are wrestling words, words designed to wrest away from interlopers the control of a story about a community that belongs *to* the community, is *about* the community, and should be told *by* the community.

"This is us" is a pronouncement that fifth graders get what the media is doing, and they will not tolerate misrepresentation of their story or the appropriation of their story by those likely to gain by cherry picking a limited, sordid-filled version of the truth. These fifth graders know that even if the intention of the media is to make things better by reporting what is happening in their South Side Chicago community—something I personally do not think is motivating the media—that is not what happens. When a story is seized and retold by others, it is a robbery. It is a violation.

Allies use their privilege to amplify the voices of others. Linsey Rose is a true ally. She, like many other teachers and caring adults, used what was happening in her students' community as a vehicle to engage students in observing and critiquing sociopolitical issues. Students are much more perceptive than we often give them credit for. Educators who are allies pry open spaces for students to think through their perceptions, to discuss deeply what troubles them, and to find a venue for expressing their reflections and emotions.

Allies orchestrate opportunities for all students to excel. Those of us who have spent time "teaching" writing can only imagine the deep conversations that preceded and sustained the piece that was eventually produced and published by these students. Vivid descriptions, stunning observations, dramatic vignettes do not find their way into a collective piece of writing without deep processing, merciless editing, and crystal-clear purpose.

Allies do not take the easy way out. Even before I had a chance to speak to Linsey Rose, I detected the guiding hand of a dedicated educator behind the end product, someone who embraced allyhood. When we did speak, and I heard first hand from her how the process unfolded, my detection was confirmed and my admiration for the work of allies and what the students accomplished was magnified.

The backstory says it all. This op-ed piece was written during the last week of school in June 2014, when most educators and students are starting to check out. The week's worth of activities included reading a model text from Sandra Cisneros, coming up with a list of negative and positive aspects of their neighborhood, writing individual pieces based upon the model text and their discussions, and then working together to find, combine, and edit the phrases, images, and sentences that they felt best captured what they wanted to communicate.

Allies let the process unfold. For all of its brilliance and sophistication, the *Chicago Tribune* piece retains the voice of the fifth-grade writers, and that is a good thing. By not taking over the process of writing this piece, Linsey Rose opened up a space for her students to find their own voice, to liberate themselves from a hostile takeover by outside media interests, to fight back with their own words and ideas.

Allies resist taking over the process, so that those whom they are supporting can experience the joy of self-expression and self-liberation. Fortunately for us, their youthful, hopeful voices have been recorded. You can watch a video of the students reading their op-ed piece and telling their own story by using the following link: https://www.youtube.com/watch?v=W279eqUdiEU. You will not be disappointed.

The Importance **12** of Allies

O nce potential allies recognize the fog in which they live and they begin to seek out and embrace the dissonance they experience as the fog starts to lift, they are often anxious to begin the actual work of being an ally. To do this well, they need to examine and embrace what allyhood means.

The chapter will consider what it means to be an ally from multiple perspectives. It will question whether it is possible or even worthwhile to become an ally. The chapter will present the anatomy of an ally, as a way of explicating the prerequisites and characteristics that go into making responsible allies. It will end with a story about allies in action.

WHAT DOES IT MEAN TO BE AN ALLY? MULTIPLE PERSPECTIVES

What does it mean to be an ally? What are the roles and functions of allies? How does one "become" an ally? These may seem like simple questions at first. After all, the dictionary, common usage, and history provide us with a pretty clear sense of what it means to be an ally. Right? Well, not exactly. There are additional definitions, usages, and histories that can and should inform how people of privilege think about and think through what it means to be an ally. Ideally, they should do so before they launch into social justice work.

Many critiques of the notion that people of privilege could be allies also exist. These critiques make it clear that allies need to understand more deeply how critically important it is to read, to listen to, and to be open to the voices of the marginalized. The experiences of the marginalized with people who claim to be allies is significantly more important in social justice work than how you or I, as a person of privilege, choose to think about being an ally. Taking the time to read, listen to, and be open to the voices of the oppressed as they relate their experiences with allies—good and not so good—can help develop a more nuanced understanding of what it means to be an ally, what the roles and functions of allies are, and how one "becomes" an ally.

Like all lessons worth learning, this one did not come without a fair amount of discomfort. Nor is it complete.

The Power Factor in Ally Work

Before I found out more, I thought of *ally* as a positive—or at least neutral—term. I thought an ally was someone who worked with another for mutual benefit. What I did not recognize is that *mutual benefit* is difficult to achieve in a social context in which one ally has more power than another. One could argue—and believe me, I did—that people of privilege and oppressed people mutually benefit from the creation of a more just society.

This recognition does not mitigate the fact that certain allies have abused their power and privilege at the expense of those with whom they purport to be allied. In the process, they have transformed the word *ally* into a charged, often negative, word.

Allies: A Critique. The word *ally* and its associated forms *allyship* and *allyhood* have been the subject of numerous—sometimes virulent—critiques in recent years. Some activist writers claim allyship is a myth. Others have penned pieces in which they make the case *against* allies. The writer, activist, and founder of the website Black Girl Dangerous, Mia McKenzie, states unequivocally that she is "done" with allies.

What is going on? The issue, as I currently understand it, is not so much the fault of the word, as much as it is the fault of how some people have taken up the term. McKenzie says it best:

> *"Ally" cannot be a label that someone stamps onto you—or, god forbid, that you stamp on to yourself—so you can then go around claiming it as some kind of identity. It's not an identity. It's a practice. It's an active thing that must be done over and over again, in the largest and smallest ways, every day.*

What strikes me about McKenzie's take is that *ally* is more verb than noun, more way of life rather than nametag. It is not an honor to be conferred but an obligation to be met with relentless attention, constant soul searching, and inexhaustible patience. Indeed, McKenzie goes on to point out that the work of an ally *should* be exhausting because, as she puts it, being oppressed is exhausting. Any time they want, allies can walk away from the toll being an ally takes on them. The oppressed have no choice (McKenzie, 2015).

McKenzie's insights, hard as they may be to swallow initially, can continue to help to inform how you think about your role in anti-oppression work.

"Dining Off My People's Oppressions"

Unfortunately, it is easy to self-proclaim your status as an ally, to set yourself up as an expert on the lives of the oppressed, and to benefit from that identification. Many have done so. Still other self-congratulatory types, as well as grossly underprepared "allies," have taken a lot of heat recently, as well they should. Some people have made a living off being a spokesperson for the oppressed. One Black activist said in a workshop I attended that she was tired of those who "dine off my people's oppressions." What a powerful image to explain a totally unethical practice.

I-driven allies—those who put their egos before others—are suspect, disingenuous, and ultimately dangerous. *We-driven* allies—those who do the right thing for the benefit of all—are trustworthy, genuine, and potentially helpful.

Herein lies what might be viewed as a contradiction. In order to become a *we-driven ally*, potential allies need to do a fair amount of *I work*. At a minimum, they need to think through how their position makes them complicit in perpetuating injustice, and they need to think through and critique their reactions to past and present unjust incidents. These two tasks involve a lot of *I work*. In a sense, this is what I have been doing throughout this book: writing through my experiences, not to put me in the center of the work but rather to demonstrate how I have worked hard—and continue to work hard—to put myself in the background. I am convinced that this *I work* is essential. Ultimately, it forms a strong starting point for a journey that will eventually allow potential allies to be more *we-driven*.

BECOMING AN ALLY—IS IT POSSIBLE? IS IT WORTH IT?

Is it possible, or even worth it, to become an ally? My answer is yes. How allies understand what allies are; how allies decide to position themselves; and how allies choose to understand their role, function, and limitations, make all the difference in the world.

Several years ago, I read Anne Bishop's definition of an ally. It was not until I read the criticisms of allies, however, that I really understood the depth and breadth of what she was saying. According to Anne Bishop, "Allies are people who recognize the unearned privilege they receive from society's patterns of injustice and take responsibility for changing these patterns" (Bishop, 2002).

If we take apart this definition and contrast it to some of the criticism levied against purported allies, the picture becomes clearer. Anne Bishop says that allies are people who do two things intentionally. They *recognize* the privilege they receive from an unjust system and they *take responsibility* for changing those patterns. *Recognize* implies deep understanding, a good amount of soul searching, and a heavy dose of honesty. Coupling this recognition with the notion of *taking responsibility* for changing these patterns puts the emphasis on the fact that allies are always in a state of action, of becoming, of doing.

THE RESPONSIBLE ALLY

Acting responsibly could imply many things depending upon where you are in relation to privilege and oppression. One thing it does *not* mean is allies moving in with their own schemes to rescue the oppressed, which generally involves taking over; imposing their outsider views; showing up with a holier-than-thou, know-it-all attitude, part and parcel of the savior syndrome. Responsible allies studiously avoid the savior syndrome.

It is very instructive to see how a group of first nations peoples from Vancouver articulate the responsibilities of allyship. They maintain an excellent website called the Anti-Oppression Network (https:// theantioppressionnetwork.wordpress.com). One section deals directly with allyship.

The first point they make in their discussion of allyship is that allies—and they count themselves as allies—do not act out of guilt, but, similar to Anne Bishop's characterization, allies act out of responsibility. They then go on to flesh out what they believe becoming a responsible ally looks like. The section on allyship was written for PeerNetBC and used with informed consent and in a slightly altered form by the Anti-Oppression Network.

With the permission of the author, the formatting and punctuation used in the list of eight ways in which allies act responsibly has been maintained. This was done for two reasons. The first is out of respect for their work and the work of the others with whom they collaborated. The second is to emphasize that they made deliberate and symbolic choices in formatting the list. According to the author of the piece, venessa, using the pronoun *we* is intended to imply that everyone is in this work together and that the author is not "exempt" from learning. Eliminating capital letters is, as venessa says, "a way to mess with academic perfectionism, intellectualism, etc." (2016, personal correspondence).

Allyship Responsibilities

- **We actively acknowledge our privileges and openly discuss them:** we recognize that as recipients of privilege we will always be capable of perpetuating systems of oppression from which our privilege came
- **We listen more and speak less:** we hold back on our ideas, opinions, and ideologies, and resist the urge to "save" the people we seek to work with as they will figure out their own solutions that meet their needs
- **We do our work with integrity and direct communication:** we take guidance and direction from the people we seek to work with (not the other way around), and we keep our word
- **We do not expect to be educated by others**: we continuously do our own research on the oppressions experienced by the people we seek to work with, including herstory/history, current news, and what realities created by systems of oppression look, feel, smell, taste and sound like
- **We build our capacity to receive criticism,** to be honest and accountable with our mistakes, and recognize that being called out for making a mistake is a gift—that it is an honour of trust to receive a chance to be a better person, to learn, to grow, and to do things differently
- **We embrace the emotions that come out of the process of allyship**, understanding that we will feel uncomfortable, challenged, and hurt
- **Our needs are secondary to the people we seek to work with:** we are responsible for our self-care and recognize that part of the privilege of our identity is that we have a choice about whether or not to resist oppression; we do not expect the people we seek to work with to provide emotional support
- **We do not expect awards or special recognition** for confronting issues that people have to live with every day

This description of what it means to be a responsible ally is succinct, comprehensive, and doable, almost a GPS system for potential allies to avoid going down blind alleys, getting lost, and needing to double back in order to get on the right track. Referencing this guidance system is important for potential allies who want to act responsibly.

Figure 12.1 Activity: Becoming a Responsible Ally

The Anti-Oppression Network identifies itself as "a community collective dedicated to helping individuals, community collectives, groups, non profit organizations and society as a whole re-evaluate, unlearn, relearn, and understand, in a deep and meaningful way, the importance of decolonization and anti-oppression principles and policy. We are interested in building self-capacity in order to fully support and utilize privileges in the best interest of marginalized beings and mother earth."

It takes deliberate moves and concerted thought to reevaluate, unlearn, relearn, and understand in deep and meaningful ways. This activity is designed to provide a process to do so.

Directions:

- Select at least two of the responsibilities of allies identified and described by the Anti-Oppression Network.
- For each, consider: In what ways might their articulation of this responsibility help you to "re-evaluate, unlearn, relearn and/or understand, in a deep and meaningful way" what it means to be an ally?
- For each, consider: In what ways might consistent, faithful, and widespread application of this responsibility contribute to building "self-capacity of marginalized beings"?
- Use the table below to record your answers.

What Responsible Allies Do	How does this responsibility help me "re-evaluate, unlearn, relearn, and/understand, in a deep and meaningful way" what it means to be an ally?	In what ways might consistent, faithful, and widespread application of this responsibility contribute to building "self-capacity of marginalized beings"?
we actively acknowledge our privileges and openly discuss them		
we listen more and speak less		
we do our work with integrity and direct communication		
we do not expect to be educated by others		
we build our capacity to receive criticism		

we embrace the emotions that come out of the process of allyship		
our needs are secondary to the people we seek to work with		
we do not expect awards or special recognition		

THE ANATOMY OF AN ALLY: THE POSITION AND THE PERSON

When people move into a new role, generally two key questions concern them. What does the job entail and do I have the right stuff to do the job adequately?

What the Position Entails

- ***Allies Act.*** According to the Department of Education, in 2011 in the United States, there were almost 133 million public schools, over 3 million public school teachers, serving 50 million students. Coupled with the administrators, students, and families associated with these schools, educators, and those most closely associated with education, are a force to be reckoned with. We have numbers on our side.

Educators also have standing within the community. Most importantly, regardless of the policies imposed by state and federal mandates, which often dictate what needs to be done in an educational setting, educators maintain control over how these policies will be implemented. In other words, the culture of the school is created and sustained by how educators orient themselves to the work, the conditions under which they want to see the school function, the relationships and linkages that they create with students and the community.

Educators can position themselves as responsible allies or they can remain impassive or quietly angry over the injustices they see in their schools and communities. Responsible allies orient themselves to the work by showing support for others, by demonstrating commitment to end oppression, and by responding to invitations to use their privilege to dismantle unfair systems.

Responsible allies also recognize that

- ***Allies Band Together.*** The battle against oppression, marginalization, and injustice is a fierce one that requires strategic use
  of every resource available. In so many ways, educators working
  in conjunction with marginalized groups and like-minded allies
  from a wide swath of society represent an untapped, enormously
  valuable resource. Working together provides the energy and
  weight needed to dismantle unjust systems as they play out in
  schools and society.
- ***Allies Have Access.*** In addition to numbers, allies possess talents, knowledge, and access that can be used to support efforts
  to reduce prejudice and beef up justice. Most social justice efforts
  have had to depend upon allies who were not members of the
  marginalized group for support. Allies use their access and skills
  to support marginalized peoples in their efforts to think through
  their lived experiences, tell their stories, and lobby for change.

Multiple opportunities for being responsible allies present themselves
to educators. They can be proactive in the classroom, in the faculty
room, and in the community.

- ***Allies Bring Groups Together.*** Allies do not need to look far
  to find individuals and groups who suffer from marginalization.
  Educators, then, also have the ability to bring these students
  together so that they can join forces to fight marginalization and
  prejudice no matter how it manifests itself. Frequently, marginalized groups spend all of their time and resources on their own
  issues rather than banding together to fight the common problem.
  It is true that different groups experience different forms of prejudice, but in the end, the root causes cut across all groups experiencing bias, exclusion, and other forms of injustice.

The systems that support inequity are deeply ingrained, powerful, and
highly resistant to change. Combined efforts and a pronounced sense
of solidarity have a much better chance of dismantling these systems
than do individual or small-scale efforts.

- ***Allies Broker Change.*** By definition, those who are not marginalized possess and exercise more power than those who are
  marginalized. Because of this power, allies can broker change.
  They can speak out in places and under circumstances that are
  not accessible to those marginalized.

The teacher who stands up to a colleague who makes an insensitive comment in the faculty room and offers to have an extended conversation about why the comment is insensitive is an ally brokering change in a space inaccessible to a marginalized student. The teacher who offers to sponsor an LGBTQ club and discussion group is exercising a power not granted to students. The member of a discipline committee who points out the disproportionate number of males and students of color who receive discipline referrals and makes suggestions on how this information could be shared and policies changed is using his or her position of privilege to undercut and challenge discriminatory practices.

The Anatomy of an Ally: Prerequisites and Characteristics

No two allies in the battle for social justice are the same. Their circumstances and contexts are different. Their skills and talents are different. Their possibilities and limitations are different. How they are asked to help is different. But, in the end, there is a foundation and orientation to the work of being an ally that enables allies to be effective, and, at the same time, it enables them to thrive in a climate that is often uninformed, resistant, and hostile.

There is an anatomy of an ally that is basic, recursive, and essential to ensure that bias and marginalization are reduced, that equity and justice flourish, and that the ally survives and thrives in the process.

Securely Anchored and Unreservedly Active. The anatomy of allies in the battle for social justice consists of two seemingly contradictory characteristics. They are simultaneously securely anchored and unreservedly active. The two complement each other and are more powerful for it.

Allies who are anchored in a firm knowledge and appreciation of their own identity, history, and sociopolitical culture are not challenged by diversity. Instead, those with secure self-identity are able to joyfully embrace, celebrate, and negotiate other identity groups and the diversity they represent with empathy, curiosity, and delight.

This grounding in self-awareness and respect is a foundation and launching pad for social justice action, the second characteristic of allies. Allies take individual and collective steps to withstand the pernicious effects of injustice levied against themselves and others. Buoyed by deep self-awareness, profound respect for others, and the fortitude to withstand the attacks of those who wish to maintain the status quo, allies are spurred to individual and collective action to oppose prejudice, dismantle unjust systems, and fight against narrow interests and destructive ways of being.

Although the characteristics of social justice allies (being anchored and being active) are presented as two aspects of the anatomy of an ally, they should be considered to be interrelated and mutually supportive rather than two unique and separate traits to be developed in an isolated or sequential manner.

For allies who also happen to be educators, these descriptions can also represent the goals of the learning and teaching activities and orientation that they bring to the classroom or school. In other words, educator-allies intentionally aim to anchor students in a strong sense of self that enables celebration of others and that ultimately leads to students becoming active in combating injustice as they see and experience it.

Figure 12.2 below summarizes the anatomy of an ally. It also demonstrates the relationship among and between each of the elements that make up the anatomy of an ally.

Figure 12.2 Anatomy of an Ally

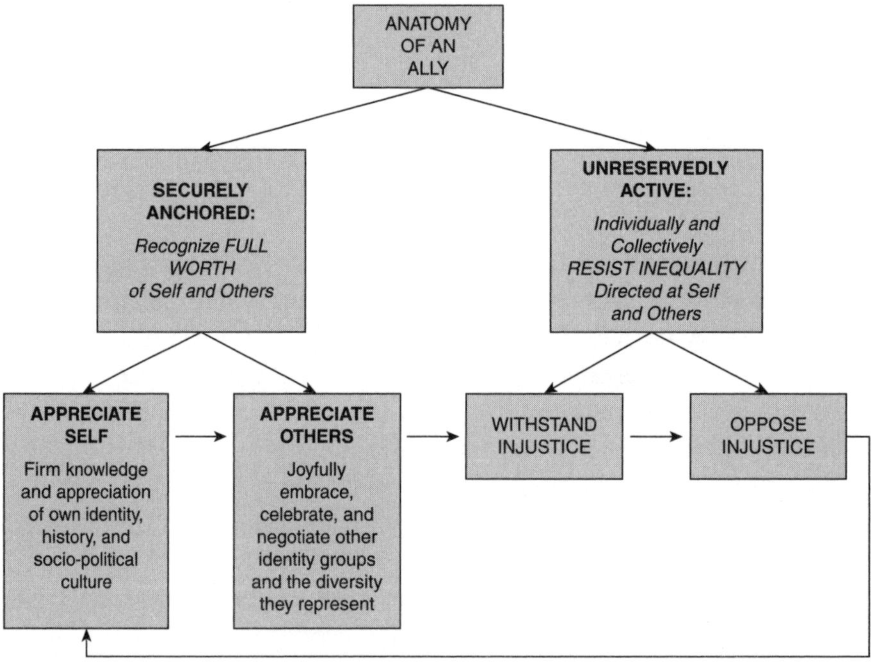

Allies who appreciate themselves do not feel threatened by others. Lack of fear of others enables them to develop compassion and empathy. Compassion and empathy enables allies to understand fully the political, social, cultural, and historical implications of injustice. This understanding spurs them to stand up to inequity, so that they can actively engage in identifying and opposing manifestations of injustice no matter what form they take. Furthermore, the process is reciprocal and recursive. Each time an ally strengthens self-appreciation, appreciation of others deepens, which enables the ally to withstand and oppose justice in continuously stronger ways.

The preceding discussion suggests that allies are both securely anchored and unreservedly active. Potential allies might well be curious about where they stand in relation to these characteristics. The activity in Figure 12.3 will help you make this assessment.

Figure 12.3   Activity: Anatomy of an Ally Self-Assessment

Directions: The table below summarizes what it means to be securely anchored and unreservedly active. Read each description and complete the self-assessment associated with each one.

ANATOMY OF AN ALLY: SELF-ASSESSMENT	
SECURELY ANCHORED	
To be anchored means to appreciate yourself and others in a way that is centered, unwavering, and thorough. <ul><li>*Appreciation* is a complex term.</li><li>It means recognizing your worth and the worth of others.</li><li>It also means possessing a heightened understanding of the implications of the political, social, historical, and cultural factors that influence your personal identity and social standing, as well as those of others.</li></ul>	
Directions: Think through the ways in which you are securely anchored as an ally, using the following descriptions and questions as an aid.	
Probing Questions	***Self-Assessment***
1. A. In what ways do you **recognize** the full worth of yourself and others? Give specific examples of how you currently <ul><li>**Value** yourself and others.</li><li>**Treasure** yourself and others.</li><li>**Admire** yourself and others.</li></ul> B. In what additional ways **could** you more fully recognize the full worth of yourself and others?	

(Continued)

Figure 12.3 (Continued)

Probing Questions	Self-Assessment
2. A. In what ways do you currently demonstrate that you understand the implications of the political, social, historical, and cultural factors that shape identity and establish social positioning? Give specific examples that demonstrate that you • **Acknowledge** the historical legacies that affect yourself and others. • **Are conscious of** and **sensitive to** these legacies. • **Refuse to ignore** them, **minimize** them, or in any other way **deny** the power of these legacies. B. In what additional ways **could** you more fully demonstrate that you understand the implications of the political, social, and cultural factors that shape identity and establish social positioning?	

UNRESERVEDLY ACTIVE
Social justice work requires allies to engage in individual and collective action **with** others, **alongside** others, **on behalf** of others. • Social justice action centers on resistance to inequality, whether the inequality is directed at allies themselves and the groups they belong to or others. • *Resist*, as used in this context, has multiple meanings. It means to both **withstand** and **oppose** inequality.
Directions: Think through the ways in which you are **unreservedly active** as an ally, using the following descriptions and questions as an aid.

Probing Questions	Self-Assessment
1. A. In what ways do you withstand inequality? Give specific examples of how you currently • **Withstand** the inevitable pushback, resistance, and anger that are directed at you and others.	

Probing Questions	Self-Assessment
B. In what additional ways **could** you withstand inequality?	
2. A. In what ways do you **oppose** inequality? Give specific examples of how you individually or with others effectively plan, execute, and evaluate strategies that whittle away at or completely dismantle the unjust systems, the accepted beliefs, and the taken-for-granted actions that exclude certain groups, that diminish self-worth, that are patently unfair. B. In what additional ways **could** you oppose inequality?	

Extension and Team Activity

Working with at least one other colleague, conduct the same analysis, considering the ways in which your school as an institution possesses the anatomy of an ally. Using the same probing questions you used for your self-assessment, consider the ways in which your school is securely anchored and unreservedly active.

ALLIES IN ACTION

A major premise of this chapter is that when responsible allies subjugate personal interests to the greater good, band together with other like-minded people, and work purposefully to oppose injustice, change can happen. The following anecdote is one story of allies who put all of these moves together to work on behalf of students.

The Context. In successive waves beginning in the 1970s, the public pastime in many parts of the country was teacher bashing coupled with a virulent anti-tax movement. This translated into failed school budgets, shattered morale, and a general malaise among educators. In one school district where the attacks on school personnel were particularly virulent over a period of years, a small group of unlikely, but equally outraged, citizens decided to fight back.

What Allies Were Up Against. Putting aside all of their historic and deeply felt real differences, they decided to find common ground and from that build a coalition to fight the real enemy: the tax-pac groups that were stripping schools of critical funding, measuring classrooms to determine how many students could physically fit into how many square feet of space, spending countless hours figuring out how to cut the petty cash funds to bring down the tax rate increase by a negligible sum, publishing the salaries of teachers in the local papers, publically denouncing school administrators as "blood sucking sloths," refusing to negotiate expired contracts, and more. In short, this small but influential group was systematically grinding down the life of the school.

What Allies Did. Leaders of the counterattack understood that among all of the vilified groups in the community, there was a common interest in returning the schools to places in which the focus was on learning and where children could thrive. In the end, they won. The lesson was instructive. Teachers and teachers unions, families and community groups, administrators and boards of education have distinct, long-standing roles, responsibilities, and constituent groups. However, when being manipulated for counterproductive ends, they could—and should—band together to fight the real threats that are trying to tear apart their communities and what their communities stand for.

KEY CONSIDERATIONS FOR ALLIES

- What it means to be a responsible ally is informed by multiple points of view, historical perspectives, and fearless consideration of critiques of allies.
- Allies consciously recognize the privilege they receive from unjust situations and they commit to responsibly counteracting injustice.
- Because allies are securely anchored and unreservedly active, they willingly accept the challenge to reevaluate, learn, unlearn, and deeply understand the importance of decolonization and anti-oppression principles and policies.
- Allies are important.
- **Looking Ahead.** Becoming an effective and responsible ally often involves navigating through and learning from mistakes and challenging situations. The next chapter will provide some examples of the problems that might be encountered and some methods of learning from them and getting past them.

False Starts, Missteps, and Minefields 13

Allies are not immune from making mistakes. It is part of the learning process. This chapter begins with one such mistake and then analyzes the lessons learned from it. It then looks at three enemies of allies: pride, impatience, and vacillating commitment. The chapter ends with another anecdote. In this story, the ideology of *color blindness* is challenged and the merit of waging strategic battles is demonstrated.

ALLIES MAKE MISTAKES

Several years ago, I was collaborating with a group of teachers and administrators on the topic of equity-informed leadership. The major point of the session was that equity-informed leadership required as much heart work as head work. I spent a good deal of time developing an activity that I thought would be eye opening. I presented participants with five leaders known for having made significant contributions to the advancement of social justice: Nelson Mandela, Mahatma Gandhi, Malala Yousafzai, Desmond Tutu, and Martin Luther King Jr. I asked participants to compare any two leaders to see what characteristics they had in common, then to compare those comparisons with the ones their colleagues came up with. In the end, the goal was to isolate a handful of common characteristics shared by highly regarded champions of social justice. What I had in mind were qualities such as empathy, love, and respect, along with courage, single-mindedness, and clear thinking.

The group I was working with consisted of White and Black educators, some of whom were deeply engaged in and well versed about social justice work, and others who were still trying to figure out why any of this mattered. One of the better-informed, highly active, and more critical thinkers in the group was a Black male high-school principal. He waited until the directions had been given, raised his hand slowly, and asked, "Who chose these examples?" I acknowledged it was me. "Why, then," he continued, "did you not choose someone like Malcolm X?" Or, I later questioned myself, why did I not select Cesar Chavez or Che Guevara?

The room went quiet. All eyes were on me. I tried to think of something to say.

I could have sidestepped the situation, offered lame excuses, and went on with the activity as planned. Instead, I acknowledged that the principal raised an interesting question and I admitted that I needed to think about why I made the selection I did. Then I did something I never would have done in the past. I scrapped the planned activity and opened up the floor for discussion. Engaging in an open, unrehearsed, collective rethinking of the choices I made had other benefits, too, since many different perspectives were held by those present in the room.

My plan was obviously a false start, I made a major misstep, and I stepped on a minefield. Instead of evading the issue and making excuses—proving that I had good reason to do what I did—I decided that openness, honesty, and humility were the best ways of handling the situation. I realized that without thinking this through thoroughly, I had no hope of learning from the experience, and I wagered the same was true for the majority of the participants.

What followed was a free-flowing, fruitful, and fascinating discussion. Some participants indicated they saw nothing wrong with my list. Others accused me of consciously or unconsciously trying to keep the conversation "safe," likely for my benefit and the benefit of the other White people in the room. Some said that there could be no discussion of putting heart into equity work without acknowledging the anger that inequity breeds. What, then, someone asked, constitutes a responsible response to years of marginalization, systemic racism, and crippling classism? What forms of protest should we allow or expect on our streets, in our communities, and in our schools? What about the role of the media? Why are some protests called acts of civil disobedience and others riots?

As these questions emerged and were batted about, much emotion bubbled to the surface. Anger, disbelief, intransigence, sharp words, hostile words, dismissive words were all part of the mix. It was clear that, despite all the work that the district had done up to this point, there remained social justice nooks and crannies that had somehow been avoided in the past. With some, newfound clarity emerged. With others, not so much—yet. A lot depended upon where people were in their coming to understand injustice and oppression. What did become clear, however, was that having time dedicated to talk through and think through injustice is necessary, should be repeated often if an organization is to have a chance at getting social justice right, and to do so requires a heavy dose of courage.

Lessons Learned—So Far

I learned much about equity work and my own prejudices during this session.

- ***Honesty and humility are friends of those becoming allies.*** We do sometimes get it wrong, not for want of trying, but for lack of experience or knowledge or careful thought. Covering up mistakes is the real mistake in this work.
- ***Openness is the door to learning.*** The principal was very open about the discomfort he felt about my carefully edited list of leaders to be considered. Good for him. I was open to the fact that I may have been operating with a single-minded goal that left out an important part of the story. If I was willing to acknowledge that leadership required heart, I also had to acknowledge that hearts can harbor a variety of emotions, including anger, rage, and hopelessness. Everyone who participated in the exchanges demonstrated openness to say what they thought, to challenge each other, to expand the discussion to larger social issues.
- ***Avoid rerouting the discussion.*** Talking about race is often uncomfortable, something many of us have been programmed to avoid. Wading in is much more fruitful.
- ***Open forums need to be created for a genuine exchange of ideas.*** District leadership had made it clear that addressing inequity and racism were key to the development of the district, that overcoming a history of inequity and racism is a process, and that open discussion was the key element in the change process.
- ***Do not hide from discomfort, yours and others.*** Discussions around race raise emotions. That is a given. Allies push themselves and others to think through the reasons for this discomfort so that they can get past it. Sometimes the discomfort comes from simply not knowing how to talk about race. Fear of saying the wrong thing is a strong deterrent to pushing past this discomfort. Allies provide opportunities for those in a dominant position to understand terms and stances that are offensive to those marginalized, including explanations of why some terms are to be avoided and others employed.

- ***Do not hide from vulnerability, yours and others***. The stakes are very high in anti-oppression work. Uncovering and interrogating the ways in which oppression operates exposes the raw nerves, the unhealed wounds, the deep hurts of the victims of oppression. At the same time, those in privileged positions can experience powerful avoidance emotions: silence, denial, guilt, shame.

One of the most significant fault lines in antiracism work is what has been labeled "White fragility," the withdrawal, the tears, the breakdown that White people often experience when confronted by the painful reality of racial injustice (DiAngelo, 2011). Those becoming allies need to recognize the many manifestations of "race-based stress" in order to get beyond their own low threshold for discomfort and help others to get beyond it, too. One anti-oppression activist I know referenced her frustration in having to deal with what she called "White women's tears."

False Starts, Missteps, and Minefields Abound

In retrospect, I see that my choice of social justice leaders known for their nonviolent approach to change demonstrated what Martin Luther King Jr. so aptly described in his *Letter from Birmingham Jail* as the White moderate's devotion to "order" rather than to justice, a common mistake, Dr. King says, among people of "good will." My choices suggested that I agreed with the goal of social justice, but like the White moderate and people of good will Dr. King described, at that moment, my choices proved that I valued the "absence of tension" and wanted to avoid, at all costs, direct, confrontational, socially upsetting action.

Dr. King, however, reminded us that neither I nor any other person of good will had any right to set the conditions upon which the system of oppression should be unraveled. In trying to do so, was I also in some roundabout way trying to "set the timetable for another man's freedom" (King, 1963)? I certainly hope not, although honesty compels me to say that no person of privilege can feel the same sense of urgency for oppressive systems to topple than those who toil under the weight of oppression every moment of their lives.

Clearly, my structuring of the activity landed me squarely in a trap of privilege. This realization left me embarrassed, humbled, and more committed than ever to think through the ways in which my position continually works to blunt my understanding of what it takes to dismantle oppressive systems. False starts, missteps, and minefields do, indeed, abound.

ENEMIES OF ALLIES: PRIDE, IMPATIENCE, AND ON-AGAIN, OFF-AGAIN COMMITMENT

As educators, we have devoted ourselves to the learning-teaching process, trying, to the best of our ability, to figure out how this complex process actually works. Sometimes we are successful, often for reasons we cannot articulate.

We also know that the more complex the concepts, the more emotionally charged the subject matter, and the more ingrained the ways of thinking and doing are, the more challenging the learning-teaching process will be. The concepts that make up social justice—oppression, privilege, and power—are complex, emotionally charged, and fraught with unquestioned and habitual ways of thinking and acting. What this suggests, then, is that coming to grips with social justice issues is fraught with false starts, missteps, and minefields.

As educators, we are working on two fronts: our own learning and the learning of others. Throughout the book, I have presented many examples of the kinds of false starts and missteps that I have made and the minefields that I have stepped on in my ongoing quest to reevaluate, unlearn, relearn, and understand deeply and meaningfully concepts and ways of being and doing that are incompletely understood by me or others. Rather than repeat these examples here, I would like to summarize what I see as three key pitfalls that those becoming allies in the battle for social justice can become prey to, which can lead them into taking false steps, making missteps, and/or triggering minefields too numerous to mention.

Pride: "Surely, We Know What Their Problems Are"

Sadly, a first nations community in Canada made the national news when a young member of the community opened fire in a school, killing several people. My sadness over these events was compounded by anger when I heard a comment made by a popular news anchor.

A group of invited political commentators—not one of whom represented the first nations communities—was discussing the many ways in which the lives of first nations peoples have been compromised by long-standing government policies, resulting in poor living conditions and numerous social problems. Everyone, including the anchor, acknowledged that conditions can—and must—be improved. To his credit, one of the commentators posited that the best way to begin to turn things around was to ask the community what they felt their problems, challenges, and needs were. The anchor, who believes being hard hitting and uncompromising are important qualities, vehemently interjected, "*Surely*, we know what their problems are!" The anchor then moved on to another issue.

Privilege-fueled pride makes comments like this one possible and turns marginalized peoples away from any desire to work with people of privilege. The bald truth is that no one can—or should—speak for another. People of privilege have tried to impose their will on marginalized people for centuries—often by force, sometimes in more subtle ways—and it has yet to work. Privilege-fueled pride calls us to insert ourselves where we have not been invited or needed, to speak louder and longer than is our right, to blab publicly about our efforts on behalf of others.

Privilege-fueled pride can often make two other mistakes. The first is to think that our minor skirmishes with feeling left out or momentarily being a minority are even remotely similar to a lifetime living inescapably on the margins. A week spent in a wheelchair may sensitize you to the condescension, challenges, and discrimination faced by differently abled people, but it would be inappropriate for you to equate that experience with that of a person with lifelong physical challenges or to claim you "totally understand" what differently abled people go through or that you have any authority to speak for them.

Privilege-fueled pride can become an impediment, too, if you put yourself forward as an ally and your offer is refused—and it could happen. The movement of liberation, full inclusion, and anti-oppression does not belong to those in positions of privilege. It belongs to and needs to be run by those who have a legitimate claim to the cruelty of oppression. When, and if, they determine they need or want help, they will ask for it.

Accept that some marginalized people may be angry and you may be a target of that anger, not because of who you are personally, but by virtue of what and whom you represent. So be it.

Accept that your major social justice work among marginalized groups might be in building trust before working side by side dismantling systems of oppression. Accept that you may have to redirect your energies to working among those members of your identity group before you will be accepted as a partner in a united attack against injustice.

Humility may be one of the best allies to becoming an effective ally.

Impatience

The fervor of a convert can often overtake people who embrace social justice as a personal calling. Often, newcomers do not understand how steep the learning curve actually is for themselves and others. This can cause them to become impatient with themselves or others as they engage in the work and face head-on the inevitable leaps forward and the enormous backward dives that make up the trajectory of coming to understand and articulate injustice, of negotiating a useful and responsible role, and of seeing with clarity what the marginalized see vividly. Those becoming allies beat back the frustration that impatience generates.

On-Again, Off-Again Commitment

Those becoming allies do not quit, do not look for quick fixes, and do not hold back.

Injustice, unfairness, bias, and prejudice rarely go on vacation. Nor do their victims. Oppression *is* a pressure, a constant, unrelenting weight. Becoming an ally in the battle for social justice requires unrelenting commitment to the work, whether marginalized people are within earshot or not.

If you are present in the faculty room when a group of teachers complains about the large numbers of classified students in their classes, you need to challenge them. Ableism, manifested in negative and prejudicial attitudes toward the differently abled, is pervasive in many schools. Even though there may not be a differently abled person in earshot, complaints about the number of classified students can be used to challenge accepted ableist assumptions. For instance, the literature is clear that inclusion has had largely positive effects for classified students, especially with regard to the larger goal of social integration of classified children. It has also contributed to all children learning that diversity is a natural part of the human condition (Hehir, 2003).

Undertaking a challenge such as the one suggested above is not without risks. Your tone of voice and your choice of words matter as much as the content of what you say. Beginning your challenge with statements such as, "You know, I was just reading about inclusion and it got me thinking that there may be another way to look at this," helps to make you sound less strident, so others might actually listen. Having facts and figures generally helps to anchor the challenge in what is perceived to be objective, authoritative data. Positioning your arguments in what is best for students—social integration of the differently abled and a keener understanding of the human condition by all students—tends to appeal to most educators.

One word of caution needs to be sounded. Allies need to avoid having colleagues roll their eyes, saying, "Here she goes again." Think strategically about when and how to address a hurtful comment or to challenge a prevailing notion or to beat back an oppressive policy. Allies may need the time to think through what transpired, to find the "data" to support their position, or to find other like-minded people who may be helpful in addressing any given situation.

Strategically postponing a challenge is not the same as ignoring or avoiding addressing a wrong, as the following anecdote helps to illuminate.

WAGE STRATEGIC BATTLES

One of the terms that trips up well-meaning White people is the term *color-blind.* How problematic this term is came into sharp focus recently and opened up a space for a healthy discussion of why this term is problematic. The discussion took a while to unfold and it is still a work in progress.

A letter to the editor that was intended to praise a grant-funded after-school care program became an abject lesson in race relations when the mother of one of the participants wrote a letter to the editor thanking the mostly Black staff for teaching her son to be "color-blind." In the letter, the mother identified herself as White and her child as "very privileged." She also indicated that initially she did not want to send her son to this particular afterschool program because it is situated in a historically Black part of town and did not have a pool and a water safety program. In the end, however, its location had some other logistical advantages for her ex-husband and herself.

When the president of the PTA, a White woman, read the letter, she copied it and proudly disseminated it to the all-White PTA executive board, the school staff, and the afterschool program staff. She had plans to make it available at the next PTA meeting.

The recently hired principal was far less happy.

She was concerned that Black families could be bothered—justifiably—by the way their community was represented, by the fact that a White person of means was taking up a valuable spot in the program, and especially by the use of the term *color-blind.* She was well aware that the school needed to address the racial and class issues raised by this letter. Among them were questions about how families were selected to participate in the program, how many other families that did not meet the economic means test or were out of the school catchment area were in the program, and why in a school with a mixed racial and ethnic background the PTA executive board was all White. The principal also wondered about what other long-standing legacies of injustice and inequity might be part of the history of this school.

The principal viewed the appearance of the letter as an opportunity to jumpstart the process of delving into these issues, but the steps she took were deliberate. She began with the immediate one: the letter.

In a private meeting with the PTA president, she brought it up. The principal listened carefully to what the PTA president had to say about why she wanted to disseminate the letter further, agreed that it is always nice to have "positive" press about their school, and then, in true ally form, asked the PTA president to consider a few things that the principal found troubling about the letter. The principal indicated that she had concerns about how members of the community might take the letter. At first baffled, the PTA president listened. Much to her credit, the president of the PTA agreed that the letter could seem insulting and condescending. The principal then asked the PTA president what she understood *color-blind* to mean. Like the well-meaning mother who wrote the letter, the PTA president thought being color-blind was a virtue. The principal explained how claiming to not see color could be interpreted by a person *of* color. Color, the principal pointed out, is very real. It shapes life experiences and figures prominently in many injustices, including unprovoked murders, as the news of multiple race-related killings by White police officers tragically makes evident.

To her credit, the president of the PTA thanked the principal for sharing her insights, admitted that she never thought through any of the points the principal made, and asked the principal to continue her efforts to educate her, the rest of the board, and anyone else on the staff and in the community that might need it. The president of the PTA clearly signaled that she was willing to take opportunities to learn, a stance Anne Bishop equates with an important step in becoming an ally (Bishop, 2002).

Although still a work in progress, tentative plans to address race and class issues at the school include engaging leadership, staff, students, and community members in a discussion about how to best address the way race plays out in their school and in the community.

This story contains important lessons for allies. To act is important, but when and how are equally important. The principal chose to address the PTA president in private and in a respectful way. She strategically asked questions that would lead the PTA president to see the letter from a different perspective. She explained why the term *color-blind* is troublesome. She jumped at the opportunity when the president left the door open for further discussion of racial issues with a wider audience.

Reevaluating, Unlearning, Relearning, and Understanding Color Blindness

What transpired in this scenario is not uncommon. A well-meaning individual—or group of individuals—goes out on a limb to "do the right thing," only to find out that the effort reinforces hierarchical and oppressive arrangements, attitudes, and actions. In this case, the arrangements, attitudes, and actions surrounding the concept *color blindness* need to be reevaluated, unlearned, relearned, and understood more deeply.

The mother who wrote the letter is not alone in thinking that "color blindness" is a noble goal. A 2014 study of millennials' attitudes toward bias indicates that most young people think racism is a problem of the past and that society would improve if race were not considered. Indeed, they also believe that focusing on race prevents color blindness, which they view as a condition to which society should aspire (MTV Strategic Insights & David Binder Research, 2014).

Figure 13.1 provides an aide to reevaluate, unlearn, relearn, and understand *color blindness*. The first column contains the types of comments that people who say they are *color-blind* often make. The second column presents an alternate reading. The third column addresses how the concept of *color blindness* contributes to racism by demonstrating the larger psychological, cultural, and historical issues raised by the comments.

A Tool for Considering Other Perspectives

An extraordinarily effective way to avoid false starts, missteps, and minefields is to think through how marginalized individuals might react to or see a situation like the letter mentioned above. Doing so intentionally in a prescribed manner can help. One intentional way is to compose a dialogue poem. Writing a dialogue poem forces the writer to confront two opposing worlds and, by doing so, to see the world through different lenses.

Dialogue Poem. Dialogue poems, or poems in two voices, have existed since the Middle Ages. They can also be highly effective tools for understanding inequality (Christiansen, 2015).

Figure 13.1 Reevaluating, Unlearning, Relearning, and Understanding *Color Blindness*

What happens when you say to a person of color . . .	Are you really saying . . .	In which case you may actually contribute to racism by doing one or any combination of the following:
I forget you are Black.	It's a compliment not to be Black?	Equating color with something negative
I am color-blind.	You do not see red or green or orange?	Erasing people's identity, rejecting their heritage, invalidating their culture
I don't see race.	Your eyesight has failed you?	Overlooking deep racial wounds
Black or White, all people are the same.	You do not see any difference in different people's skin color?	Ignoring racial experiences and long-standing systemic injustices

"Rich Woman, Poor Woman" is a dialogue poem written in 1973 by a working-class Chilean woman after the overthrow of Salvador Allende. The poem contrasts the vastly different effects of the same historical events on the lives of two women. Much of its power comes from the way in which the lines echo each other in terms of grammar and structure, but the content and typeface are drastically different. One says, "I am a woman born of a woman whose man owned a factory." The other says, "*I am a woman born of a woman whose man labored in a factory.*" The poem continues in this fashion. The first woman says her man "wore silk suits and constantly watched his weight." The second says her man "*wore tattered clothing*" and his "*heart was constantly strangled by hunger.*" The first watches two babies grow into "beautiful children," while the other watches two babies "*die because there was no milk.*" The poem continues in this fashion, revealing details of the fluctuating fortunes of each woman as a result of political shifts. The complete poem can be found at the following website: http://carla.umn.edu/cobaltt/lessonplans/attachments/139/poem.pdf.

What follows is a dialogue poem based upon details included in the letter written by the mother praising the community center for teaching her son to be "color-blind."

I Am a Mother

I am a mother.

I am a mother.

I have an ex who does not live with us, but he supports his son.

I have a man who does not live with us, and who has fathered my son and his five siblings.

I worry about water safety skills for my White, very privileged son.

I worry about profiling safety for my Black, not-so-privileged son.

I send my son to an afterschool program in a historically Black community for the sake of convenience.

I send my son to an afterschool program in MY historically Black community for the sake of survival.

I have a son who noticed after seven years that almost all of his friends were Black.

I have a son who knew from day one that he was Black.

I have a son who was introduced to Black history, rights, and equality by the staff of the community center.

I have a son who was introduced to Black history, rights, and equality at our kitchen table.

I have a son who was given the gift of color blindness.

I have a son who was given the gift of color, for which he would like to be acknowledged.

Figure 13.2 Activity: Dialogue Poem

Reflection: The purpose of a dialogue poem is to present two contrasting experiences as a means of highlighting and understanding inequality. What do you see as the social justice issues raised by this poem that an ally might address?

Extension Activities: Writing a Dialogue Poem

- Using details from the poem "Two Mothers," write a dialogue poem from the perspective of the two sons.
- Watch the TED Talk by Naty Rico, Overcoming Ableism: What You Don't Know About Ableism as an Able Bodied Person (https://www.youtube.com/watch?v=X1xnyVCBYNQ), in which she recounts her struggles attending UC Irvine as a first-generation, low-income, Latina, differently abled student. Write a dialogue poem from her perspective and from the perspective of an able bodied student.
- Think of an unjust situation that has moved you or find one in the media.
  - Note the details of the injustice. Where it takes place. Who is involved. The precise nature of the injustice.
  - Decide whose voices will tell the story.
  - Write a dialogue poem from their perspectives.

KEY CONSIDERATIONS FOR ALLIES

- Ally work is fraught with almost unavoidable false steps, missteps, and minefields, which can become exacerbated by pride, impatience, and intermittent commitment.
- *Color blindness* is a concept and ideology that encourages ongoing racism.
- Reevaluating, unlearning, relearning, and understanding social justice issues require allies to see the world from the perspective of the oppressed.
- **Looking Ahead**: Prepared allies make effective allies. Some of the ways in which allies can prepare themselves to become effective will be covered in the next chapter.

Reflection, Resources, Resilience, and Position

14

Allyhood is a process—a process of becoming. Potential allies, then, are always and forever in the process of moving to the next level of understanding, moving to the next level of attitude, and moving to the next level of action.

Responsible allies are reflective, they amass, carefully consider, and employ a variety of resources, and they are resilient in the face of setbacks. Responsible allies also think through how and where to position themselves in the quest for a more just world. Reflection, resources, resilience, and positioning are intertwined and recursive. They feed into and support the dynamic movement of big-hearted people who embrace the notion of becoming an ally. How reflection, resources, resilience, and positioning interact will be discussed in this chapter.

REFLECTION IN ALLY WORK

Responsible allies see the world from a different vantage point. How they sharpen their ability to do so involves a two-step process: amassing information and sifting through that information using a social justice lens. Listening helps.

Listen for a Change

Listening is a powerful social justice tool, a precursor to, and a form of reflection. Consider the title of the 2016 Trinity Institute on social justice,

Listen for a Change. Depending upon how you read the title, the sense subtly shifts. *Listen* for a change, could be an exacerbated plea: Be quiet and listen for a change instead of dominating a discussion, giving your opinions, hearing only yourself. Listen for a *change,* on the other hand, is more of a rallying cry: Listen, and change has a chance of occurring. Without listening, there is no hope for change.

Those becoming allies in the battle for social justice understand that listening is critical to their development as allies and fundamental to dismantling unjust systems. To *listen* has multiple meanings, and allies embrace them all.

Allies *make a conscious effort to hear* what the oppressed have to say. They *pay attention to* the ways in which members of the privileged class respond, so that they can intervene appropriately. They *take note of* the ways in which classrooms and meetings are set up, who sets the agenda, who gets to speak, and whose voices are heard. They *heed* the advice of those who have devoted themselves to anti-oppression work, research, and thought. They *attend* to the stated and unstated biases, attitudes, and perspectives of those who benefit from being privileged.

Reflective Listening

Listening in this context is much more than the physical act of hearing, as the five italicized verbs in the paragraph above indicate. Indeed, making a conscious effort *to hear, to pay attention, to take note, to take heed,* and *to attend to* are all facets of reflecting, of careful thought, of deep consideration. Furthermore, they are repetitive actions, recursive actions, ongoing actions. When potential allies listen for a change, they reap the benefits of repetitive, recursive, and ongoing listening, which, in turn, supports them in the process of becoming an ally.

Reflective Listening in Action

Much can be learned about attitudes, hidden and overt agendas, and underlying values by attending carefully to who says what. I did exactly that recently at an annual statewide conference intended for ESL supervisors and ESL teachers.

I paid attention to what was being discussed, by whom, the makeup of the audience, the format of the presentations. Teachers, administrators, and state officials discussed everything from scaffolding to differentiation, from web-based learning to lowering language barriers, from ESL assessment to ESL counseling.

All of this concerted listening and reflecting led to several observations:

- As the ESL population grows, so do the number of acronyms used to describe and categorize these students, to assess and sort them, and to describe and assign programs and learning goals.
- The number of acronyms used goes up depending upon who is presenting. State officials tend to use the most. Teachers tend to use the fewest.
- When discussing students, state officials refer only to groups and they only use acronyms. Teachers reference individual students and they use their names.
- State officials and supervisors are more likely to be concerned with legal requirements, standards, and assessments. Teachers are more likely to be concerned with kid-friendly dictionaries, interactive notebooks, and cooperative-learning techniques.
- Teachers, administrators, and state officials continually refer-enced "service models" for ESL students. I could not help think that *things* get serviced: cars, boilers, and air conditioners. People are provided *with* services.

My deep listening and reflecting left me troubled, which was why I was pleased that I had built my presentation around the following question: What would happen if we dramatically changed the way we think about, talk about, and interact with our English Language Learners? (In a small gesture of protest, I intentionally did not refer to students as ELLs, choosing, instead, to spell out the acronym.) I posited that our English Language Learners come from all over the world and thus represent a world of possibilities. I also posited that focusing on possibilities rather than problems would enable English Language Learners and their teachers to thrive: to grow and prosper. Finally, I posited that this shift would eradicate what I have previously called the crime of squandered potential (Jackson &McDermott, 2012). In other words, I was advocating a social justice agenda rather than a compliance agenda.

I wonder how effective state officials can be as allies when they resort to acronym-rich, individual-denying statements about ACCESS scores of LEPS and SLIFEs, or how WIDA ELD standards align with SOLs for ELLs.

GATHERING AND KEEPING TRACK OF HIGH-QUALITY RESOURCES

Reflection develops and sustains potential allies. Reflection that draws upon high-quality resources is the surest way to support allies in the making.

Figure 14.1 Social Justice Resources Guide Template

Title	Author	Type	Where Found	Summary	Use/Comments
"White Fragility"	R. DiAngelo	Article	http://libjournal .unceg.edu/ jjcp/article/ view/249/116	Explains social arrangements that keep White Americans feeling comfortable and insulated from "race-based stress" and how they can sometimes react when confronted with racial realities.	Excellent resource Provocative Not for newcomers
Anti-Oppression Network	Maintained by several first nations peoples from Vancouver	Website	https://theanti oppression network .wordpress.com	Compilation of anti-oppression brochures and toolkits, a list of documentaries, a list of terminologies of oppression, and additional websites	Clear definition of allyship, including responsibilities of allies Clear definitions of varioius types of oppression Newcomer-friendly
Teaching Tolerance	Southern Poverty Law Center	Website	http://www .tolerance.org	Teaching Tolerance is dedicated to reducing prejudice, improving intergroup relations, and supporting equitable school experiences for our nation's children. Website offers a vast array of free materials, including lesson plans, articles, and webinars.	Student-friendly materials on a vast array of social justice issues Excellent teacher resources for understanding social justice issues and how to integrate them into classroom discussions and activities

Reading through the Social Justice Resources Guide is different than actually using it. Using the prompts below, add your own entries to determine if the template needs to be modified to suit your needs.

Developing a list of suggested ongoing educational resources is an excellent way to begin the process of reflection. Maintaining a record of resources consulted over time is an effective way to track your progress in pursuing high-quality resources. This record can also be used to quickly access or review needed information. Commenting on and updating the list is a way to keep it fresh and usable.

Figure 14.1 shows a template that can be used to develop and maintain a handy social justice resource guide that you can quickly consult to jog your memory about articles you have read, websites you have visited, or videos you have watched that support the work of becoming an ally, whether you are focusing on your own growth or you are helping others to grow into the role. (See page 202.) The template is purposely designed to be brief so that it is easy to complete and easy to consult. The template can be easily modified to suit your needs. For instance, it could be maintained collaboratively by a group of people, in which case it may be good to indicate who submitted the resource. It could be done on a spreadsheet so that it can be electronically manipulated and searched.

By way of demonstration, I have populated the template with a few examples from references previously referred to in the book. These sample entries are drawn from a variety of articles, videos, and websites.

By following the directions included in Activity 14.2, you can begin to add resources of your own to the Social Justice Resources Guide template.

Figure 14.2   Activity: Adding to the Social Justice Resources Guide Template

- Add at least two resources to your personal Social Justice Resources Guide. You may want to consider references mentioned in this book or others that you have used in the past.
- Select one or two of the following outstanding resources. Spend time on the website. Add to your Social Justice Resources Guide.
  - Rethinking Schools: http://www.rethinkingschools.org.
  - Diane Ravitch's Blog: http://dianeravitch.net.
  - Education Opportunity Network: http://educationopportunitynetwork.org.
- Debrief the experience of completing an entry in the guide. What did you find helpful? Challenging? How might you modify the entries to suit your needs?

TWO SIDES OF RESILENCE

Resilience, the ability to keep going in the face of inevitable setbacks, is another characteristic that supports the development of allies. Before talking about how, I would like to be an ally by showing support to all of the marginalized students who may be hurt by this concept.

Another Reading on Resilience

I have come to resist the recent emphasis on resilience and its counterpart, grit, especially as these terms have come to be applied to marginalized students. To my mind, the concept of resiliency and grit, sticking with your goals through thick and thin, fails to account for the variation in the kinds of adversity students face. For those with all of the benefits aligned and the major obstacles out of the way, sticking with goals is substantially easier than for those students who are less favorably placed. Thick and thin take on new meanings in this context. Marginalized students have a much thicker layer of adversities to overcome than do their more favorably treated counterparts.

What I object to is that one reading of the notion of resiliency and grit places enormous and undue pressure on the individual to do all it takes to overcome adversity. The image of the heroic individual does not account for the ways in which the system gangs up on certain students. Too often, the message that is given is that with enough resilience and grit anyone can succeed. The message is also clear about "failure": not achieving is directly attributable to personal failings. It is important to understand that society is made up of a complex array of interactions among people, institutions, contexts, and opportunities that support certain students and hinder others. Without recognizing and accounting for this alternate reading, the application of the concept of resilience to marginalized students could be harmful.

The Resilience Factor in Becoming an Ally

Despite my resistance to applying the concept of resilience and grit to marginalized students, I embrace it—with some clear parameters—as it relates to those wishing to become allies.

Resilience can and should be part of the toolkit and attitude of anyone wishing to become an ally in the battle for social justice, as long as the ally in question understands that the work of becoming an ally requires bouncing back from the inevitable setbacks that the ally will encounter. The only sure way to do so is to ensure that the ally is working *in conjunction* with other allies, including members of marginalized groups. Mutual support is critical to becoming an ally. Lone rangers will generally flounder and give up.

REFLECTION, RESOURCES, AND RESILENCE WORKING TOGETHER

I am embarrassed to tell this story, but if I don't, two things will happen. I will not be able to claim I am being honest with you, and we will have lost an opportunity to think through how reflection, resources, and resilience aid the process of becoming an ally.

I was riding to the airport with one of my Black colleagues. Our relationship was never close, and, as I look back, I suspect neither one of us understood the other very well. Stuff like this happens.

Suddenly, her cell phone rang. During the conversation, I gathered that an opportunity to write was being offered. My colleague was very excited about the prospect and assured the caller that there were plenty of people in the organization who could write and write well. She then began to name several, all of whom were people of color and none of whom had ever written a book. I half expected and very much wanted her to mention me. After all, I had just published my first book, I was sitting right next to her, and we had spent the week working together. Instead, I was completely overlooked. In fact, during the bulk of the conversation, my colleague turned her back to me and turned her head toward the window, which I read as physically excluding me.

I was furious. I was hurt. I was truly insulted. We got to the airport and parted. I took the first opportunity I could to rant to a trusted confidante. You can imagine the things I said, but what stopped the rant was my loud assertion that my Black colleague was exercising "reverse racism." "It does not exist," my confidante quietly interrupted. "What doesn't exist?" I demanded mid-rant. "Reverse racism," she clarified.

I stopped, but I was too angry and upset to pursue this further. Maybe I was secretly wallowing in my wounded pride. I certainly was not ready for insight and clarity.

Insight and clarity did come eventually, thanks in no small measure to several discussions about "reverse racism" that appear in the book *Is Everyone Really Equal?* The authors assert that "reverse racism," like "reverse sexism," are "misnomers." They do not exist. They further explained what I already knew but somehow chose to forget: "Isms" refer to power relations that are steeped in history, are intricately woven into societal patterns, and are inescapable and pervasive. They reminded me that there is no seesaw of power and oppression. Power and oppression do not flip back and forth. Historic holders of power in the United States and Canada continue to wield power. I knew this, of course, but somehow I fell prey to my emotions and almost completely undid all the work I had been doing over so many years to come to think through the ways in which power and oppression interact.

I am certain I could come up with a host of reasons for my lapse, but that is not the point. The point is that the trajectory to undo a lifetime of understandings and ways of doing business does not happen overnight, nor does it proceed smoothly. As someone hoping to embrace becoming an ally, I have to expect setbacks. I do not have to throw up my hands in despair. I do not need to stay in my retracted position. I have to practice resilience; to continuously and purposefully reflect; to continuously and purposefully find, use, and listen to resources. Continuous and purposeful use of reflection and resources enables a potential ally to resiliently bounce back.

Thinking Through Reflection, Resources, and Resilience

Reflection was not on the agenda when my confidante first told me "reverse racism" does not exist. I was too taken aback by the apparent rebuke (mild as it was) and too emotionally charged at that moment to hear anything more. As potential allies, we need to recognize that timing is crucial and patience is a virtue in dealing with our own ally trajectory, as well as the trajectory of others.

Reflection did not end with the reading of *Is Everyone Really Equal?* As I revisited other familiar books and articles, I could not help but do so through the lens of my "reverse racism" faux pas. These reflections helped me to read even more deeply into these familiar texts and to understand, on a deeper level, a concept I thought I understood, racism.

My reflections took me back to other experiences, other exchanges that I was part of or that I witnessed. Again, rethinking "reverse racism" shed more nuanced light on these experiences and exchanges.

The constellation of resources that I immediately sought out after this incident—and that I continue to seek out years later—is made up of the books, articles, videos, experiences, exchanges, and people I interact with daily. I did, of course, eventually discuss my "reverse racism" comment with my confidante. She obviously is an important resource, one with whom I try to maintain an open and honest relationship. People definitely are resources.

My embarrassment at succumbing to a waft of negative emotions, my uncensored expression of White fragility, my completely off-the-mark reaction could have caused me to retreat from anti-oppression work. Shame is powerful and I felt ashamed at having responded the way I did. Stubbornness is also powerful and I knew that one mistake would not negate years of trying to dismantle unjust systems.

This incident also taught me to rethink how I wanted to position myself in social justice work versus how responsible allies position themselves. At the moment this incident occurred, I was literally sitting in the back seat of the car heading to the airport. Much as I hate to admit it, the back seat was—and is—where I belonged.

WHERE ALLIES SHOULD BE POSITIONED: ON THE FRONT LINE FROM THE SIDELINE

The phone call looking for writers was a turning point for me. I wanted to be acknowledged for my abilities and successes. I wanted to lead or at least be part of the project. In other words, I wanted to insert myself where I clearly was not needed or wanted. This is a hard lesson for members of the dominant group. We often are used to being consulted, to being asked to participate, to sharing our opinions requested or not.

Allies understand that the real work of liberation belongs to those seeking liberation. The role of members of a dominant group who want to be allies is to wait quietly in the wings to be called upon when others determine we are needed. This is a hard pill to swallow. It is a complete reversal of the social order as members of a dominant group have experienced it, but it is essential.

Waiting to be called upon does not mean doing nothing. Allies continually educate themselves. Allies continually educate others, especially other members of their dominant group. Allies continually build relationships with members of marginalized groups as a means of building trust.

One thing allies avoid is burdening members of marginalized groups with the responsibility of teaching allies about their lives. Reliving unsavory experiences for the benefit of others is a true imposition. Instead, allies can educate themselves about the experiences of others by reading widely.

When Allies Position Themselves in the Center of the Work

How potential allies position themselves in ally work is critical. Unfortunately, it is sometimes done incorrectly, as the following examples will demonstrate.

"Pet" Projects. Members of marginalized groups know when members of the dominant group have arrived on the scene to "save" them. I shudder when I read about the ways in which some wealthy people fund certain charitable efforts. Think of the words and the message. They often talk about adopting "pet" projects. How insulting! How condescending! No group of people should be thought of as "pets," nor should they be subjected to the donor's reading of their situation coupled with the donor's preferred solution.

The world of education has been victimized by "pet" project thinking. Consider two examples. The Gates Foundation and Mark Zuckerberg have donated enormous amounts of money to the education sector to help "fix" failing schools. These funds come with strings attached; that is to say implementation of the Gates or Zuckerberg theory of learning and teaching. (The funds also come with a good bit of return on the investment, since their approach to education often makes use of the products and services they sell.)

Efforts such as these corrode true allyship by commandeering, controlling, and undercutting the efforts of those whose lives are directly affected by failing schools. They set unrealistic timetables. They impose rather than draw out. They foster turnover instead of building stability. They demonstrate impatience instead of patience. No wonder they rarely work, as is the case in Newark, New Jersey, compared to its neighboring town of Union City. Twenty-five years ago, both cities were plagued by poor student outcomes. In a short amount of time, Newark got the attention of politicians and the money of outsiders like Zuckerberg. Union City worked with the talent and resources they had. They planned. They did their homework. They grew their educational program to meet the context of the lives of the people who live in the community. Union City employed what the *New York Times* called "home grown gradualism" rather than charismatic leaders bent on flipping the district. In 2014, 81 percent of Union City students graduated from high school. In Newark, the number was 69 percent (Kirp, 2016).

The White Savior Industrial Complex and "Peternalism." Contrast the politicians and philanthropists' approach to that of P. K. Subban, a well-loved professional hockey player, who donated $10 million to the Montreal Children's Hospital. The only stipulation he put on the donation was the proviso that the hospital use the funds as the hospital sees fit. Some might label the proviso a statement of trust in the capacity of the hospital leaders to know what their needs are, as well as a statement of humility on the part of P. K. Subban that he knows how to ice skate and handle a puck, but he knows precious little about how hospitals function. There is something else, too, to be considered about P. K. Subban. He is Black. A Black player in the world of the National Hockey League is a rare commodity. Black players represent less than 5 percent of the total roster. One has to wonder if being Black plays into P. K. Subban's approach to philanthropy.

Writer Teju Cole puts another spin on the efforts of billionaires—White male billionaires like Gates and Zuckerberg—and their charitable donations. He minces no words in describing what he calls the fastest growth industry in the United States, the White Savior Industrial Complex, in which the White savior "supports brutal policies in the morning, attends charity functions in the afternoon, and receives awards in the evening." He goes on to say that the White Savior Industrial Complex is about having "a big emotional experience that validates privilege" (Cole, 2012). These are strong words and they received plenty of attention when they first appeared.

One of the most familiar manifestations of the savior syndrome is paternalism, that attitude in which persons of privilege position themselves to laud it over those in subordinate positions. Call it the Father Knows Best syndrome. Part and parcel of paternalism is restricting the freedom and responsibilities of those in subordinate positions, supposedly because those in privileged positions know what is best. Those in privileged positions enjoy disproportionate respect and advantages, which they want to exercise in ways that relegate those in lesser positions to roles of dependence and inferiority. Paternalism allows those in power to "save" others.

Those blessed by privilege, such as Gates and Zuckerberg, exercise a form of paternalism in the way they position themselves as saviors of the educational system or any other pet project their money and influence allows them to champion. They find causes they can back, elevate them to their "pet" projects, and come up with solutions to address the disaster du jour. Teju Cole warns, "If we are going to interfere in the lives of others, a little due diligence is required." Without a nuanced understanding of the realities and intricacies of complicated social or political situations, adopting pet projects becomes nothing more than those in privileged positions exercising a form of paternalism, which I see as "*pet*ernalism."

Most educators do not have the resources that the people in the examples above have, but we do sometimes adopt a savior mentality when addressing the inequities we see. Allies need to be able to guard against falling victim to the savior syndrome, paternalism, and *pet*ernalism.

The Position of Educators and Education in Combatting Marginalization.

Combatting marginalization in any of its forms has to start somewhere, and educators can play an important role. Indeed, one major educational research organization maintains that the work of combatting racism *should* begin in schools.

After the racially motivated shooting of nine prayer group members that took place in Charleston, South Carolina, the American Education Research Association (AERA) published a position paper asserting why and how schools should play a role in antiracism work. Although targeting racism directly, and for very good reason, the document can also be used as a blueprint for combatting marginalization of any kind.

Figure 14.3   Activity: The Position of Educators as Allies

Directions:

- Read the AERA statement, which can be found using the following link: http://www.aera.net/Newsroom/News-Releases-and-Statements/AERA -Statement-on-the-Charleston-Shootings-and-Racism-in-America.
- What does the statement say about why antiracism education is necessary, why school should be a place for antiracism education, and what the educational community can do to combat racism?
- How might this statement inform your work as an ally?

KEY CONSIDERATIONS FOR ALLIES

- Deep reflection, quality and organized resources, a heavy dose of resiliency, and thinking through how to position yourself as an ally provide allies with the means to avoid making damaging mistakes, to continue to grow in the work, and to become a valuable part of the change movement.
- Listening is a powerful change agent.
- "Reverse racism" does not exist.
- Schools and educators can play an important role in social justice efforts.
- **Looking Ahead**: There is no shortage of ways in which individuals and groups of educators can contribute to dismantling and counteracting injustice. The next chapter will provide multiple examples.

The Many Faces 15
of Activism in
Action

When I first moved to Canada, I was often amazed at the number of times I heard Canadians use the term *social contract*, their shorthand for society considering and promoting the common good. And they are serious about it, too.

THE SOCIAL CONTRACT AND ALLIES

My first spring in Montreal, there was widespread university student unrest over proposed tuition hikes (tuition throughout Canada is shockingly low, at least from an American perspective). One day I caught a call-in radio show devoted to the student unrest. A woman who identified herself as retired called in. *Oh boy*, I thought. *Here it comes.* I expected to hear: *I am on a fixed income. Why are my tax dollars going to support young people?*

Instead, the caller said the exact opposite. *Young people need a break. Why should they pay more tuition? It is hard enough for them.* Then, she said what I know I never heard in the United States as I was fighting to get school budgets passed: *Why doesn't the government take BACK the tax break they just gave us elderly folk and use it to keep tuition down? Isn't that what the social contract is all about?*

At that moment, I knew I wasn't in Kansas anymore. Where I had spent my life, *tax* was a four-letter word and elderly people were the bane of any attempt to increase school taxes. I recall well-orchestrated campaigns to round up retired people on school budget vote days and bus them to polling places with the express purpose of defeating school budgets.

Affix your social justice signature to the social contract. At that moment, I decided the *social contract* is a wonderful thing. Like all contracts, it requires a commitment often symbolized by affixing your name to the contract in the form of your unique signature. We do so at important life moments: marriage, buying a house, adopting a child, accepting a job. Signatures matter.

How wonderful it would be if each of us deliberately and thoughtfully inscribed our unique social justice signature on today's social contract. This chapter is about the myriad ways people with a range of talents, different forms of currency, and variable levels of commitment have, in fact, added their unique signatures to the social contract, attesting to their willingness to be activists for a new order.

Pick a slice of the pie. Allies come in all shapes and sizes and work best when they put their unique talents to a small slice of the cause. Waneek Horn-Miller, a Mohawk and a celebrated aboriginal rights activist in Canada, reminds Canadians not to look at aboriginal issues and think that the issues, which are huge and long-standing, are too big to be taken on. Instead, she advises, pick a slice of the pie—a tiny slice—and then dedicate yourself to it. This support can be as simple as celebrating indigenous history, supporting indigenous businesses, buying handmade jewelry and learning about the artist and the meaning behind the creation, or speaking out on issues of equitable funding for education.

Don't wait a single moment. When and how can allies begin the work of being an activist for social change? According to the youthful optimism of Anne Frank, the time is now. "How wonderful it is that nobody need wait a single moment before starting to improve the world," she wrote, not long before the circumstances of her birth and virulent hatred brought her to an untimely death. Young as she was, her words were profound. We need not wait a single moment before starting to improve the world. We are ready right now, because each and every one of us has something valuable to offer, some talent or skill that can shift the balance of power, make someone's life more tolerable, disrupt the culture of inequity that constrains so many lives.

EXAMPLES AND PROFILES OF ALLIES IN ACTION

The possibilities for ally work are endless because each of us is unique and each of us is capable of contributing something to the advancement of justice. What follows are a number of examples and profiles of the many ways others have embraced the urgent call to change the world—to work on behalf of political and human freedoms, socioeconomic rights, value systems, and identity. These examples are in no way inclusive. Instead, they are presented as ideas from which you can take your unique ability and apply it purposefully as an ally in the battle for social justice. They are also provided with the belief that together we have the ability to fill in the fissures of race, gender, class, geography, etc., in order to make the world more whole for all.

The examples will begin and end with two profiles. Both have been advocates for social justice for many years. The first has made anti-oppression work the primary focus of her career. The second is an artist who has used her incredible talent to fight for many causes but especially for women's rights around the world. The first profile contains very specific steps that could be taken in any school to address a variety of social justice issues. The second is presented to inspire potential allies to put to work whatever talents they possess in the service of social justice.

As the adage goes, *we* are the people we have been waiting for.

Work *Inside* the Confines of Formal Structures

The Context. Liza Talusan is an adaptable, and persistent, ally. For many years, she worked at the university level promoting understanding of gender equity, multicultural affairs, and experiences of underrepresented populations in higher education, the workplace, and in mainstream American culture. Liza, who identifies as Filipina American, recently moved from the world of higher education to the world of elementary/middle-school education. She currently is Director of Diversity, Equity, and Inclusion at a school that serves preK to Grade 8 students. The challenge: how to adapt critical social justice concepts, scores of workshop activities, and important understandings so that children can understand them.

The Response. She has done just that, and, along the way, she has worked within the institution to tweak the way things are done so that the theories behind social justice work are translated into practical applications.

- Today, applicants for a position at the school are asked additional pre-interview questions that deal with their preferred gender pronoun, their preferred method of getting around the building to provide greater access, and any needs they may have for additional time to address medical or lactation issues.
- In a break from the way things had been done in the past, professional development activities are open to faculty and staff, not just faculty.

- A weekly open forum, Conversation Circles, takes place for twenty-five minutes, in which faculty and staff can share their responses to social justice issues in the news, such as their take on the Flint Michigan water crisis or Oscars So White. For those who cannot physically be present, comments are posted on social media and a school-sponsored blog.

- Schoolwide campaigns on social justice issues occur regularly. A recent one invited everyone to not only think about social justice issues but to actually DO something to make the world a better place. Among the topics students discussed were ways to make their school more equitable, accessible, and welcoming. A campaign to do something each day to make someone at the school smile was a highlight and made more meaningful by discussing the ways in which smiles build connections, and connections are the soul of social justice work.

- Parents and teachers use Liza as a resource when issues develop at home and in school that make adults uncomfortable. While young children rarely enact racism intentionally, Liza believes strongly it is never too early to discuss issues of social justice and equity. Adults often have questions when they overhear a young child make a comment like, "You cannot be the princess because you have Black skin," or "Only boys play with trucks." Liza helps adults think through and plan how they could and should intentionally talk about social justice issues with children.

- Over the years, Liza has provided workshops on many aspects of anti-oppression work. She has created and adapted numerous strategies and workshop ideas and discussion starters, which she collected in a downloadable document that is available free to anyone who wants to use them. The document, which was written when Liza worked at Stonehill College, is titled *Practicing Inclusion: Icebreakers and Team Builders for Diversity.* Each strategy/activity is presented in lesson-plan format, which can easily be adapted to fit individual contexts. It can be found at http://www.stonehill.edu/files/resources/talusandiversityteambuilders.pdf.

Takeaways. In her role as Director of Diversity, Equity, and Inclusion, Liza has drawn upon and rejiggered material and methods that worked well at the college level, found ways of enhancing and building upon where her new school is in terms of social justice work, and she freely shares what she knows and what she has created. Her efforts prove that allies need to be adaptable, creative, generous, and persistent. They also need a simple, clear message.

Liza's message *is* clear and could easily serve as a mantra for allies:

- *Diversity* is who we are.
- *Equity* is what we strive to provide.
- *Inclusion* is how we achieve our goals.

Work *Outside* the Confines of Formal Structures

The Context. In Montreal today, accessibility for the differently abled is still a huge issue. Only recently have metro stations begun the process of being retrofitted to include elevators, and the majority of restaurants, bars, and businesses are not accessible.

The Response. Omar Lachheb, a quadriplegic as the result of a diving accident, is well aware of the situation. He decided to do something about access. He started a not-for-profit organization that donates lightweight ramps to businesses. In a true spirit of cooperation, another organization partnered with him to construct the ramps. This organization assists young people who have left school develop a trade, contribute to society, and, along the way, find a career path. Many business owners happily employ the ramps as a visible welcome mat for those who find getting around to be difficult.

Takeaways. All it takes is a good idea to rally support from various sectors. Despite the lack of comprehensive legislative support to address an unjust situation, committed people can find ways outside of the formal system to address a pressing need. Creative solutions can improve the situation for those affected, highlight the injustice of official policies, and garner growing support to demand an official and comprehensive response.

Create a Curriculum, Unit, or Lesson

The Context. On December 6, 1989, twenty-five-year-old Marc Lépine entered a classroom at the École Polytechnique in Montreal, separated the male students from the female students, announced that he was "fighting feminism," and proceeded to open fire on the women, leaving fourteen of them dead. Today, December 6 is remembered throughout Canada as a National Day of Remembrance and Action on Violence Against Women. Throughout Canada, municipalities and groups have organized events and commemorations with the aim of raising awareness about violence and discrimination against women.

The Response. Two teachers and a journalist, greatly moved by the horrific massacre and convinced that the place to begin to stem the tide of violence against women begins in school, responded by creating a violence-prevention curriculum that has been used throughout the world. Their organization, Men for Change, is a perfect example of teachers becoming allies in the battle for social justice. Who better to research, organize, publish, and implement a curriculum than teachers themselves?

Takeaways. Teachers who are not up to creating an entire curriculum, however, have plenty of opportunities to develop units and lessons with a social justice bent. Ideas abound on previously mentioned websites like Teaching Tolerance and, in Canada, the Human Rights Museum in Winnipeg. Teaching Tolerance is so well regarded that by the end of 2015, the website had 15,000 anti-bias lesson plans online.

Read Talk Write, sponsored by the International Literacy Association and The National Council of Teachers of English, is another treasure trove of social justice lessons, rubrics, and handouts that can be searched by grade level and topic. Furthermore, these websites encourage teachers to submit their own units and lessons, reading lists, and comments.

Create a Movement

The Context. In the early 1990s, if there were any talk about LGBTQ people or issues in school, it is likely that it would have been in the form of snide remarks made in hallways, insensitive jokes overheard in locker rooms, or hurtful banter and off-handed comments made in the context of a classroom lesson. Life for LGBTQ students was not easy. Many lived behind a veil of silence and fear.

Also at that time, there were only two gay-straight alliances in the United States, one state with a policy directly addressing protection of LGBT students, and precious few resources available for educators to use to create safe, welcoming, bullying-free schools. A high school history teacher, Kevin Jennings, himself a victim of bullying and harassment due to his sexual identity, took action and a movement was born.

The Response. On June 2, 2015, the Gay, Lesbian, and Straight Education Network (GLSEN), the movement Kevin Jennings created, celebrated its twenty-fifth anniversary. Its list of achievements is impressive. The organization has affected policy, created classroom materials, and produced reports designed to create awareness about LGBTQ issues. Its reach is equally impressive. Where once there were two gay-straight alliances nationwide, there are now over 4,000 registered high school alliances. The organization sponsors three annual national "Days of Action." They maintain a website rich in resources, revealing reports, and remarkable stories. Volunteers, educators, students, and families are part of the organization. GLSEN's perspective and expertise has helped shaped national and state policy. GLSEN has certainly helped to change the way LGBTQ people and issues are addressed in schools.

Takeaways. GLSEN began as an alliance between a gay teacher and a female student and it has remained an alliance. Alliances are built around common interests. Alliances bring allies together. Alliances have staying power, which is a much-needed commodity in any movement. GLSEN created a national movement keeping these principles in mind. GLSEN understood and attended to the group processes that strengthen and drive change movements. GLSEN also tackled issues over time, building upon past successes and learning from past errors. Schools can implement similar group processes and multi-year plans built around a common focus.

Identify and Activate Strengths

The Context. Many members of society, including some teachers, view differently abled students like those on the autism spectrum as challenges, as problems, or as deficient in some way.

The Response. Former special education teachers Liam O'Rourke and Dan Tenveen began their work as allies for students on the autism spectrum by seeing the potential these students possess and finding ways to cultivate that potential.

When they were teaching, they often used media as an additional tool for students to acquire concepts. They were so impressed by what students could do, they decided to find ways to empower students to use and grow their talents. What has resulted is Spectrum Productions, a fully functioning media house whose creators, technicians, directors, actors, animators, and camera people are all on the autism spectrum. For many, this is the first time that their unique artistic and technical skills have been recognized and cultivated.

Takeaways. Allies can learn a lot from them about starting from strengths. By intentionally and deliberately identifying the strengths of their autistic students, they were able to conceive a way to activate and develop those strengths, resulting in opening up a world of possibilities for a group of students who might otherwise be kept on the margins in terms of self-esteem, skill development, and opportunities for employment. Identifying and activating strengths is a powerful mind shift that bears tremendous fruit for both students and teachers (Jackson & McDermott, 2015).

Engage the Hard Questions

The Context. It would be hard to find a more challenging, emotional, provocative question than "I'm not racist. . . Am I?" Yet, that is exactly the question that twelve New York City high-school students from a variety of backgrounds addressed in a year-long conversation and series of workshops that delved into the heart of racism and privilege and that changed each one of the participants. The year's events were captured in a powerful and memorable feature documentary, *I'm Not Racist . . . Am I?* (http://notracistmovie.com).

The Response. Who these students are, how they understand and experience race and privilege, and who they became as a result of this experience are all part of the film. More importantly, the audience also gets to consider who *they* are, how *they* understand race and privilege, and who *they* became as a result of watching and discussing the film.

There are numerous striking and unforgettable moments in the film. Getting to know the various students and their range of experiences is one. Observing powerful moments and seismic changes that took place in the various workshops is another.

Takeaways. Allies fearlessly engage hard questions. This film kept a hard question as its focus and engaged many fearless allies willing to explore this hard question from a number of vantage points. The fearless allies who participated in the project included:

- the members of the Calhoun School who wrote and won a W. K. Kellogg Foundation grant specifically designed to engage young people in deconstructing race,
- the filmmakers from Point Made Films, who are dedicated to tell the stories that will change the world (http://wp.pointmade .com),
- the workshop facilitators, who did not hesitate to ask the really tough questions and who were prepared to respond to the intense emotional reactions the questions generated. (Information regarding the workshops and the leaders is found on the film's website: http://notracistmovie.com/workshops.)

Finally, there are the numerous organizations and schools that have arranged a viewing and the workshops that accompany the film, thus bringing the tough questions into their own communities, contexts, and lives.

Use 21st Century Tools

The Context. Three strangers with vastly different backgrounds came together as allies on behalf of Syrian children living in refugee camps through a mutual interest in making a positive social change and the tools of the 21st century. Here is how their effort played out.

The first ever GROOC, a massive open online course for a group, was offered by McGill University in the fall of 2015 and involved over 5,000 people from more than one hundred countries around the world interested in the topic "Social Learning for Social Impact." One of the requirements of the course was to collaborate on a real-world social initiative to create a positive change.

The Response. Three students—a Syrian living in a refugee camp in Iraq, a Moroccan with a degree in operations and strategic management, and a British teacher currently living in Turkey who has taught English in over twenty countries—combined their expertise and experiences to come up with their project. The result was a successful crowdfunding campaign to provide a mobile classroom that could be used to teach English to Syrian refugee children.

The expertise and experiences of the three GROOC students is evident in the project. The site of the mobile classroom is where the Syrian refugee was living at the time. The crowdfunding was managed by the Moroccan with the business degree. The English teacher provided advice on the content of the English course, as well as contacts with possible volunteer teachers. The entire project came to pass virtually. The course and crowdfunding initiative was made possible through the Internet. Facebook and Skype made communication across countries possible.

Takeaways. What some of the work of allies will look like in the future is unimaginable now, since none of us know what additional virtual tools may be available. The example from the GROOC suggests that allies have not yet fully exploited the power of 21st century technology to support the work of allies. Allies with an interest and a facility with these tools may want to think through the ways in which their work could be made possible or enhanced by technology.

Build Trust; Find Like-Minded Spirits; Stand Firm

The Context. The Coatesville Area School District is located forty miles west of Philadelphia, and, for a time, it was many miles away from being a respected, trusted partner when it came to educating children with disabilities and/or children of color. Today, a team of allies is working together to change all of that.

The details are unsavory. The former superintendent resigned in 2013, after it was revealed that he had exchanged numerous sexist and racist text messages with a staff member. In addition, allegations were made that district officials discriminated against students with disabilities and students of color. Thanks to a courageous leader, an unlikely coalition of allies, and a robust plan to address what many see as grievous institutional wrongs, things are changing.

The Response. The new superintendent, Cathy Taschner, is the courageous leader. She determined that her first task was to rebuild trust with the community. To do so, she embarked upon a month-long listening tour. But her work did not end there. She also took advantage of a lucky happenstance. Rob Marshall, a community member and divinity school student, was looking for a community-service project he needed to complete to meet graduation requirements.

The two formed a partnership, Citizens Who S. E. E. (Citizens Who Seek Educational Equity), a group of trained volunteers who serve as advocates for parents of students with disabilities. Not only do they attend CSE meetings to provide moral and technical support, they also work with parents to help them understand their rights and to be better prepared and less overwhelmed when they get to meetings. The volunteers include a former school superintendent, a retired school psychologist, and a former youth-justice specialist. This unlikely coalition of allies is making a change in terms of parents' ability to advocate on behalf of their children.

For any of us who have sat in on CSE meetings and have taken the time to think about the meeting from the perspective of a parent, we have to be honest and say it is not a pleasant experience. Parents are at a clear disadvantage. They are outnumbered and often outranked by a group of people who hold multiple degrees and lots of power over the lives of their children. Many of these decision makers are strangers to parents, distant, disconnected district officials brought in for the event. If these aspects do not reduce parents to the rank of bystanders in the decision-making process, the formality, language, and perfunctory manner in which these meetings are conducted often do.

In Coatesville, parents love what the group has done for them. They report feeling less intimidated and more empowered when they go to meetings. Not too surprisingly, some district officials, used to doing business unchallenged by parents in the know, are less enthusiastic (Samuels, 2016).

Takeaways. The message for potential allies is clear. Do not run from problems. Get to the heart of them by building trust through listening, finding, and working with like-minded people with a range of skills, and have a plan that encourages and supports others to work on their own behalf.

Embrace the Social and Sacred Obligation of Having a Talent

The Context. Artist Cheryl Braganza is clear: Her weapon against injustice is her paintbrush. "Given a talent," she says, "I believe we have a social and sacred obligation to use it wisely, as much for ourselves as for the greater good."

The Response. Cheryl has lived this belief, turning her artistic talent into art activism. Her reaction to global catastrophes, especially those that involve unfair and cruel treatment of women, has fuelled many of her most evocative paintings and has inspired others to become activists. That is the power of art, be it music, literature, or graphic in nature.

Takeaways. All of us have talents and they are all different. Thank goodness, too, because when put together in the service of social justice, they form an intricately woven, mutually supportive, powerful force capable of withstanding pushback and concerted efforts likely to be launched to crush social movements. Allies are willing to use their talents as an expression of their activism. Cheryl's talents have resulted in her winning multiple awards and recognitions, which she parlays into further activism. In her humble, self-effacing, and quiet way, she exhorts us to action. "A dab of paint or a scribble are small gestures but miles better than doing nothing at all."

Figure 15.1 Activity: The Many Faces of Allies in Action: Reactions and Commitments

The eight examples and profiles presented above contain lots of information regarding the work each ally has undertaken. This activity will ask you to consider what resonated with you and what ideas for action the example or profile suggest that you can undertake on behalf of social justice.

Directions:

- Select at least two examples or profiles.
- For each, consider what resonated with you about the particular context, response, or takeaways that were presented. Record your reactions in the second column of the chart below.
- In the third column, record some ideas that you can take away from each example or profile that you might be able to enhance, alter, or borrow wholesale to advance the cause of social justice.

THE MANY FACES OF ALLIES IN ACTION: REACTIONS AND COMMITMENTS		
Example/Profile	*What Resonated With You?*	*Ideas for Action*
Work Inside the Confines of Formal Structures		
Work Outside the Confines of Formal Structures		

(Continued)

Figure 15.1 (Continued)

Example/Profile	What Resonated With You?	Ideas for Action
Create a Curriculum, Unit, or Lesson		
Create a Movement		
Identify and Activate Strengths		
Engage the Hard Questions		
Use 21st-Century Tools		
Build Trust; Find Like-Minded Spirits; Stand Firm		
Embrace the Social and Sacred Obligation of Having a Talent		

Extension and Team Activities:

- Select one of the ideas you came up with. What is the context? What steps might you need to take to implement your idea?
- Work with a partner or group to complete the chart above.

KEY CONSIDERATIONS FOR ALLIES

- There is no shortage of ways allies can put their unique abilities, interests, and talents to work in the service of social justice.
- **Looking Forward:** The social contract is ready for your unique signature.

Afterword

"USE YOUR WORDS"

On September 13, 2012, the world shifted—cosmically. My first grand-child, Ida, was born.

Ida's arrival signaled the birth of several new identities accompanied by new responsibilities, new roles, and new names. Our daughter and son-in-law became parents, Mommy and Daddy. My husband and I became grand-parents, Papa and Nana. My father, the only remaining member of the previous generation, became a great-grandfather for the first time. He died one month after we snapped a picture of him clad in a hospital gown, sitting in a wheelchair in the lobby of the hospital, cradling and cuddling and caressing Ida, while his grandchildren looked on and an IV sustained him. This photograph is powerful, unforgettable, and pregnant with meaning.

This is how it goes in the cycle of life. The web is intricate. Ida's birth heralded a new era, a new iteration of who our family is, a new version of how we are connected to the world, a new take on whom each one of us is. In my father's day, his marriage to my mother was considered shock-ing. After all, her family came from a totally different part of Italy than my father's! I can still remember hushed conversations that took place around both sets of families' tables regarding the food the others ate, the dialect they spoke, and the values they represented. This was identity politics on a familial level, and, quite frankly, I did not get it. To me, both sets of grandparents were important, were loving, were part of me and I of them.

By the time my generation came around, the circle widened. Neither my husband nor my brother's wife has Italian blood in them. We were, however, connected by faith. Our son's marriage took place under a Hoopah, the Jewish wedding tent. When my husband and I met with the caterer who was eventually hired to cater our daughter's wedding dinner, the first question he asked was, "Tell me a little about the bride and groom." We indicated that both the bride and groom were PhD candi-dates working in the world of anti-racism education, that our daughter is American of Irish and Italian descent, and our soon-to-be son-in-law is from Trinidad of East Indian and Afro-Caribbean heritage. "What are you going to do with that?" I asked. "Have fun!" he responded. And he did. And so do we. What a blessing it is to have grandchildren who have the history and heritage of three continents flowing through their veins. What richness. What connections. What miracles.

In October 2013, *Time* magazine published an article, "The Changing Face of America," which begins by saying that the United States is no longer a country "in which race is so black and white." To prove this point, they include statistics from the U.S. Census that indicate that one of the fastest-growing categories on the 2010 census was the one that allowed people to choose multiple racial designations, an opportunity, by the way, that only began in 2000. Also included is a gallery of photographs of people young and old with captions indicating how they self-identify and how they are categorized on the census.

Is the multi-race option a step forward? Some people would argue absolutely not, since the categories themselves are based on a very flawed idea that race is rooted in biology, when it is clearly a social construct. Still categorizing lives and identities goes on. Categorizing provides easy answers, pathways to articulate the very complex process of coming to understand and name who you are. People whose faces do not match rigidly defined racial expectations often maintain a fluid identity depending upon circumstances, most notably how others might use that information. Some take a playful root, blending labels: Blackanese, Filitino, Korgentinian.

But, they are still labels. They are still words that carry with them the legacy of division, the horrors of hierarchy, the politics of exclusion.

When Ida was just beginning to talk, she was often coaxed and encouraged by her parents, "Use your words." Now that our second grandchild, Leo, is starting to talk, he, too, has been encouraged to use his words. Words matter. They define. They highlight. They insinuate. Finding the right words is a weighty matter and it is often very hard.

Ida and Leo live in Canada, where their skin color and facial features earn them the identity of a "visible minority." These words conjure up for me an image of my grandchildren being always and forever visible, out in the open, members of a minority and thus less than.

Visible minority. Ouch. That hurts my American ears; my grandmother's protective instincts; my life's work to reduce barriers, to eliminate oppression, to give all children unfettered access to everything they need to thrive. Visible minority: defined by the Canadian government as "persons, other than aboriginal peoples, who are non-Caucasian in race or non-white in color." I bristle at the notion that my grandchildren—that any child—can be officially defined by what they are NOT, rather than what they ARE. That is why I chose to write this book. It was—and will remain—my attempt to change things through the one means I know I have at my disposal. I will use my words.

References

Adair. J. K. (2015, September). *The impact of discrimination on the early schooling experiences of children from immigrant families.* Retrieved from http://www.migrationpolicy.org/research/impact-discrimination-early-schooling-experiences-children-immigrant-families

Adichie, C. (2009, July). The danger of a single story [Video file]. Retrieved from https://www.ted.com/talks/chimamanda_adichie_the_danger_of_a_single_story?language=en

Advancement Project. (2010, March). *Test, punish, and push out: How "zero tolerance" and high-stakes testing funnel youth into the school-to-prison pipeline.* Retrieved from http://www.advancementproject.org/resources/entry/test-punish-and-push-out-how-zero-tolerance-and-high-stakes-testing-funnel

Apple, M. W. (2006). Interrupting the right: On doing critical education work in conservative times. In G. Ladson-Billings and W. F. Tate (Eds.), *Education research in the public interest: Social justice, action, and policy.* New York, NY: Teachers College Press.

Arnold, R., Burke, B., James, C., Martin, D., & Thomas, B. (1991). *Educating for a change.* Toronto, Ontario, Canada: Doris Marshall Institute for Education and Action and Between the Lines Press.

Ashton-Warner, S. (1963). *Teacher.* New York, NY: Simon and Schuster.

Baptist, E. E. (2014). *The half has never been told: Slavery and the making of American capitalism.* New York, NY: Basic Books.

Berliner, D. C., & Biddle, B. J. (1995). *The manufactured crisis: Myths, frauds, and the attack on America's public schools.* New York, NY: Perseus Books.

Berliner, D. C., & Glass, G. V. (2014). *Myths and lies that threaten America's public schools: The real crises in education.* New York, NY: Teachers College Press.

Bishop, A. (2002). *Becoming an ally: Breaking the cycle of oppression in people.* London, England: Zed Books.

Bomer, R., Dworin, J. E., May, L., & Semingson, R. (2008). Miseducating teachers about the poor: A critical analysis of Ruby Payne's claims about poverty. *Teachers College Record, 110,* 2497–2531. Retrieved from http://www.tcrecord.org/Content.asp?ContentId=14591

Christiansen, L. (2015). Learning about inequality: A poem for two voices. *Rethinking Schools, 29*(4), 38–43.

Cohen-Rottenberg, R. (2014). Doing social justice: 10 reasons to give up ableist language. Retrieved from http://www.huffingtonpost.com/rachel-cohenrottenberg/doing-social-justice-thou_b_5476271.html

Cole, T. (2012, March 21). The White-savior-industrial complex. *The Atlantic.* Retrieved from http://www.theatlantic.com/international/archive/2012/03/the-white-savior-industrial-complex/254843/

Cooper, E. J. (2005). It begins with belief: Social demography is not destiny. *Voices from the Middle, 13*(1), 25–33.

Crenshaw, K. (1989). Demarginalizing the intersection of race and sex: A Black feminist critique of antidiscrimination doctrine, feminist theory, and antiracist politics. *The University of Chicago Legal Forum, 140,* 139–167.

Cruz, B. C., Ellerbrock, C. R., Vasquez, A. & Howes, E. V. (Eds.). (2014). *Talking diversity with teachers and teacher educators: Exercises and critical conversations across the curriculum.* New York, NY: Teachers College Press.

Delpit, L. (1995). *Other people's children.* New York, NY: W. W. Norton & Co.

DiAngelo, R. (2011). White fragility. *International Journal of Critical Pedagogy, 3*(3), 54–70.

Duncan-Andrade, J. M., & Morrell, E. (2008). *The art of critical pedagogy: Possibilities for moving from theory to practice in urban schools.* New York, NY: Peter Lang.

Du Bois, W. E. B. (1903). *The souls of Black folk.* Chicago, IL: A. C. McClurg & Co. Retrieved from http://www.bartleby.com/114/

Du Bois, W. E. B. (1935). *Black reconstruction: An essay toward a history of the part which Black folk played in the attempt to reconstruct democracy in America, 1860–1880.* New York, NY: Harcourt Brace.

Etcoff, N. (1999). *Survival of the prettiest: The science of beauty.* New York, NY: Anchor Books.

Feuerverger, G. (2007). *Teaching, learning and other miracles.* Rotterdam, The Netherlands: Sense Publishers.

Freire, P. (1985). Reading the world and reading the word: An interview with Paulo Freire. *Language Arts, 62*(1), 15–21.

Freire, P. (2008). *Pedagogy of the oppressed.* (30th anniversary edition). New York, NY: Continuum. (Original work published 1970)

Garmston, R. J., & Wellman, B. M. (2009). *The adaptive school: A sourcebook for developing collaborative groups.* Norwood, MA: Christopher-Gordon.

Gilmore, S. (2015, January 22). Canada's race problem? It's even worse than America's. *Maclean's.* Retrieved from http://www.macleans.ca/news/canada/out-of-sight-out-of-mind-2/

Gilroy, P., & Yancy, G. (2015, October 1). What "'Black Lives" means in Britain. *New York Times.* Retrieved from http://opinionator.blogs.nytimes.com/2015/10/01/paul-gilroy-what-black-means-in-britain/?_r=0

Gordon, R., & Crosnoe, R. (2013). In school, good looks help and good looks hurt (But they mostly help). *Council on Contemporary Families.* Retrieved from https://contemporaryfamilies.org/good-looks-help-report/

Gorski, P. C. (2008). The myth of the culture of poverty. *Educational Leadership, 65*(7), 32–36.

Gorski, P. C. (2009). Cognitive dissonance as a strategy in social justice teaching. *Multicultural Education, 17*(1), 54–57.

Gorski, P. C., & Swalwell, K. (2015). Equity literacy for all. *Educational Leadership, 72*(6), 34–40.

Halford, J. T., & Hsu, S. H. C. (2014, December 19). *Beauty is wealth: CEO appearance and shareholder value.* http://ssrn.com/abstract=2357756 or http://dx.doi.org/10.2139/ssrn.2357756

Handy, K. (2013). Healing the hidden wounds of racial trauma. *Reclaiming youth and children, 22*(1), 24–28.

Harvey, D. (2005). *A brief history of neoliberalism.* Oxford, England: Oxford University Press.

Hehir, T. (2003). Beyond inclusion. *School Administrator, 60*(3), 36–39.

Hesse, D. E. (2005, January-February). How do teachers' political views influence teaching about controversial issues? *Social Education, 69*(1), 47–48.

Hesse, D. E., & McAvoy, P. (2015). *The political classroom: Evidence and ethics in democratic education.* New York, NY: Routledge.

Hilliard, A. G. (2003). No mystery: Closing the achievement gap between Africans and excellence. In T. Perry, C. Steele, & A. G. Hilliard (Eds.), *Young, gifted, and Black: Promoting high achievement among African-American students.* Boston, MA: Beacon Press.

Howard, G. R. (1999). *You can't teach what you don't know: White teachers, multiracial schools.* New York, NY: Teachers College Press.

Hyerle, D. (2004). *Student successes with thinking maps.* Thousand Oaks, CA: Corwin.

Jackson, Y. (2011). *The Pedagogy of confidence: Inspiring high intellectual performances in urban schools.* New York, NY: Teachers College Press.

Jackson, Y., & McDermott, V. (2009). Fearless leading. *Educational Leadership, 67*(2), 34–39.

Jackson, Y., & McDermott, V. (2012). *Aim high, achieve more: How to transform urban schools through fearless leadership.* Alexandria, VA: ASCD.

Jackson, Y., & McDermott, V. (2015). *Unlocking student potential: How do I identify and activate student strengths?* Alexandria, VA: ASCD.

Jackson, Y., McDermott, V., McDermott, M., & Simmons, M. (2015). Creating a culture of confidence: Re-conceptualizing urban educational leadership. In M. Khalifa, N. W. Arnold, A. F. Osanlo, & C. M. Grant (Eds.), *Handbook of urban leadership* (pp. 62–70). Lanham, MD: Rowman & Littlefield.

King, M. L., Jr. (1963, April 16). Letter from Birmingham jail. *Martin Luther King, Jr. Papers Project.* The Estate of Martin Luther King, Jr. Retrieved from http://kingencyclopedia.stanford.edu/kingweb/popular_requests/frequentdocs/birmingham.pdf

King, T. (2012). *The inconvenient Indian: A curious account of native people in North America.* Toronto, Ontario, Canada: Doubleday Canada.

Kirp, D. L. (2016). How to fix the country's failing schools and how not to. *New York Times.* Retrieved from http://nyti.ms/1RBbt4c

Kohn, A. (1993). *Punished by rewards: The trouble with gold stars, incentive plans, A's, praise and other bribes.* New York, NY: Houghton-Mifflin.

Laughland, O., & Ackerman, S. (2015). For a teen aspiring to be president, being Muslim is a hurdle in post-9/11 America. *The Guardian.* Retrieved from https://www.theguardian.com/us-news/2015/sep/26/muslim-teen-president-america-islamophobia-911

McIntosh, P. (1988). *White privilege and male privilege: A personal account of coming to see correspondences through work in women's studies.* Center for Research on Women. Wellesley, MA: Wellesley College.

McIntosh, P. (1989, July/August). White privilege: Unpacking the invisible knapsack. *Peace and Freedom Magazine,* 10–12.

McKenzie, M. (2015). Black Girl Dangerous. http://www.blackgirldangerous.org

Metcalf, S. (2002). Reading between the lines. *The Nation.* Retrieved from https://www.thenation.com/article/reading-between-lines/

Michael, A., & Bartoli, E. (2014, Summer). What White children need to know about racism. *Independent School Magazine.* Retrieved from http://www.nais .org/Magazines-Newsletters/ISMagazine/Pages/What-White-Children -Need-to-Know-About-Race.aspx

Moll, L., Amanti, C., Neff, D., & Gonzalez, N. (1992). Funds of knowledge for teaching: Using a qualitative approach to connect homes and classrooms. *Theory Into Practice, 31*(2), 132–141.

MTV Strategic Insights & David Binder Research (2014). *MTV Bias Survey.* Retrieved from http://cdn.lookdifferent.org/content/studies/000/000/002/ DBR_MTV_Bias_Survey_Full_Report_I.pdf?1398858309

Ng, W-I. (2004). (Ed.). A tool for everyone: Revelations from the "Power Flower." In *That all may be one – A resource for educating toward racial justice* (pp. 53–55). Toronto, Ontario, Canada: Justice, Global and Ecumenical Relations Unit, The United Church of Canada.

Obidah, J. E., & Manheim Teel, K. (2001). *Because of the kids: Facing racial and cultural differences in schools.* New York, NY: Teachers College Press.

Osta, K., & Perrow, M. (2008). *Coaching for educational equity: The BayCES coaching framework.* Retrieved from http://www.bayces.org

Pink, D. H. (2011). *Drive: The surprising truth about what motivates us.* New York, NY: Riverhead Books.

Pollock, M. (Ed.). (2008). *Everyday antiracism: Getting real about race in school.* New York, NY: The New Press.

Rawls, J. (1971). *A theory of justice.* Cambridge, MA: Harvard University Press.

Samuels, C. A. (2016). Group aims to boost advocacy skills for parents of students with disabilities. *Education Week.* Retrieved from http://www.edweek.org/ew/ articles/2016/02/10/group-aims-to-boost-advocacy-skills-for-parents.html

Saul, J. R. (2014). *The comeback: How aboriginals are reclaiming power and influence.* Toronto, Ontario, Canada: Penguin Random House Canada.

Schweik, C. (2011). Kicked to the curb: Ugly law then and now. *Harvard Civil Rights-Civil Liberties Law Review, 46*(1), 1–16.

Sensoy, O., & DiAngelo, R. (2012). *Is everyone really equal? An introduction to key concepts in social justice education.* New York, NY: Teachers College Press.

Slaughter, A. (2015, September 18). A toxic work environment. *New York Times.* Retrieved from http://www.nytimes.com/2015/09/20/opinion/sunday/ a-toxic-work-world.html?emc=eta1

Smyth, J. (2004). Social capital and the "socially just school." *British Journal of Sociology of Education, 25*(1), 19–33. Retrieved from http://www.jstor.org/ stable/4128657

Steele, C. M. (2010). *Whistling Vivaldi and other clues to how stereotype threats affect us.* New York, NY: Norton.

Steele, D. M, & Cohn-Vargas, B. (2013). *Identity safe classrooms: Places to belong and learn.* Thousand Oaks, CA: Corwin.

Style, E. (1988). Curriculum as window and mirror. *Listening for All Voices.* Summit, NJ: Oak Knoll School Monograph.

Taylor, K. (2015, April 6). At Success Academy Charter Schools, high scores and polarizing tactics. *New York Times.* Retrieved from http://www .nytimes.com/2015/04/07/nyregion/at-success-academy-charter-schools -polarizing-methods-and-superior-results.html

Truth and Reconciliation Commission of Canada. (2015). Honouring the truth, reconciling for the future: Summary of the final report of the Truth and Reconciliation Commission of Canada.

Tyack, D., & Cuban, L. (1995). *Tinkering toward utopia: A century of public school reform.* Boston, MA: Harvard University Press.

Vega, T. (2014, March 21). Students see many slights as racial "microaggressions." *New York Times.* Retrieved from http://nyti.ms/1r2vWBr

Walker, A., Shafer, J., & Iiams, M. (2004, Winter). "Not in my classroom." Teachers' attitudes toward English language learners. *NABE Journal of Research and Practice, 1*(2), 130–160.

Wells, G. (1987). *The meaning makers: Children learning language and using language to learn.* London, England: Hodder and Stoughton.

Woodson, J. (2014). The pain of the watermelon joke. *New York Times.* Retrieved from http://www.nytimes.com/2014/11/29/opinion/the-pain-of-the-watermelon-joke.html

Wright, R. (2008). *What is America? A short history of the new world order.* Toronto, Ontario, Canada: Alfred A. Knopf.

Yancy, G. (2012, March 23). *How can you teach me if you don't know me: Embedded racism and White opacity.* Address at the Philosophy of Education Society (PES). Retrieved from http://ojs.ed.uiuc.edu/index.php/pes/article/view/3600/1221

Index